REREADING CONRAD

ALSO BY DANIEL R. SCHWARZ

AUTHOR:

Imagining the Holocaust (1999)

Reconfiguring Modernism: Explorations in the Relationship between Modern Art and Modern Literature (1997)

Narrative and Representation in the Poetry of Wallace Stevens (1993)

The Case for a Humanistic Poetics (1991)

The Transformation of the English Novel, 1890–1930 (1989; revised edition 1995)

Reading Joyce's "Ulysses" (1987)

The Humanistic Heritage: Critical Theories of the English Novel from James to Hillis Miller (1986)

Conrad: The Later Fiction (1982)

Conrad: "Almayer's Folly" to "Under Western Eyes" (1980)

Disraeli's Fiction (1979)

EDITOR:

The Secret Sharer (Bedford Case Studies in Contemporary Criticism; 1997)

The Dead (Bedford Case Studies in Contemporary Criticism; 1994)

Narrative and Culture (co-editor) (1994)

Rereading Conrad

DANIEL R. SCHWARZ

UNIVERSITY OF MISSOURI PRESS
COLUMBIA AND LONDON

Library of Congress Cataloging-in-Publication Data

Schwarz, Daniel R.
   Rereading Conrad / Daniel R. Schwarz.
      p.   cm.
   Includes bibliographical references and index.
   ISBN 0-8262-1326-X (alk. paper) — ISBN 0-8262-1327-8 (alk. paper)
   1. Conrad, Joseph, 1857–1924—Criticism and interpretation.   I. Title.

PR6005.O4 Z79273   2001
823'.912—dc21   00-066600

Text design: Stephanie Foley
Jacket design: Susan Ferber
Typesetter: The Composing Room of Michigan, Inc.
Printer and binder: Thomson-Shore, Inc.
Typefaces: Minion, Rapier, and CG Metropolis

For my wife, Marcia Jacobson, and my sons,
David Schwarz and Jeffrey Schwarz

CONTENTS

ACKNOWLEDGMENTS

My most profound debt is to my wonderful and gifted Cornell students, with whom I have been reading Conrad these past thirty-three years. It has been a pleasure not only to teach them but also to learn from them. I should add my gratitude to the participants in my five NEH seminars for College Teachers and to students at various universities where I visited and audiences to whom I lectured. I wish to thank Gillian Klempner, Bernhard Schriebl, and Victoria Walker for their fine editorial assistance. It has been my privilege to work with Jane Lago and Beverly Jarrett at the University of Missouri Press. My best reader and my best friend is my wife, Marcia Jacobson, who is always there for me.

REREADING CONRAD

Introduction

Rereading Conrad is a collection of my essays on Conrad written after my *Conrad: "Almayer's Folly" to "Under Western Eyes"* (1980) and *Conrad: The Later Fiction* (1982). This collection touches on virtually the entire canon, but the focus is on the masterworks to which I have returned in my writing, often in response to invitations to lecture or to contribute to a volume. In the essays that follow I write as teacher in the interrogative spirit of "This is true, isn't it?" Often I stress the pedagogical issues with the hope of sharing with colleagues and students my experience as a teacher of Conrad for thirty-five years.

Why, no matter what the critical fashion, has Conrad spoken to readers for a century? If it is in large part his psychological subtlety and political complexity, it is also because we recognize on every page parallels to both our private lives and our public reality. We recognize our reality in his ironic skepticism toward all dogma. Conrad always writes as the outsider, the marginalized figure who does not quite belong. For example, in *Under Western Eyes* (1911) he sees the peculiar parallel between the solitary and lonely betrayer, Razumov, and the fastidious Western language teacher and narrator. With a perspective that anticipates contemporary views of cultural production, he also understands the difference between the rationality and morality of Western democracy and the fanaticism and cynicism produced by Russian autocracy. He understands how politics is a mosaic of individual motives. Rereading *Nostromo* (1904), we see how each person projects his or her own expectations and desires upon the Italian chief of the cargadores who has been given by others the title that translates as "our man," although Nostromo is virtually anonymous and has only the vaguest hints of a personal past or national identity. How other characters give meaning to Nostromo anticipates the way we attribute values to sports heroes, actors, and rock stars about whom we know nothing. At times life imitates art. The disjunction between the Goulds' public stature and their dysfunctional private life—Charles Gould obsessed with wrenching silver from the mines; his wife caught in the sterile formalism of a marriage gone awry—is a fictional foreshadowing of the Clintons' marriage.

Conrad never allows his reader to find a comfortable position; by testing a wide variety of attitudes in his fiction, he demands that his reader do the same. Just as his narrators and characters struggle to come to terms with experience, so must his readers. While we cannot be sure that Conrad is devoid of racial prejudice, *The Nigger of the "Narcissus"* (1897) tests us as moral human beings because it shows that the protagonist, James Wait, is an invalid and malingerer as well as the victim of stereotypical racist views. Given the renewed interest in ethics in the curriculum, we can find still another reason to predict safely Conrad's prominence in the twenty-first century.

Finally, Conrad recognizes the distinction between how events occur and how we remember them, and between how we remember them and the verbal constructions we discover to tell them. He realizes that our versions of events, like the versions of Marlow, the captain-narrator in "The Secret Sharer" (1910), and Jim in *Lord Jim* (1900) are self-created constructions that fulfill their psychic and moral needs. Put another way, to quote Marlow in *Heart of Darkness* (1899), "we live, as we dream—alone."

Perhaps our continuing interest in Conrad reminds us that modernism is a continuing part of our present, and that consigning writers or artists to historical periods is often a pointless exercise in archaeology. Indeed modernism originally was not a period preceded by Victorianism or Edwardianism and followed by a period we now denote as postmodernism, but an ongoing tradition of experimentation in literature, dance, architecture, music, painting, sculpture, photography, and film. If modernism is considered the *end* of historical periods, the last gasp of historicism, what can come next? Because each period thinks of itself in a state of crisis, modernism is really not so much a period as a state of mind. To be sure, modernist narrative is different in degree rather than kind from prior narratives and builds upon such techniques as interior monologue, stream of consciousness, nineteenth-century journalism, psychoanalysis, and naturalism. Postmodernism's audacious claims of originality and uniqueness not only *measure* the very claims of modernism decades ago but remind us that challenges to unity, fragmentation, radical disjunctions and inconsistency in point of view, multiple perspectives on reality, and moral paralysis reach back to modernism.

Conrad's genius depended in large part upon his inventing a brilliantly suitable form for many kinds of novels. How different is the narrator's cynical perspective and taut style when presenting the political world of London in *The Secret Agent* from the more convoluted structure, epic scope, and more circumlocutious style with which the narrator in *Nostromo* renders the uneasy marriage between the rapacity of empire and the violent political maelstrom of emerging nations? How different is the oblique but lucid style of the retrospective teller of "The Secret Sharer," trying to come to terms with the bizarre encounter that becomes the bridge to a mature captaincy and integration of self, from the meditative, obsessive style with which in *Heart of Darkness* Marlow tries to makes sense of his journey into the Congo, his disillusionment with the pretensions of European imperialism, and his confrontation with Kurtz?

My essays take account of recent developments in theory and cultural studies, including postcolonial, feminist, gay, and ecological perspectives, and show how reading Conrad has changed in the face of the theoretical explosion over the past two decades. My essays are the history of the way my own criticism has changed and the way that literary studies have changed. While still a formalist interested in the inextricable relationship of form and content within an imagined ontology, I stress the historical and theoretical framework a bit more. That is not to say I have abandoned prior positions, but rather that I have often reformulated in a more inclusive way the positions I took in the earlier books. In every essay I test some of the claims of recent theory, even while articulating the humanistic poetics that have underlain my entire critical project for more than three decades. For example, in the essay entitled "Reading *Lord Jim:* Reading Texts, Reading Lives," I now propose a complementary reading to the one in *Conrad: "Almayer's Folly" to "Under Western Eyes";* in this newer reading, I establish a dialogue between humanistic and deconstructive (read: more skeptical) readings and focus more attention on the novel's evolving tripartite form. I also stress the structural importance of the dialectic between the friendship ring and the gun in resolving the novel and give more attention to the role of that odd fin-de-siècle figure, Stein. Finally I argue that the very essence of *Lord Jim* is its aesthetic unity that is inextricably tied to asserting its moral judgments.

In my new discussion of "The Secret Sharer," I not only see the text in terms of a homoerotic perspective but explore the insights of Lacan as well as the potential for discussing the relationship between literary and visual narratives. In both of the essays on *Heart of Darkness* in this volume, I stress Conrad's interest in racial and cultural diversity and his compelling political protest against racism, exploitation, and environmental rapacity, even while, as a resistant reader, maintaining an awareness of where Conrad falls short in terms of contemporary values.

I am especially interested in the process and aesthetics of reading. I am struck by the way so many of Conrad's novels take us from the opening sentence into a unique imagined world. Upon rereading, we see how the opening paragraphs establish a grammar of psychological, political, and moral cause and effect. For example, let us turn to *The Secret Agent* (1907): "Mr. Verloc, going out in the morning, left his shop nominally in charge of his brother-in-law. It could be done, because there was very little business at any time, and practically none at all before evening. Mr. Verloc cared but little about his ostensible business. And, moreover, his wife was in charge of his brother-in-law." The disjunction between behavior and motive—a disjunction that is at the center of private and political life in Conrad's turn-of-the-century London—is foreshadowed in this opening paragraph. Verloc's real business is spying, although the soft porn he peddles in his shop serves as a cover for his illicit relationship with Vladimir and the British police. Pretending to be an anarchist, he is actually in the pay of the embassy of an unnamed authoritarian country. We learn that everyone is in charge, or thinks he is, of others, but that those *in the charge of those in charge* often have their own secret plans. "Ostensible" business is a disguise for a more complex group of motives. Written large in the above passages are essential Conradian themes: (1) the discrepancy between, on the one hand, dimly acknowledged needs, obsessions, and compulsions and, on the other, actual behavior; (2) the distinction between actual behavior and articulated motive—that is, the story we tell ourselves about ourselves.

Conrad's conservative desire for a few simple moral and political ideas is at odds with his oft-remarked skepticism. Yet he is not a cynic or a nihilist; he believes that, within a morally neutral universe, humans can create islands of tentative meaning, even if from an objective perspective those islands are illusions. *The Secret Agent*'s meaning depends on a self-dramatizing narrator willfully separating himself from a world he despises, only to gradually emerge in his telling as a character with his own humanistic values. Conrad creates a narrator whose cold, detached style aggressively reduces the characters to formal elements. Yet the narrator is always evaluating, controlling, and restraining the nihilism of the world he describes with such disdain.

Recently there have been calls for a new formalism that foregrounds close reading without sacrificing some of the interests of cultural studies. That the pleasure of reading derives from our understanding of a text's unity and how the parts relate to the whole is particularly true for Conrad's texts. The consonance between Conrad's beginnings and endings is remarkable and one of the reason his works are so satisfying. Every aspect functions in terms of an aesthetic whole. As *The Secret Agent* concludes with the psychotic figure known as the Professor we think not only of Stevie's last fatal walk in Greenwich but also of Verloc's walk to the Embassy of an unnamed totalitarian regime where he is intimidated—indeed terrorized—by Vladimir, the regime's political operative in England, into planning the bombing, which will arouse a desire for repression: "And the incorruptible Professor walked, too, averting his eyes from the odious multitude of mankind. He had no future. He disdained it. He was a force. His thoughts caressed the images of ruin and destruction. He walked, frail, insignificant, shabby, miserable—and terrible in the simplicity of his idea calling madness and despair to the regeneration of the world. Nobody looked at him. He passed on unsuspected and deadly, like a pest in the street full of men." Does not the psychotic, narcissistic Professor—walking around as a perambulatory explosive—make us aware of the ironic disjunction between those espousing radical politics and the human life they supposedly wish to improve? Does not his cynicism recall that of the debonair Vladimir, who also revels in images of mindless violence even while being treasured as a social pet by British high society? The Professor emphasizes the nocturnal and self-serving activities of society's protectors, Inspector Heat and the Assistant Commissioner, who themselves mysteriously walk about London driven by their own private motives. Their behavior recalls the tolerance of Nazi sympathizers by the British in the 1930s, which Kazuo Ishiguro has highlighted in *The Remains of the Day,* a novel with Conradian resonance.

The novel's central anarchic incident is based upon the Greenwich Bomb Outrage of 1894, when a man named Martial Bourdin had, like Stevie Verloc, killed himself setting off a bomb in Greenwich Park near the Royal Observatory. Bourdin's brother-in-law, H. B. Samuels, like Verloc, was a police agent. In keeping with the renewed emphasis on historical context, much has been made of the source material for the anarchists. But whether detailed knowledge of source material is essential to understanding how Conrad imaginatively transmuted factual material is moot. Rather, Conrad's characterizations in *The Secret Agent* depend on discovering apt tropes for recognizable political types of the right and left, types that barely need contextual explanation.

New historicism and its theoretical cousin, postcolonial studies, have brought renewed interest to Conrad's political vision. *Heart of Darkness* is a visionary text that exposed the abuses of King Leopold of Belgium's exploitation of the Congo and, by implication, colonial imperialism. Kurtz's nationality is never specified. When we read of the terrorists in *The Secret Agent,* we recognize them from the daily newspaper stories about psychotic racists, violent anti-abortionists, plane hijackers, and political terrorists seeking to destroy regimes they dislike, including the right-wing fanatics who bombed a federal building in Oklahoma City. Listen to Yundt, one of the anarchists in *The Secret Agent:* "No pity for anything on earth, including themselves, and death enlisted for good and ill in the service of humanity—that's what I would have liked to see." The Professor dreams of delivering a "startling" violent "blow fit to open the first crack in the imposing edifice of legal conceptions sheltering the atrocious injustice of society."

An orphan and émigré, Conrad is a dark figure haunted by insecurity, self-doubt, neurosis, illness, and debt. He wrote prolifically, yet complained constantly about his inability to write. He never felt comfortable in his adopted land. His writing life—his ability to construct imagined worlds from elusive worlds—was often more real than his actual life, even after his marriage to Jessie in 1898 at the age of thirty-eight and the subsequent birth of his two sons.

My earlier books on Conrad proposed a taut relationship between Conrad's work and life at a time when such an approach was less in vogue than it is today. His eloquent letters and nonfiction prose give us important insight into his mind. They provide contexts by which we can better understand his work.

As a Pole living first in France and then in England, Conrad was fascinated by cultural difference. In his fiction, the East plays a prominent role; the Malay culture, like the Congo, is depicted as mysterious, passionate, libidinous, intuitive, and passive-aggressive. In *Lord Jim,* Conrad is fascinated with the exoticism of Bugi culture, including the male bonding of the warriors in Patusan. *Under Western Eyes,* written in 1910–1911, juxtaposes East and West, using Russia as an example of difference, exoticism, mysticism, and passion. The son of parents sent into exile by authorities who distrusted political activity, Conrad was also fascinated with the tolerance for diverse views that marked British political life. In *The Secret Agent,* Vladimir's disdain for democracy—"This country is absurd with its sentimental regard for individual liberty"—is what he knew of the Russians from his own experience.

We might recall Conrad's eloquent words in *A Personal Record* (1908): "And what is a novel if not a conviction of our fellow-men's existence strong enough to take upon itself a form of imagined life clearer than reality and whose accumulated verisimilitude of selected episodes puts to shame the pride of documentary history?" He understood that what many of his contemporaries in the late nineties saw as a division between subject and object was specious, and that the *making of the subject is both the subject and object of art.* Most important, Conrad's writing enabled him to create and re-create himself. As a result of his early maritime career, he thought of the production of each work of fiction as a voyage to be completed; it was often the navigation of that writing voyage that sustained him in his battles with depression and despair: "I dare say I am compelled, unconsciously compelled, now to write volume after volume; as in past years I was compelled to go to sea, voyage after voyage. Leaves must follow upon each other as leagues used to follow in the days gone by."[1]

Some years ago I was asked to be part of an MLA panel on teaching *Heart of Darkness.* The organizer asked me how many would come, and I guessed that a room for thirty would be sufficient, but more than a hundred packed into the room. The reason is that *Heart of Darkness* renews itself for each generation of readers, and so do Conrad's other major texts: *Lord Jim, The Secret Agent, Nostromo, Under Western Eyes,* and "The Secret Sharer." Were *The Nigger of the "Narcissus"* not burdened with a revolting title, it, too, would be in the canon of major texts. While "The End of the Tether" (1902), *The Shadow-Line* (1916), *Chance* (1912), *Victory* (1915), and *The Rover* (1923) have had oscillations in their reputations, they are all wonderful texts to read and to teach. Other than "The Secret Sharer" and *Heart of Darkness,* "Youth" and "Typhoon" are probably the most frequently anthologized of Conrad's stories, but one is likely when thumbing through anthologies to find among the selections such Conrad stories as "An Outpost to Progress," "Falk: A Reminiscence," "Amy Foster," "Il Conde," "Karain: A Memory," "The Lagoon," "The Duel," and "The Tale."

I I

As in all my work from the past three decades, I stress in the following pages that literary works are by humans, about humans, and for humans, and I stress close reading within a historically contextual framework. I am interested in modes of narration and representation. A place is once again being cleared for literary criticism informed but not driven by theoretical hypothesis. For me literary

1. *A Personal Record,* 15, 18. All quotations from Conrad's works are from the Kent Edition.

criticism means an empathetic reading of a text to discover the conscious and unconscious patterns of language that the text conveys to both the reader for whom it was written and the contemporary reader. Literary criticism necessarily depends on an awareness of what, in the transaction of reading, a particular reader does to a text. I seek a pluralistic approach that allows for multiple perspectives and a dialogic approach among those perspectives. Such a criticism leaves room for resistant readings—feminist, ethnic, and gay—without allowing the text to be appropriated by theoretical or political agendas. It means teaching our students that reading is an evolving process requiring attention to what the text is saying, to the structure of effects the text generates, and to how authors make conscious and unconscious choices to create their structure of effects.

An aesthetics and ethics of reading need account for changes in the way we read an author. In a sense, Conrad changes even though he writes no more words. The interpretative history of a text is a trialogue among (1) the text as an object that critics write about; (2) the subjective interests of individual critics; and (3) the predisposition and assumptions of the culture in which those critics write.

The literary canon enriches itself because each generation brings something different to major authors and texts. As my teaching has evolved in response to changes in literary and cultural perspectives, the texts that I teach have changed as well. For example, until 1980 few critics thought about the homoeroticism of the male bonding in "The Secret Sharer"; now it is a foregrounded subject. Thus, in my edition of the "The Secret Sharer" in the Case Studies in Contemporary Criticism series, every contributor took up the subject in one way or another. I now see "The Secret Sharer" in the context of other works that focus on seeing and being seen, including Henry James's *The Turn of the Screw* and Thomas Mann's *Death in Venice,* and also trace that focus back to the seminal nineteenth-century painter Édouard Manet, and especially his *Déjeuner sur l'herbe.* Moreover, while I have always read "The Secret Sharer" as a confessional psychodrama requiring psychological and at times a Freudian-based psychoanalytic criticism, the insights of Lacan play a role in my current response. Finally, I see continuity between "The Secret Sharer" and other novels of bachelor figures at the turn of the century, a period that regarded male bachelors with a certain suspicion as insidious and even pernicious secret agents within the social order.

The history of Conrad criticism is a miniature of the history of Anglo-American criticism in the postwar period. Thus in the criticism of the 1950s and

1960s we see two major aspects of formalism: the New Criticism, a formalism that eschewed biography and the reader's response and emphasized the *isness* of the text; and Aristotelian criticism, a formalism that stressed what we might call the *doesness* of the text—that is, the structure of effects upon the reader as a result of the creation, consciously or unconsciously, by the *author* of these effects in the text. Until recent years, Anglo-American criticism of English fiction has in part derived from the very tradition of manners and morals that the English fiction addresses. Perhaps from a historical perspective this criticism should be seen as a response to British fiction's interest in content and its moral effects on readers. Thus Anglo-American criticism of British fiction has tended to focus on the moral context of texts, viewing aesthetic matters as subservient.

We might recall how the study of English emerged in the late nineteenth and early twentieth centuries from the classics and from philology in the face of great resistance. In the nineteenth century, one read vernacular literature in one's own tongue for pleasure, but did not study it. Even then, if one studied modern literature at all, it was to establish canonical texts. Indeed, as late as the early sixties, English studies at major universities in Britain and America resisted the acknowledgment of modernism, a field that began with the writers after Hardy and sometimes with Hardy and Hopkins.

The tradition of close reading fostered by the New Criticism was particularly appropriate to modernist texts that resisted easy understanding. To be sure, at times the New Criticism—whose philosophical underpinnings included the early critical essays of T. S. Eliot, himself an Anglo-Catholic, and his example of the religious poet and Anglican priest John Donne—may have been appropriated by some as a bulwark for bolstering orthodox religious values, but the emphasis was on powerful close reading of complex texts. Even if the New Critical readings were at times reductive efforts to resolve tension, irony, and ambiguity in overly positivistic and (w)holistic readings—readings in which the teleology of an organic whole mimed the organic "plot" of Christianity stretching from Genesis to Apocalypse—it was more often the case that the New Criticism was a secular and skeptical tool in the service of closely examining the words in a text and, in the hands of such practitioners as William Empson, a method of seeing the need for opening the doors and windows of possibilities. The New Criticism and Aristotelian criticism installed the Kantian category of the aesthetic as central; the aesthetic ideal holds that artistic experience is different in kind from other experiences, and that art is not simply art-as-such, that is, art as sociology or art as biography, but rather that art is unique in itself.

Accompanying the rise of English studies was the development of highly sophisticated modes of reading. The Anglo-American critical tradition, I have argued, has yielded an important theory and method. Indeed, did not the modern tradition—the tradition of Joyce, Eliot, Conrad, and Stevens—*depend* upon powerful close formalist reading, based on attention to the text as aesthetic object, to explicate its texts and to make them accessible to college and university students and other serious readers?

Even when Anglo-American criticism through the 1980s is primarily interested in aesthetic issues, that criticism never really abandons humanism. Notwithstanding the theoretical explosion in the last decades of the century, concerns of that criticism remain the accuracy, the inclusiveness, and the quality—the maturity and sincerity—of mimesis in the novel, particularly how people live in a social community. Indeed, Anglo-American criticism has usually subscribed to the view that art is about something other than art and that subject matter is important. To be sure, Anglo-American novel criticism takes seriously the importance of form, but its interest in form is inextricably tied to an interest in values. For Anglo-American novel criticism believes that the doing—technique, structure, and style—is important *because* it reveals or discusses the meaning inherent in the subject.

The differences that separate various strands of Anglo-American criticism—formalist and historical—prior to the theoretical revolution of the 1970s seem less significant than they once did. Now we are able to see that the New Critics, Aristotelians, the *Partisan Review* group, contextualists, and literary historians share a number of important assumptions: authors write to express their ideas and emotions; how humans live and the values for which they live are of fundamental interest to authors and readers; literature expresses insights about human life and responses to human situations, and that is the main reason we read, teach, and think about literature. While the emphasis varies from critic to critic, we can identify several concepts that define Anglo-American criticism in general, and we can see that until the theoretical revolution of the 1970s all shared similar humanistic assumptions:

(1) The form of the novel—style, structure, and narrative technique—expresses its value system. Put another way: form discovers the meaning of content.

(2) A work of literature is also a creative gesture of the author and the result of historical context. Understanding the process of imitating the external world gives us an insight into the artistry and meaning of the work.

(3) A novel imitates a world that precedes the text, and the critic should recapture that world primarily by formal analysis of the text, although knowledge of the historical context and author is often important.

(4) Humanistic criticism believes that there is an original meaning, a center, that can be approached, and often almost reached, by perceptive reading. The goal is to discover what authors said to their intended audience *then,* as well as what they say to us now. Acts of interpretation at their best—subtle, lucid, inclusive, perceptive—can bring that goal into sight.

(5) Human behavior is central to most works and should be the major concern of analysis. In particular, humanistic criticism is usually interested in how people behave—what they fear, desire, doubt, need. Although modes of characterization differ, the psychology and morality of characters must be understood as if they were real people; for understanding others like ourselves helps us to understand ourselves.

(6) The inclusiveness of the novel's vision in terms of depth and range is a measure of the work's quality.

Following Wayne Booth's eloquent insistence on asking "who is speaking to whom" and "for what purpose," Conrad scholars focused in the 1960s and 1970s on the narrator, particularly the role of Marlow in the turn-of-the-century works such as "Youth," *Heart of Darkness,* and *Lord Jim* and the later *Chance,* as well as the captain-narrator's act of telling in "The Secret Sharer" and *The Shadow Line.* Intense scrutiny of the complexity of Conrad's tellers also extended to the fastidious language teacher in *Under Western Eyes* and the supposedly omniscient narrators of *The Secret Agent* and *Nostromo.*

The theoretical explosion of the past two decades has dramatically reshaped the way we read Conrad. Bakhtin's *The Dialogic Imagination* has given us better tools to discuss pluralistic perspectives in the fiction and taught us to be attentive to a novel as a dialogue among perspectives. In the wake of new historicism's return to mimesis and the implications of representation, cultural criticism needs to enter into a dialogue with older forms of contextualism. While trained as a formalist, I have always regarded literary texts as cultural artifacts. In my books such as *Reconfiguring Modernism: Explorations in the Relationship between Modern Art and Modern Literature* (1997) and *The Case for a Humanistic Poetics* (1991), I have advocated a wider cultural criticism that moves beyond micropolitical and macropolitical issues and includes inquiries into cultural configurations—such as the place of Picasso, Joyce, and Wallace Stevens in the genealogy of modernism. I am interested in why and how readers choose the critical narratives they do at a given time; I am interested in these choices as interpretive history, as socioeconomic production, and as a history of individual values and temperaments. A dialogue between the neglected under-belly of socioeconomic forces—including micropolitical relations within gen-ders and suppressed classes—and the dominant paradigm of intellectual and social history will necessarily create new multilayered cultural and literary his-tory as well as vigorous analysis of representations of works. For example, when we understand the homoerotic nature of male bonding among the Malay war-rior culture, the suicide of Jim in *Lord Jim* becomes not only Jim's abandonment of Jewel but also his ritualistic acceptance of punishment for violating a con-summated intimacy with Dain Waris.

Rather than a noun that names positions, cultural criticism needs to be thought of as a verb, as a process of inquiring, teaching, and reading. Cultural criticism needs to address the category of the aesthetic and its relationship to the political and the ethical. Now that literary studies have returned in the past fifteen years or so to a criticism that focuses on contexts, we need to ask what is the place of the aesthetic in cultural criticism; why do we find some works beau-tiful, moving, and pleasing; and why do we respond to the quality and integri-ty of mimesis—the way the parts of a work are unified—as well as to other formal ingredients of a work, including narrative voice, verbal texture, and char-acterization? How can we speak of ethical and political value without surren-dering the value of the aesthetic? We do not have to subscribe to the view that all art is a separate ontology, its value intrinsic to itself, to ask how we can main-tain a place for the aesthetic.

Rereading Conrad explicitly and implicitly proposes the ingredients of a hu-manistic cultural criticism that has a place for the aesthetic. It seeks to define cultural configurations and to re-create the economic, social, and political world Conrad, and by implication all authors, inhabits. It tries to define an awareness of the cultural position of the critic and to understand interpretive history not only as a history of awareness—of aesthetic assumptions, political interests, worldviews—but also as an idiosyncratic history of individual critics. It seeks a dialogue among various social, economic, and historical factors, be-tween literature and history, between literature and the arts. It tries to operate in a dialogic manner but insists on retaining a place for the aesthetic.

I argue for a cultural criticism that explores similarities that go beyond the borderlines between art forms and between national literatures. At the same time that Conrad and other modernists were making similar experiments in fic-

tion, Picasso was embarking on cubism—on scrambling the distinction between foreground and background, on freeing color from the morphology of
representation, and on including multiple perspectives on the same subject. In
a sense, color in painting provides the kind of energy and differentiation that
Conrad's adjectives provide in his fiction. My essay "The Influence of Gauguin
on *Heart of Darkness*" suggests how Gauguin's Tahitian experience shaped Conrad. And Gauguin, Picasso, and Matisse, among others, were exploring man's
primitive and atavistic antecedents during the approximate decade that Conrad
was writing *Heart of Darkness* (1898), *Lord Jim* (1900), his Malay novels (including *The Rescue,* which he did not publish until 1919), *Nostromo* (1904), and
"The Secret Sharer" (1910). Do we not need more courses that juxtapose paintings such as Matisse's 1910 *Dance II* and its sequel *Music*—with their vermilion
figures, blue sky, and green hill—not merely to major texts of British literature
but to roughly contemporary texts of other literatures, such as Mann's *Death in
Venice* (1912)?

Like figures in *Lord Jim,* Matisse's figures are poised between a realistic and
an aesthetic world. *Dance II* enacts the primitive fantasy that informs Conrad's
Congo and Patusan, including the female figures of the savage mistress and Jewel. In *Heart of Darkness* Marlow speaks about how he was tempted to go ashore
for "a howl and a dance" with the savages. Matisse and Picasso—whose *Three
Musicians* (1921) and *Three Dancers* (1925) are his comments on Matisse's
Dance II and *Music*—would have endorsed Marlow's words in *Heart of Darkness:* "The mind of man is capable of anything—because everything is in it, all
the past as well as all the future." Just as Matisse's reflective *Music* and libidinous
and fantastic *Dance II* give meaning to one another, so, too, in *Lord Jim* do the
realist perspective of the *Patna* collision and of Jim's subsequent trial after the
officers desert the ship and the romance perspective of Patusan inform one another. In *Heart of Darkness,* we see a similar dialogue between disparate aspects
of modernism in Kurtz's reversion to savagery and Marlow's often reflective
(and, later, retrospective) psychological responses.

I I I

I began thinking about Conrad when I was an undergraduate; he was the focus
of my undergraduate honors thesis and later of my doctoral dissertation. As a
Jew in a field with few Jews, I was attracted to him because he was an outsider;

as an American studying English and European cultures who occasionally resisted expectations to culturally cross-dress, I empathized with his position as a
Pole within the alien British culture.

The opening essay of *Rereading Conrad*, originally written for Columbia
University Press's *History of the British Novel*, gives an overview of Conrad's life
and achievement and becomes a necessary reference point for what follows.
"The Secret Sharer" essays originated in projects that focused on teaching that
text, while the essay entitled "Signing the Frame, Framing the Sign: Multicul-
turalism, Canonicity, Pluralism, and the Ethics of Reading *Heart of Darkness*"
speaks to both pedagogical and theoretical issues. The essay entitled "Reading
Lord Jim: Reading Texts, Reading Lives" derives, as I have noted, from a sub-
stantial rethinking of my chapter in *Conrad: "Almayer's Folly" to "Under Western Eyes."* "Conrad's Quarrel with Politics in *Nostromo*" examines Marxist readings of Conrad's anti-imperialistic novel before reaffirming the importance of
individual behavior and motives in determining sociopolitical events. At the
same time I suggest nonideological ways of reading Conrad's novels.

"Abroad as Metaphor: Conrad's Imaginative Transformation of Place" discusses how Conrad transformed experience into imaginative constructs and
how his settings become a seam where author and reader meet. "The Continuity of Conrad's Later Novels" stresses the thematic and formal continuities
among his later works. Taking issue with the notion that the later works are symbolic tales and allegories, different in kind from his prior work, I stress that,
rather than asserting a particular value system, Conrad remained interested to
the last in dramatizing states of consciousness and in exploring how humankind
copes in an amoral cosmos. In my essay on the later fiction, I turn to *Chance* as
my paradigmatic text not only to demonstrate that Marlow still serves for Conrad as an alter ego to whom Conrad transfers the problems of writing and understanding but also to show that the London of *The Secret Agent* still exists in
all its shabby and ugly decadence. The first novel after the three major political
novels—*The Secret Agent, Nostromo,* and *Under Western Eyes*—*Chance* sustains
and intensifies the stress on private life and passionate love as the only alternatives to a world threatened by materialism, political ideology, and uncontrollable historical forces. Like many older artists, Conrad's later work revives earlier forms and themes of past successes while dramatizing, in his characters and
images, a nostalgia for earlier periods of life and hopes for meaningful final
years. Thus it is appropriate that I conclude my essay and *Rereading Conrad* with
a discussion of the vastly underrated *The Rover* in terms of how Peyrol—a man

of action who sacrifices himself for the happiness of others and who mistrusts democracy—is a surrogate for Conrad's fantasy of a significant death climaxing an heroic old age.

A final word: While I have excised much replication from these essays, on occasion, to retain the spirit of the original occasion, I repeat sentences that are crucial to the argument of individual essays. At times I use the interrogative mode to encourage an openness to discussion and the dialogic nature of my readings. When we get an intimation of what seems true or right by examining evidence and developing reasoned arguments, we should want to express it for others and ourselves, not in the spirit of shouting down or in the dismissiveness of some recent academic discourse, but in the spirit of participating in a community of inquiry. When we attend to what others are saying and writing, we are learning; when we argue about meaning (as Plato knew), we come to understand how we know what we know.

Joseph Conrad

Joseph Conrad is not only one of the greatest novelists who has written in English, but he is particularly important for understanding twentieth-century British culture. Although English was his third language, Conrad combined his unique personal background as a Polish émigré and as a seaman with the traditions of his adopted country to change permanently the English novel. He brought a new psychological and moral intensity to the English novel and its traditions of manners and morals. He recognized the role in human conduct of repressed desires, unconscious motives, and unacknowledged impulses. Because he wanted to dramatize how a writer comes to terms with words and meaning, he focused on the teller as much as the tale. Focusing on the problems of how we understand, communicate, and signify experience, he anticipated essential themes in the philosophy, linguistics, criticism, and literature of our era. He understood the potential of the novel for political and historical insights and thus enlarged the subject matter of the English novel. When he dramatized the dilemma of seeking meaning in an amoral universe, he addressed the central epistemological problem of the twentieth century. To achieve a more intense presentation of theme and a more thorough analysis of characters' moral behavior, he adopted innovative techniques, including nonlinear chronology and the meditative self-dramatizing narrator he called Marlow.

Lacking a father, a bachelor until he was thirty-eight, an exile from his native land who felt guilty for deserting not only his homeland but also his father's political heritage, Conrad is particularly concerned with loneliness and isolation. Perhaps the passage from the German writer Novalis that serves as the epigraph to *Lord Jim* and is repeated in *A Personal Record* should serve as the epigraph to Conrad's whole career: "It is certain my conviction gains infinitely the moment

Originally published in *The Columbia History of the British Novel,* ed. John Richetti (New York: Columbia University Press, 1994), 685–714.

another soul will believe in it." The desperate reaching out to an alter ego who might sympathetically respond to his frustrations—the pattern of his letters to Edward Garnett and R. B. Cunninghame Graham—defines a central structural and thematic component of his work: a lonely soul—be it Marlow, Jim, the captain in "The Secret Sharer," Razumov, Heyst, or Captain Anthony—reaches out for another who, he hopes, will recognize, understand, and authenticate him.

In the 1890 to 1930 period, the author's struggle with his subject becomes a major determinant of the novels' form. Thus, in the 1898 to 1900 Marlow tales—as in D. H. Lawrence's *The Rainbow* (1915), James Joyce's *Ulysses* (1922), and Virginia Woolf's *Mrs. Dalloway* (1925)—the author writes to define himself or herself. The writer does not strive for the rhetorical finish of earlier novels but, instead, like Rodin in such sculptures as *Balzac* (1895), invites the reader to perceive a relationship between the creator and the artistic work and to experience the dialogue between the creative process and the raw material. While the Victorian novelist believed that he had a coherent self and that his characters could achieve coherence, the modernist is conscious of disunity in his own life and the world in which he lives. The novelist becomes a divided self. He is both creator and seeker, the prophet who would convert others and the agonizing doubter who would convince himself while engaging in introspective self-examination. Even while the writer stands detached, creating characters, we experience his or her urgent effort to create a self. Thus the reader must maintain a double vision. He must apprehend the narrative and the process of creating that narrative. In such diverse works as the Marlow tales, *The Rainbow,* and *To the Lighthouse* (1927), the process of writing, of defining the subject, of evaluating character, of searching for truth, becomes part of the novel. Yet, as Woolf writes in "Mr. Bennett and Mrs. Brown" (1924), "where so much strength is spent on finding a way of telling the truth, the truth itself is bound to reach us in rather an exhausted and chaotic condition."[1] "Finding a way"—the quest for values and for aesthetic form—becomes a major modernist subject.

Conrad believed that "another man's truth is a dismal lie to me." To understand why Conrad thinks each of us is locked into her or his own perceptions and that all values are ultimately illusions, perhaps we should examine Conrad's ironic image of the cosmos as created by an indifferent knitting machine—an

---

1. *The Captain's Death Bed and Other Essays,* 117.

image he proposed in an 1897 letter to his optimistic socialist friend Cunninghame Graham:

> There is a—let us say—a machine. It evolved itself (I am severely scientif-
> ic) out of a chaos of scraps of iron and behold!—it knits. I am horrified at
> the horrible work and stand appalled. I feel it ought to embroider—but it
> goes on knitting. You come and say: "this is all right: it's only a question of
> the right kind of oil. Let us use this—for instance—celestial oil and the ma-
> chine shall embroider a most beautiful design in purple and gold". Will it?
> Alas no. You cannot by any special lubrication make embroidery with a
> knitting machine. And the most withering thought is that the infamous
> thing has made itself; made itself without thought, without conscience,
> without foresight, without eyes, without heart. . . .[2]

Conrad uses this elaborate ironic trope to speak to the late-Victorian belief that
the industrial revolution is part of an upwardly evolving teleology; this belief is
really a kind of social Darwinism. According to Conrad, humankind would like
to believe in a providentially ordered world vertically descending from a benevolent God—that is, to believe in an embroidered world. But we actually inhabit a temporally defined horizontal dimension within an amoral, indifferent universe—or what Conrad calls "the remorseless process."

Conrad dramatizes that humans always judge one another in terms of their
own psychic and moral needs at the time that they are making judgments. But
notwithstanding the fallibility of all judgments, we must strive to make objective judgments and to sustain values and ideals, even if we know that we will always fall short of them. Thus, when Conrad writes that all is illusion, he means
that all we can do is make working arrangements with the cosmos, and that
there are no absolute values derived from an external source. But he does not
mean that all values are equal. Similarly, merely because we cannot discover an
absolute, final, original reading, it does not follow that all readings are equal.
Rather, as readers, even while acknowledging that our readings are a function
of our limitations, we must strive to establish judgments and values within complex texts. By affirming the value of the search for meaning in the lives of his
characters within his imagined world, Conrad is rhetorically enacting the value of this search in reading texts.

---

2. Letter of December 20, 1897, in *Collected Letters of Joseph Conrad, vol. 1, 1861–1897*, ed. Frederick Karl and Laurence Davies, 425.

BEGINNINGS

Conrad's first two novels, *Almayer's Folly* (1895) and *An Outcast of the Is-lands* (1896), reflect his state of mind and reveal his values. In these early nov-els, narrated by a conventional omniscient narrator, Conrad tests and refines themes and techniques that he will use in his subsequent fiction. In a way that will become characteristic of Conrad's early works, he uses fictional material from his own adventures as his source material. He not only draws upon his ex-perience when he sailed as mate with the *Vidar* (1887–1888) but also bases the title character of his first novel on a man he actually knew. While these two nov-els seem to be about remote events, they actually dramatize his central concerns.

Before he created Marlow, Conrad had difficulty controlling the personal turmoil that we see in his letters of 1894 to 1896; he feels isolated in a mean-ingless universe; he is cynical about man's motives and purposes on this earth; he senses that he is an artistic failure; he doubts his ability to communicate even while expressing his desperate need to be understood. If his speaker's com-mentary is not always appropriate to the dramatic action that evokes it, it is be-cause Conrad is using his speaker to explore his own bafflement in a universe he regards as amoral, indifferent, and at times hostile.

In the first two novels, when Conrad uses the narrator as a surrogate for him-self to place an episode in an intellectual and moral context, he is often testing and probing to discover what the episode means. Conrad subsequently learns to capitalize on his reluctance to be dogmatic; he dramatizes Marlow's process of moral discovery and shows how Marlow continually formulates, discards, and redefines his beliefs through experience. But because in 1894 and 1895 Con-rad had difficulty embracing a consistent set of values, his narrator's commen-tary does not always move toward a consistent philosophic position, but rather may posit contradictory perspectives. Quite frequently, the omniscient voice of the first two novels, *Almayer's Folly* and *An Outcast of the Islands*, explores char-acters and action from the perspective of a man committed to family ties, the work ethic, sexual constraint, individual responsibility, and racial understand-ing. Yet these basic humanistic values are often at odds with the artistic tenta-tiveness and moral confusion that derive from Conrad's uncertainty and anxi-ety. The unresolved tension between, on the one hand, Conrad's own personal concerns and, on the other, his attempt to objectify moral issues is revealed in conflicts between the values expressed by the narrator and the implications of his plot and setting.

Conrad's early artistic code, the original preface to *The Nigger of the "Narcissus"* (1897), is remarkable for its emphasis on creating a community of readers. Seen in the context of his own fear of loneliness and of not communicating, it reflects his decision that fiction will not only enable him to arrest the flux and turmoil within himself but also relieve him of his sense of isolation. Conrad defines art as "a single-minded attempt to render the highest kind of justice to the visible universe, by bringing to light the truth, manifold and one, underlying its every aspect" (vii).[3] The artist's mission is to reveal the experience that unites all men and, in particular, to make the reader aware of the common humanity each shares with mankind. Conrad hopes for a community of responsive temperaments to verify the effectiveness of *his* creation; this hope may be behind the intensity of the famous but elusive assertion, "My task which I am trying to achieve is, by the power of the written word, to make you hear, to make you feel—it is, before all, to make you *see*" (viii).

Conrad's 1914 preface to the American edition makes clear that he meant the tale's focus to be on the crew's response to Wait: "In the book [Wait] is nothing; he is merely the centre of the ship's collective psychology and the pivot of the action" (ix). Sentimentalism is the peculiar form of egoism that preys upon the crew's response to Donkin's poverty at the outset and that causes the men to sacrifice their integrity in a desperate and pathetic effort to forestall Wait's inevitable death. Neither Wait nor Donkin has an identity independent of that conferred by the crew's sentimentalism; they flourish *because* the crew responds to them. Wait is in a parasitic relationship with the crew: "Each, going out, seemed to leave behind a little of his own vitality, surrender some of his own strength, renew the assurance of life—the indestructible thing!" (147–48). Once the crew responds to Donkin with a "wave of sentimental pity," "the development of the destitute Donkin aroused interest" (12–13). When he responds to Wait and Donkin against his better judgment, the sailor-speaker embodies Conrad's own fear of sentimentalism. After he had completed *The Nigger* but before it had begun to appear in the *New Review,* Conrad wrote, "I feel horribly sentimental. . . . I want to rush into print whereby my sentimentalism, my incorrect attitude to life . . . shall be disclosed to the public gaze."[4] Just as the eternal truths of Singleton and Allistoun triumph over the "temporary formulas" of Donkin and the crew's misguided sentimentalism, the fiction writer must

---

3. Page numbers in parentheses refer to the Kent Edition of Conrad's works.
4. Letter of March 26, 1897, in *Collected Letters,* ed. Karl and Davies, 347.

eschew fashionable aesthetic philosophies: "Realism, Romanticism, Naturalism, even the unofficial Sentimentalism . . . all these gods must . . . abandon him . . . to the stammerings of his conscience and to the outspoken consciousness of the difficulties of his work," Conrad wrote in his 1897 preface (x–xi). The speaker–crew member, and possibly Conrad too, wants to believe that the crew's experience with Wait represents a confrontation with death. If he were to lower the rhetorical ante, he would be left with his nominalistic adventure tale, which boldly reveals his own mediocre behavior. Sympathy with Wait almost causes the men, including the crew member, to refuse duty. Thus their catatonic fear of death, evoked by the presence of Wait, displaces the captain as master. Although the men detest Wait as a possible malingerer, they irrationally equate preserving him with forestalling their own deaths.

Conrad discovered that the voyage experiences of his sea career could free him from the debilitating restraints of shore life and be an ordering principle for his new career as a writer. Like the passing of a period in a man's life, a ship's docking is a kind of prolepsis of her final death. But when Conrad presents his narrative to his readers, the created world and the self embodied in that world achieve a kind of immortality.

THE MARLOW TALES

Conrad was concerned with the dilemma of transforming the "freedom" of living in a purposeless world from a condition into a value. And Marlow enabled him to examine this dilemma in "Youth" (1898), *Heart of Darkness* (1899), and *Lord Jim* (1900). Writing enabled Conrad to define his values and his character. He uses his narrators and dramatic personae to objectify his feelings and values. Marlow is a surrogate through whom Conrad works out his own epistemological problems, psychic turmoil, and moral confusion; his search for values echoes Conrad's. Thus he is a means by which Conrad orders his world. He is defining not only the form of the story but also the relation between Conrad's past and present selves. The younger Marlow was explicitly committed to the same conventional values of the British Merchant Marine to which Conrad had devoted his early adulthood, but the mature Marlow has had experiences that have caused him to reevaluate completely his moral beliefs. That Marlow is a vessel for some of Conrad's doubts and anxieties and for defining the problems that made his own life difficult is clear not only from his 1890 Congo diary and the 1890 correspondence with Madame Poradowska, but even more so from the letters of the 1897 to 1899 period, selections from which have already been quoted.

The meaning of several other novels, most notably *The Nigger of the "Narcissus"* and *The Rescue* (1919), depends on understanding the way that Conrad's emotional life becomes embodied in the text. In *Nostromo* the suicidal despair of Decoud reflects a mood that Conrad had known many times in his novel-writing years. Even such an objective work as "The Secret Sharer" (1910) becomes more meaningful once we recognize that it has an autobiographical element. At the outset of his voyage, the captain not only relives emotions Conrad once felt during his first command but also reflects the uncertainty and anxiety that Conrad experienced in the period when he wrote it.

"Youth," the first short story written after *Tales of Unrest* (1898) was completed, addresses the dour view of European life presented in *Tales of Unrest*. Marlow is the heir of the white men of such early Conrad stories as "The Lagoon" (1896) and "Karain: A Memory" (1897)—those sensitive, if disillusioned, men who neither live passionately like the natives nor believe in any sustaining ideals. "Youth" is about Marlow's efforts to create a significant yesterday so that his life will not seem a meaningless concatenation of durational events. Marlow's narrative reflects his need to "arrest" time and preempt the future. Somewhere past the middle of his life, Marlow attempts to discover a symbolic meaning in the past voyage of the *Judea*. He wishes to believe that his first journey to the East was one of "those voyages that seem ordered for the illustration of life, that might stand for a symbol of existence" (3–4). As Marlow recalls his great adventure, he discovers that, in spite of the voyage's failure, it not only contains great significance for him but enables him to recapture on occasion his feeling of youthful energy. Conrad takes a good-natured, ironical view of the supposedly mature Marlow's attempts to expose his own youthful illusions. While he purports to take an objective and detached view of a meaningful experience of his youth, the mature Marlow is revealed as a romantic sentimentalist. Conrad shows us that reality is partly subjective and that our illusions and oversimplifications are as real to us as so-called objective facts.

For a contemporary reader, *Heart of Darkness* raises important questions because at first it seems to present women and blacks from a perspective that is reductive and even sexist and racist. We need to understand that the views expressed by Marlow are not Conrad's, and indeed are a dramatization of a perspective that Conrad uses ironically. Yet it is important to acknowledge that

Conrad does not adequately separate himself from Marlow's view of women, a view that assumes that women are more sentimental, myopic, and domestic than their male peers. Marlow seems to believe that it is the male role to protect women from the more searing truths and to help them live in their illusions. If we understand Marlow's patronizing attitude toward women as naive and simple, can we not use the text to show the difference between authorial and resistant readings—that is, between how texts are read when they are written and how they are read now? Does the lie to the Intended reveal Marlow's sexism? Is Conrad aware of Marlow's sexual stereotyping, even if he means the lie to the Intended to be a crucial moment of self-definition for Marlow? In a situation where opportunities for heterosexuality are limited, what does *Heart of Darkness* say about male bonding among the whites and about miscegenation? Are we offended that one of Kurtz's "abominable practices" is the taking of a savage mistress? If we can understand the agon as an enactment of how the natives' energy and instincts have been corrupted by materialistic, overly rational imperialists, we can see that the charge of racism is itself reductive.

It is useful to place *Heart of Darkness* in its cultural context. The story speaks to major turn-of-the-century concerns: the breakdown of moral certainty, the sense that each of us lives in a closed circle, and the consequent fear of solipsism. That the frame narrator can retell to his audience the story shows that Marlow has communicated with someone and offers a partial antidote to the terrifying fear of isolation and silence that haunted Conrad.

Conrad's narrative demonstrates how the Africans and Europeans share a common humanity: the English too were once natives conquered by the Romans, and England too was once one of the dark places of the earth. Moreover, Europeans not only require laws and rules to restrain their atavistic impulses, but they become more monstrous than those they profess to civilize. Finally, terms like *savage* and *barbarian* are arbitrary designations by imperialists who in fact deserve these epithets more than the natives.

The Congo experience has plunged Marlow into doubt and confusion. Sitting "apart, indistinct, and silent" in his ascetic Buddha pose, Marlow is deliberately trying to separate himself from the cynicism and hypocrisy that he associates with Europeans. As in "Youth," while Marlow is telling the story he arrests the future, places his back against the present, and becomes part of the created world of his own imagination. The tale Marlow tells becomes not only a version of but an epistemological quest into "the culminating point of my experience" (116). The experience proves recalcitrant to Marlow's efforts to understand it. Marlow's probing mind cannot impose an interpretation on Kurtz: "The thing was to know what he belonged to, how many powers of darkness claimed him for their own. That was the reflection that made you creepy all over. It was impossible—it was not good for one either—trying to imagine" (116). Part of his hostility to his audience derives from his own frustrated desire to discover the language that will make his experience comprehensible to himself. Marlow's is the voice of a man desperately trying to create meaning; unlike Kurtz, who "could get himself to believe anything," Marlow has trouble convincing himself that there is the possibility of belief. Marlow's narration is a quest for the symbols and signs to explain the darkness that still haunts his imagination. Ernst Cassirer, in *The Logic of the Humanities,* provides a helpful gloss: "The possibility and necessity of . . . a 'breaking free' of the limitations of individuality emerges nowhere so clearly and indubitably as in the phenomenon of speech. The spoken word never originates in the mere sound or utterance. For a word is an intended meaning. It is construed within the organic whole of a 'communication,' and communication 'exists' only when the word passes from one person to another."[5]

Marlow's experience in the Congo invalidated his belief that civilization equaled progress. While Kurtz, the man who seemed to embody all the accomplishments of civilization, reverted to savagery, the cannibals showed some semblance of the "restraint" that makes civilization possible. Kurtz was a poet, painter, musician, journalist, potential political leader, a "universal genius" of Europe, a man who "had come out equipped with moral ideas of some sort," and yet once he traveled to a place where the earliest beginnings of the world still survived, the wilderness awakened "brutal instincts" and "monstrous passions."

Marlow's journey from Europe to the Congo helped prepare him to sympathize with Kurtz. From the outset he was offended by the standards and perspectives of the European imperialists, and gradually he began to sympathize with the natives against the predatory colonialists. As an idle passenger on a boat taking him to the Congo, he caught glimpses of the inanity he later encountered as an involved participant. Even then, he saw the fatuity of the "civilized" French man-of-war's shelling the bush: "Pop, would go one of the six-inch guns; a small flame would dart and vanish, a little white smoke would disappear, a tiny projectile would give a feeble screech—and nothing happened" (62).

5. *The Logic of the Humanities,* trans. Clarence Smith Howe, 58.

Soon, more than Marlow's Calvinistic belief in the redemptive powers of purposeful labor was offended. He viewed the company's outer station from an ironic standpoint, noticing the neglected machinery, lying like an animal's "carcass"; the "objectless blastings"; and the native workers, their rags resembling tails, chained together as if they were a team of mules. He mocked the folly of those who put out fires with buckets that have holes in the bottom and who considered diseased and starving men "enemies" and "criminals." His original epistemological stance, dependent not upon a naive, idealized conception of the trading company's commercial ventures but simply upon his belief that European civilization represents a tradition of humane values, was shaken. He began to realize that this version of civilization is not an "emissary of light" but an instance of exploitative imperialism at its worst. After Marlow arrived at the Central Station, his quest soon focused on discovering an alternative to the amoral pragmatism and cynicism illustrated by the manager and his uncle. The manager's only objection to Kurtz's abominations was that the results were unsatisfactory.

Conrad has Marlow describe his quest to meet Kurtz in romance terms to suggest ironically Marlow's kinship with folk and legendary heroes who also search for miracles and magicians to solve their problems and relieve their anxieties. Standing in the blood of his helmsman, Marlow could only think that Kurtz was dead, and that he would never be able to speak to Kurtz. It was as if he were frustrated in a journey to consult an oracle. After discovering that Kurtz had "taken a high seat among the devils of the land," he did not renounce his existential commitment to Kurtz as "the nightmare of my choice"; Kurtz still seemed preferable to the hypocrisy and malignity of the Europeans who have deprived language of its meaning, civilization of its ideals, and life of its purpose. Marlow, formerly a representative of European civilization, desperately identified with a man he knew to be ostracized by that civilization. Ironically, Marlow turned only to a different form of greed and egotism; Kurtz's atavistic impulses—modeled perhaps on the Belgian King Leopold's predatory imperialism—have a magnitude and purity that contrast with the pettiness and niggling greed of the imperialists.

We do not know how perceptive Marlow was when he met Kurtz, but Marlow *now* knows that Kurtz was without the restraint that even the helmsman and other cannibals had: "Mr. Kurtz lacked restraint in the gratification of his various lusts . . . there was something wanting in him—some small matter which, when the pressing need arose, could not be found under his magnificent

eloquence" (131). Earlier in his narration, Marlow seems to be preparing to ex-
cuse Kurtz; he asserts that the "idea" behind an action can be redemptive for the
committed individual. However, his narrative discredits this view that the ultimate test of an action is the sincerity of the concept that motivates it. Originally, Kurtz had "set up and [bowed] down before" a benevolent idea, but when the
wilderness had "sealed his soul to its own by the inconceivable ceremonies of
some devilish initiation," Kurtz's idea became its own solipsistic parody: "My
Intended, my ivory, my station, my river, my—" (115–16).

Marlow invests Kurtz with values that fulfill his own need to embody his
threat of the jungle in one tangible creature. If Kurtz is considered the center of
the "heart of darkness," the business of following Kurtz and winning the "struggle" enabled Marlow to believe that he had conquered a symbol of the atavistic,
debilitating effects of the jungle. This belief is central to his interpretation of the
journey's significance. For Marlow, capturing Kurtz after he escapes symbolizes
a personal victory over darkness. Increasingly, Kurtz had been attracted to the
jungle by the urge to go ashore for "a howl and a dance." Having given in to his
primitive urges he appropriately crawled away on all fours. Marlow recalls how
he too was tempted by savage impulses and confused his heartbeat with the beat
of the natives' drums. Uncharacteristically, he thought of giving Kurtz a "drub-
bing." He was "strangely cocksure of himself" and enjoyed stalking his prey. His
assertion that "he left the track" indicates that he, too, was in danger now that
he was alone in the jungle; he thought that he might never get back. But when
Marlow confronted Kurtz, he recalls, "I seemed to come to my senses, I saw the
danger in its right proportion" (143). To Marlow, the confrontation represents
coming to terms with the dark potential within himself against the background
of primitive and unspeakable rites. But he did not surrender to the appeal of the
wilderness precisely because he had internalized the restraints imposed by civilization.

Conrad takes issue with Victorian assumptions about univocal truth and a
divinely ordered world. His use of Marlow's dramatized consciousness reflects
his awareness that "we live, as we dream—alone" (82), and the concomitant
awareness—seen in the development of cubism and Joyce's ventriloquy in
Ulysses—that one perspective is not enough.

As I will argue in detail in my chapter on *Lord Jim*, the process of reading
Lord Jim involves the reader in the "remorseless process"—to recall the crucial
1897 letter to Cunninghame Graham that I cited above, which proposed the
ironic trope for the cosmos of an indifferent knitting machine—of responding

to different judgments of Jim's behavior. Lost in his fantasies of heroism, Jim fails to respond to an emergency on the training ship. Jim's second failure occurs when, while serving as first mate, he loses his nerve. Conrad's narrative coding continues to create a concatenation of episodes that judges Jim's moral dereliction and psychological incapacity. Thus Jim, after he recovers from his leg injury, throws in his lot with those who eschew the "home service" of the merchant marine for easier employment. The fourth episode or vignette that inexorably illustrates that, contrary to Jim's contention, his jump was a characteristic rather than a gratuitous action is his behavior on board the *Patna;* as on the training ship his mind is wooed from his duty to the "human cargo" of pilgrims by fantasies of accomplishment. What follows is Marlow's self-revealing examination of the consequences of Jim's behavior, an examination that, as we shall see in my essay on *Lord Jim,* exposes Marlow's vulnerability and his inability to sustain absolute values in judging Jim's shortcomings. Marlow loses his belief in fixed standards and becomes an apologist for Jim even as Conrad undercuts his pretensions to moral authority.

THE POLITICAL NOVELS

Conrad's novels about politics have been viewed both as nihilistic statements and as dramatizations of a political vision. While the subject of these novels—*Nostromo* (1904), *The Secret Agent* (1907), and *Under Western Eyes* (1911)—is often politics, their values are not political. The novels affirm the primacy of family, the sanctity of the individual, the value of love, and the importance of sympathy and understanding in human relations. Conrad's concern for the working class derives not from political theory but from his experience as a seaman and from his imaginative response to the miseries of others.

The essay "Autocracy and War" (1905) helps us understand Conrad's political novels. The essay boils down to two central points. Above all, Conrad is opposed to autocracy. Secondly, he uncharacteristically affirms a belief in the evolution of both nations and mankind. Because I devote my entire fifth chapter to *Nostromo,* I shall limit my remarks here to a few observations.

In *Nostromo,* the form is a correlative to a narrative about a civilization that lacks a moral center. Motivated by intense vanity that is related to his need to compensate for a disrupted family, Nostromo has a relationship to the cargadores and natives that parallels Gould's position with the aristocrats. For Gould, the mine rather than his wife has become his primary relationship. The narrator describes the first silver that the mine produces in terms suggestive of a demonic birth. In what might now be seen as an instance of Conrad's aware-ness of the commodification of women, Mrs. Gould is midwife to silver rather than mother to children. Mrs. Gould has sublimated her sexual needs and has tacitly permitted the production of the silver to become Gould's homage to her and to substitute for intercourse.

Decoud, the man who is alternately cynic and romantic, pragmatist and ide-alist; the man whose perceptive analysis of others often goes beyond the narra-tor's understanding; the man who uses the written word to rescue his identity is, like Marlow, a character from whom Conrad is at times barely able to dis-tance himself. Decoud is Conrad's mirror, and the distance between Conrad's voice and his character dissolves when he narrates Decoud's complete inability to cope with his solitude. Decoud's final crisis approaches states of mind that Conrad experienced in the period from 1895 to 1898. Thus, in 1896 Conrad wrote to Edward Garnett:

> I am paralyzed by doubt and have just enough sense to feel the agony but am powerless to invent a way out of it. . . . I knock about blindly in it till I am positively, physically sick—and then I give up saying—tomorrow! And tomorrow comes—and brings only the renewed and futile agony. I ask my-self whether I am breaking up mentally. . . . Everything seems so abom-inably stupid. You see *the belief* is not in me—and without the belief—the brazen thick headed, thick skinned immovable belief nothing good can be done.[6]

Decoud's suicide, nihilism, and self-hate objectify qualities that Conrad de-spised in himself.

The bathetic denouement of the romance plot that composes the last three chapters is itself a comment on the possibility of reinvigorating the larger-than-life world of love and heroism embodied in romance or epic. Indeed, the hero-ic image that a man creates for himself—for example, Gould's image of himself as the bringer of justice and security, and Nostromo's image of himself as the man of incorruptible reputation—really has little to do with the basic interests of the community. Rather than heirs to a heroic tradition where men risked

6. Letter of August 5, 1896, in *Collected Letters,* ed. Karl and Davies, 296.

everything to save the community, these are men whose acts are corrupted by their motives.

The Secret Agent depends upon a tension between disintegration of content (Conrad's perception of turn-of-the-century London) and integration and cohesion of form (the language and the tightly unified narrative). Conrad creates a language that is moral, civilized, and rational, and a narrator with the intelligence and moral energy to suggest alternatives to the cynicism, amorality, and hypocrisy that dominate political relationships within London. Although the narrator, to whom the entire language of the book is assigned, at first seems isolated and detached from a world he abhors, he gradually reveals himself as a multidimensional figure whose concern and sympathy for those trapped within the cosmic chaos become part of the novel's values. The major character is the narrator; his action is to attack a world he despises. The satire in *The Secret Agent* depends upon the immense ironic distance between a civilized voice that justifiably conceives of itself as representing sanity, rationality, and morality, and the people of London who are for the most part caught in a maelstrom of violence and irrationality beyond their control.

In *The Secret Agent*, Conrad takes issue with a common Edwardian view that time inevitably equals progress. Such writers as Butler and Shaw proposed the concept of an upwardly evolving life force. Conrad regarded as cant the political euphoria of the Fabians and his socialist friend, Cunninghame Graham, and their sanguine conviction that a "benign" and "congenial" fixture awaits us once we locate and ameliorate the problems of civilization. Conrad's sense of history as a process inexorably indifferent to man's aspirations was shaped partly by his despair and indignation at the continuous suppression of Polish freedom. Thus, even the book's dedication to the utopian H. G. Wells has its ironic aspect. *The Secret Agent* proposes no solutions for the oppressive economic system or the negligent political system.

The narrator stresses that those who should protect society are as oblivious to the objective world outside themselves as are those who would destroy it. Ethelred, the "great man" and "presence," is handicapped by poor vision; he expresses himself in a vigorous manner, but in his haughtiness refuses to concern himself with—has indeed a physical horror of—details. A not entirely unsympathetic caricature of an Edwardian progressive, Ethelred takes seriously his business as a reformer and lives as if time were measuring progress toward social goals. Whatever our present attitudes toward ecology, Conrad would have wished us to see that the energy devoted to the bill for the nationalization of

fisheries was misspent and that Ethelred, with his obvious leadership capaci-
ties—his "powerful" touch and vigorous tone are stressed—is exhausting himself with trifles. (In three of Conrad's short stories of this period, we find that
Ethelred's fastidious and ineffectual counterparts are the Count and narrator of
"Il Conde" and the narrators of "An Anarchist" and "The Informer.")

It may be that the fundamental importance of *Under Western Eyes,* the
last of Conrad's major political novels, is its rejection of political commitment
in favor of personal relationships and private commitments. The language
teacher's retrospective narrative re-creates the process of coming to terms with
the terrifying Dionysian world he has confronted. By the conclusion of part one,
we have learned enough about the fanaticism, mysticism, and irrationality of
the Russians to begin to appreciate the intelligence and perspicacity with which
the narrator has edited Razumov's record. In contrast to the revolutionary fren-
zy and the autocratic regime's fanaticism, the narrator's detachment and effort
to discover the moral aspect of the tale become attractive.

Autocratic politics create a world in which personal lives are distorted by the
political abstractions served by proponents and antagonists. Russia finally
emerges as primitive and atavistic, a kind of European version of the Congo
where possibilities exist that have all but been discarded by Western countries.
On the other hand, Geneva is a civilization where the libidinous energies and
the atavistic impulses may be squelched, but violence and anarchy are under
control. It is very much to the point that the people who reside in Geneva, other than the revolutionaries, are engaged in shopkeeping, teaching, picnicking,
walking; and that these quite ordinary activities can take place in Geneva, unlike Russia, without bombs and intimidation. Geneva may have its materialistic aspect, epitomized by the rather tasteless Chateau Borel that now stands
abandoned by its absentee owners, but it makes possible the civilized world of
personal affections and the fulfillment of private aspirations that the autocratic and violent Russian world blunts. Conrad deliberately depicts Geneva as tediously geometric and rather claustrophobic. Razumov is contemptuous of its
decorum; he regards the view of the lake as "the very perfection of mediocrity
attained at last after centuries of toil and culture." The novel confirms the value of the mind's own interior space, of personal communication and private relationships; it rejects historical and geographical explanations that seek to place
moral responsibility beyond the individual conscience. The humanity and perspicacity that the narrator brings to his reminiscence *contain* and undermine
the Russian conception of a world of vast objective space.

THE LATER FICTION

We can divide Conrad's career after 1910 into three distinct phases. In the first, Conrad wanted to demonstrate that he was an English novelist, not a Slav writing in English, as some reviewers implied. The diffident, self-effacing narrator of *Under Western Eyes* owes something to this impulse. In a sense, *Under Western Eyes, Chance* (1912), and *Victory* (1915) are Conrad's English trilogy. Thus *Chance* and *Victory* focus explicitly on personal relationships and manners, and allude to contemporary issues in England. Conrad had to prove to his audience and perhaps to himself that he had become an English writer who could deal with the intricacies of personal relationships in the context of contemporary customs and values. Since I shall be speaking in some detail about the later fiction in my concluding chapter, I shall restrict my remarks in this overview of Conrad's career.

In the great 1910 story "The Secret Sharer," the captain-narrator, separated by a "distance of years" from the meeting with Leggatt, recounts a tale of initiation in which he successfully overcame debilitating emotional insecurity to command his ship. Like those of Eliot's Prufrock and Joyce's Gabriel Conroy, the integrity of the captain's personality is threatened by a disbelief in the authenticity of self. The significance of the events for the sensitive and intelligent captain is that he discovered within himself the ability to act decisively. As a younger man, the captain doubted himself, felt a "stranger" to the community to which he belonged, and wondered if he should "turn out faithful to that ideal conception of one's personality every man sets up for himself secretly." His concern *now* is to present the issues in terms of what Leggatt meant to him. Although he certainly knows that harboring an escaped murderer represents a threat to a maritime civilization and a violation of his own legal and moral commitment, his retelling ignores this.

In *Chance* and *Victory,* Conrad's subject matter is less his own life than the external world. The form and narrative technique stress his detachment and withdrawal. Even when he revives Marlow in *Chance,* that figure is no longer a surrogate who echoes his own anxieties and doubts. Although we certainly see important resemblances between Conrad and his characters Heyst and Captain Anthony, he is not primarily writing about fictional versions of himself.

Chance, the first novel after the three major political novels, sustains and intensifies the stress on private life and passionate love as the only alternatives to a world threatened by materialism, political ideology, and uncontrollable historical forces. In *Chance,* as in Conrad's earlier novels, each character is lonely, isolated and separate, and requires the recognition of another as friend, lover, parent, child, or counsel to complete him. If there is an alternative in *Chance* to repression, isolation, and self-imprisonment, it is in the possibility of sympathy and understanding, and, most significantly, passionate love.

Although London is not the setting, *Victory* is the last of Conrad's novels that analyzes contemporary European culture. As we shall see, beginning with *The Shadow-Line* (1916), the subsequent novels beat a retreat from confronting the crisis of values that Conrad believed was undermining Western civilization. For Conrad, the crisis was epitomized by imperialism, capitalism, the decline of family and national ties, and the replacement of human relationships based upon personal ties with relationships based on economic consideration. *Victory* depicts an "age in which we are camped like bewildered travellers in a garish, unrestful hotel." Schomberg's hotel becomes a mnemonic device to recall that image, and Schomberg's malice, enervation, lust, and greed are the quintessence of that age. In a world dominated by various forms of materialistic adventurism—from the coal mine in the tropics to Zangiacomo's traveling band and Schomberg's parody of a hotel—Heyst's courtesy and delicacy stand as a vestige of an older tradition. But his manners and formality also serve as a barrier not only to reaching a complete understanding with Lena but also to contending with the forces of economic barbarism—Jones, Ricardo, and Schomberg. "Outward cordiality of manner" and "consummate politeness" become Heyst's refuge. *Victory* is about the decline in civility and morality not only in what Conrad had once called "an outpost of progress" but in Western civilization. Conrad perceived, as Thomas Mann had in *Death in Venice* (1912), that something had gone wrong with the amenities and proprieties that are the glue that holds civilization together.

In the period between 1912 and 1914, when Conrad wrote *Victory,* the stable, secure England in which he had found a home was in danger of disintegration. Beset by political turmoil in the forms of labor unrest, the women's movement, and the excesses and zeal of the Conservative opposition, which threatened to undermine parliamentary government, England must have seemed to him to be increasingly in danger of becoming like his native Poland. The ironically titled *Victory* is Conrad's response to an England torn by conflicting but powerful enclaves and suffering a loss of esteem in its own eyes as well as in those of other nations.

Heyst may represent Conrad's perception that a certain kind of man—polished, tolerant, polite, considerate of others, and of impeccable integrity and the highest personal standards—was becoming obsolete in England. For all his quirks, Heyst adheres to Edwardian propriety and decorum in all his actions with the single exception of his elopement. The negativism of Heyst's father may echo the anonymous 1905 pamphlet *The Decline and Fall of the British Empire;* in any case, it is an extreme rejection of the more optimistic of the social Darwinists. It may also be a criticism of *A Commentary* (1908) by Conrad's friend John Galsworthy. *Victory* is a novel that attacks imperialistic pretensions, decadent aristocracy, and business morality, only to give those forces the laurels of victory. The title *Victory* finally implies the triumph of materialism and greed over feelings and personal relationships. By using the word *business* interchangeably with *game*, Conrad emphasizes the effort of Edwardian culture to disguise in understatements its competitive and aggressive impulses.

The second phase of Conrad's later career derives more from a personal impulse. After *Chance* and *Victory*, he returns from contemporary issues to his own memories. *The Shadow-Line* and *The Arrow of Gold* (1919), like "The Secret Sharer" and "A Smile of Fortune" (1911), are expressive of Conrad's emotions and passions, but in these works, unlike the Marlow tales, Conrad re-creates emotions of the past more than he objectifies his present inner turmoil.

Based on his command of the *Otago* in 1888, *The Shadow-Line* explores the difference between merely practicing skills and providing leadership to a community. Conrad wrote in Richard Curle's copy of the novel, "This story had been in my mind for some years. Originally I used to think of it under the name of *First Command*. When I managed in the second year of war to concentrate my mind sufficiently to begin working I turned to this subject as the easiest. But in consequence of my changed mental attitude to it, it became *The Shadow Line*."[7] By contrast, the seemingly similar "Secret Sharer" emphasized the captain-narrator's personal psychological development rather than his ability to occupy a position in terms of standards established by maritime tradition. By fulfilling the moral requirements of a clearly defined position, the captain-narrator fulfills himself; he overcomes ennui, anxiety, and anomie and merges his psychological life with the demands of the external world. To oversimplify: *The Shadow-Line* affirms that hyperconsciousness is a moral rather than—as in "The Secret Sharer"—a psychological problem. The later work demonstrates how hyperconsciousness and its symptoms can be overcome by discovering the authentic self that exists beneath self-doubt and anxiety.

7. Quoted in Frederick Karl, *Joseph Conrad: The Three Lives: A Biography*, 770.

In the final phase, Conrad looks back in *The Rover* (1923) and in the incomplete *Suspense* to the Napoleonic period and creates large historical canvases that recall the great political novels. The last novel Conrad completed, *The Rover* was written with the idea of reaching that part of the mass of mankind which was literate. In important respects, it is a synopsis of a number of major themes in his previous work. Conrad spoke of *The Rover* in terms that suggest its special importance to him: "I have wanted for a long time to do a seaman's 'return' (before my own departure)."[8] Peyrol's desire in his final voyage to merge his destiny with that of his nation may reflect Conrad's desire, as he approached death, to contribute meaningfully to Poland's destiny. His fantasy of a significant political act is embodied in Peyrol. If, like Vladimir Nabokov's, Conrad's life was embodied in his imagination, he was never comfortable that he had turned his back on politics and the heritage of his father, whom he recalled as an idealistic patriot. The novel's title also refers to himself, the twice transplanted alien who finally found a home in England and no longer felt himself something of an outsider. Peyrol re-creates himself at fifty-eight when circumstances connive with his own weariness to deprive him of his past; he creates a new identity just as surely as a younger Conrad did when he left Poland to go to sea and, later, when he turned from the sea to a writing career. *The Rover* combines Conrad's fantasy of retreat with his lifelong fantasy of a heroic return home. (Neither his first visit to Poland in 1890 nor his second at the outbreak of the war quite fulfilled this fantasy.)

Conrad's later works demonstrate the continuity of his career. Throughout his career his works are expressions of his quest for values and self-definition. Continuing the focus of the novels about politics (*Nostromo, The Secret Agent,* and *Under Western Eyes*), Conrad's later works are more concerned with family and personal relationships than are his prior works. Except for "The Secret Sharer" and *The Shadow-Line,* the later works are concerned with how and why people love one another. But they also address how historical and social forces limit and define the possibilities for love and action. Conrad never puts behind him the conviction that man is caught in a web of circumstances beyond his control. But he also believes in man's capacity to grow, to love, and to know himself. Conrad believes that, within an indifferent if not hostile universe, man's indomitable will enables him to survive despite setbacks and individual failures. Thus, he is not the nihilist and the prophet of darkness that he has been depicted in much recent criticism.

8. Letter of February 22, 1924, in Gérard Jean-Aubry, *Joseph Conrad,* 2:339.

Signing the Frame, Framing the Sign

MULTICULTURALISM, CANONICITY, PLURALISM, AND THE ETHICS OF READING *HEART OF DARKNESS*

Elie Wiesel begins *Night,* his autobiographical novel of the Holocaust, with a description of Moshe the Beadle, an insignificant figure in a small town in Transylvania who taught the narrator about the cabala:

> They called him Moshe the Beadle, as though he had never had a surname in his life. He was a man of all work at a Hasidic synagogue. The Jews of Sighet—that little town in Transylvania where I spent my childhood—were very fond of him. He was very poor and lived humbly. . . . He was a past master in the art of making himself insignificant, of seeming invisible. . . . I loved his great, dreaming eyes, their gaze lost in the distance.

But Moshe is expelled in early 1942 because he is a foreign Jew and is not heard of for several months. He unexpectedly returns to tell of his miraculous escape from a Gestapo slaughter of Jews in the Polish forests. But no one believes him. Moshe cries: "Jews, listen to me. . . . Only listen to me." But everyone assumes that he has gone mad. And the narrator—still a young boy—recalls asking him: "Why are you so anxious that people should believe what you say? In your place, I shouldn't care whether they believe me or not."[1]

Let us consider the significance of Moshe the Beadle. For one thing, Wiesel is using him as a metonymy for himself in his present role as narrator who is, as he writes, calling on us to listen to his words as he tells his relentless tale of his own miraculous escape from Nazi terror. Implicitly, he is urging us that it is our ethical responsibility not to turn away from the witnessing voice—Moshe

---

This essay, derived from the keynote address I gave at the 1993 Australian National University Conference in Canberra entitled "Renegotiating Ethics: Moral Inquiry and Literary and Cultural Discourses in the 1990s," was published in *Beyond Poststructuralism: The Speculations of Theory and the Experience of Reading,* ed. Wendell V. Harris (University Park: Penn State University Press, 1996).

1. *Night,* trans. Stella Rodway, 5.

himself, indeed all those who have seen, specifically, the Holocaust and, metonymically, for us, man's inhumanity to man—whether it occurs in Bosnia, Northern Ireland, or Somalia.

Why do I begin with *Night?* For one thing, it is a novel that depends upon and affirms the concept of individual agency; the speaker tells a wondrous and horrible tale of saving his life and shaping his role as Witness. We see dramatized the process of the narrator's developing into his role of Witness in the face of historical forces that would obliterate his humanity, his individuality, and his voice. Notwithstanding the efficiency of Nazi cultural production and the technology of the death camps and gas chambers, the narrator re-creates himself through language. In the sense of the technological fulfillment of an ordered state that subordinated individual rights to the national purpose of the State, Nazi ideology has been thought of as a product of modernism. For those who have experienced, like Wiesel, the Holocaust firsthand—for whom Auschwitz is not a metaphor but a memory—language is more than the free play of signifiers. For these people and others on the political edge, their very telling—their very living—testifies to will, agency, and the desire to survive that resists and renders morally irrelevant simple positivistic explanations which argue that an author's language is completely culturally produced. In psychoanalytic linguistic terms, the narrator's telling is a *resistance* to the way in which the word *Jew* was culturally produced to mean inferior people who were progressively discounted, deprived of basic rights as citizens, labeled with a yellow Star of David, imprisoned, enslaved, and killed.

I select this spare, rough-hewn text because it is an eloquent testimony that depends on human agency and ethical commitment. *Night* reminds us, too, that the concept of author-function as a substitute for the creating intelligence does not do justice to the way in which language and art express the individual psyche. Readers will recall that the book's signification depends on its taut structure, the underpinning for an apparently primitive testimony, and depends, too, on its spare, even sparse, style. Its eloquence derives from its apparent ingenuousness. Yet *Night* speaks on behalf of meaning, on behalf of will—the will to survive, the will to witness—and on behalf of language's signification. *Night* eloquently reminds us of a grotesque historical irony, namely, that with its use of modern technology and Enlightenment rationality, Western man's progress led to the efficiency of the Nazi transport system, Nazi work camps, and Nazi gas chambers. *Night* is a text that resists irony and deconstruction and cries out in its eloquence, pain, and anger as it enacts the *power of language.* The text traces the death of the narrator's mother, a sister, and, finally, his father; it witnesses an encroaching horrible moral NIGHT, a night that includes the speaker's loss of religious belief in the face of historical events.

Assuming in its form—especially in its prophetic voice—an ethical imagined audience, *Night* also demands an ethical response. By that I mean attention to issues that pertain to how life is lived within imagined worlds. Truth in novels takes place within the hypothesis "as if," which is another way of saying that as we think about our reading we are never completely unaware of the metaphoricity of literature. At one time, some critics may have naively ignored the metaphoricity of language and confused characterization with actual human character. But have not some theorists reached the other pole of willfully denying analogies to human life and naively repressing the possibilities of significance?

While I would be the first to acknowledge that the stakes are infinitely smaller, I think humanists and those interested in the ethical implications of writing, reading, and teaching have justifiably felt like Moshe the Beadle that their voices were for a while being ignored in the din of theoretical shouting. But in the wake of the revelations about Paul de Man's past as a Nazi collaborator and the insistence of many feminists, minorities, postcolonialists, and new historicists that we look at what literature represents, the voices of those who all along believed in the ethical and aesthetic dimensions of literature and culture are once again being heard.

By beginning my discourse with Wiesel's *Night*, I am enacting my view that each of us belongs to different interpretive communities at the same time, and that these communities are in a dialogic relationship with one another. For example, I am an American academic, an English professor at Cornell, a divorced father who for several years has been the primary parent of two young adult sons, and, despite three or four generations of assimilation, still a Jew for whom the Holocaust has profound meaning. In my chapter on Paul de Man's life and work in my book *The Case for a Humanistic Poetics*, as well as in my *Imagining the Holocaust* I write as a secular Jew who feels deep synchronic and diachronic ties to his heritage, and who tends to be drawn to those writers who have been culturally marginalized—whether by nationality, such as Conrad and Joyce, or by gender, such as Woolf—and to those in economically straitened circumstances, such as Lawrence. To situate ourselves and our interests is part of an ethics of reading.

A word more about Jewishness. Perhaps it is because the Jewish tradition— for me, at least, as a secular Jew who makes choices about how and what I believe—has always been open and exegetical that I resist theoretical dogma.

When one looks at a page of the Talmud, one sees an unresolved dialogue among diverse commentators. In Judaism, there is no Nicene Creed, no attempt to resolve issues in a concluding statement. For example, in the Passover Haggadah, the various rabbis comment upon the meaning of the Exodus story and specifically the meaning of Passover customs, but again there is no attempt at resolution. Because historically Jews have lived on the margin—in ghettos and shtetls—never sure of what pogroms tomorrow will bring—they have tended to be skeptical of sweeping universals and to dwell in the particular. Moreover, Jews have been concerned with relations between man and God and man and man, not simply the hereafter—in part because the hereafter was often a luxury while they eked out a living and awaited what seemed like arbitrary changes in the political winds. And the Jewish tradition is ethically based—think of the Talmud as a debate about law and ethics—with an emphasis on living in what Aristotle called the "ineluctable modality of the visible" (and Joyce in *Ulysses* redefined into "What you damn well have to see").

Because each of us is a nodal point where multiple major influences as well as secondary influences meet, each of us encounters the texts we read on the seam of reading—and by "seam," I am playing with S-E-A-M, S-E-E-M, and S-E-M as in semiotics and dissemination. I stress how texts shape readers and readers shape texts. I am a pragmatic Aristotelian who stresses the relationship of the text as a made object, the product of an author's conscious (and unconscious) art or craft designed to achieve foreknown ends that result from the psyche, values, and idiosyncrasies that differentiate her or him from others. Thus my version of cultural criticism would seek to create what Saul Rosenzweig, speaking of his own "Freud, Jung and Hall the King-Maker," calls the "idioverse, the universe of events that constitutes the individual," as it is realized in the artist's works.[2] I am prone to pose the question "What is your evidence?" to myself and to my students, and expect my and their answer to consist of passages from primary texts. I am conscious of how plot enacts values, and how plot is a structure of effects. I try to balance the structure of tropes with a sense that the plot represents an anterior reality. (I do not believe that citation by one theorist of another theorist constitutes an argument. Indeed, if current theory is a production of knowledge, not the reproduction, how is it that current theory relies so much on the argument from authority?)

2. "Freud, Jung and Hall the King-Maker," 1, 20.

Narrative is both the representation of external events and the telling of those events. My interest in narrative derives from my belief that we make sense of our life by ordering it and giving it shape. The stories we tell ourselves provide the continuity among the concatenation of diverse episodes in our lives, even if our stories inevitably distort and falsify. We are all continually writing and rewriting the text of our lives, revising our memories and hopes, proposing plans, filtering disappointments through our defenses and rationalizations, making adjustments in the way we present ourselves to ourselves and to others. To the degree that we are self-conscious, we live in our narratives—our discourse—about our actions, thoughts, and feelings. While there is always a gulf between imagined worlds and real ones, does not the continuity between reading lives and reading texts depend on understanding reading as a means of sharpening our perception, cultivating discriminations, and deepening our insights about ourselves? For reading is a process of cognition that depends on actively organizing the phenomena of language both in the moment of perception *and* on the fuller understanding that develops as our reading continues, as well as in our retrospective view of our completed reading.

Reading is a dialogic activity in which multiple ways of looking at a text contend with one another; each perspective implicitly suggests interrogatives to other approaches. I suggest that as readers we can and should belong to multiple interpretive communities; rather than propose unitary stories of reading and choose between the either/or of possible readings, we can and should enjoy multiplicity and diversity in our readings. The kind of pluralistic criticism I imagine sees criticism as a series of hypotheses rather than as a final product. In its healthy and open pluralism, it is inclusive rather than exclusive. Even as we answer each question and pursue each line of inquiry, we become aware that each explanation is partial. It may be time to back off from the notion that the critic is *vates* and return to the more modest Socratic question-and-answer structure in order to leave rhetorical space for other explanations. Pluralism may at times define a position passionately but always in the mode of "This is true, or is it?" and always leaving space for a response. By contrast, dogmatism asserts its position without allowing for an alternative, while relativism accepts all positions as if they were equal.

The text itself, what it represents, what it signifies, and how it enacts a meaning should always be an important part of our pedagogy. Yet, as Stephen Greenblatt understands, all reading has an element of self-fashioning, and we should be self-conscious about how self-fashioning creates angles of distortion. For example, how each of us responds to the narrative of Paul de Man's life and work depends on how we are personally situated, including the extent to which we invested in deconstruction. How we situate ourselves as individual readers and as members of interpretive communities is an important part of our reading, and, as teachers, we need to make the students aware of how we and they might acknowledge *our differences*. We need to be careful about defining our own position because we do not always see ourselves as others see us. We can get lost in a welter of self-pity and can overestimate our own worth.

As I have argued elsewhere, the largest interpretive community is one. Positioning oneself in relationship to a text is as important as positioning a text in relation to cultural contexts and our debates within the academic community about critical assumptions. Simply put, texts like Elie Wiesel's *Night* are different for those whose family disappeared in the concentration camps and different again for those fellow Jews who, like myself, by accident of place survived. Indeed, I believe that there is a place within literary studies for texts that reflect our own varied interests. Special interest has always been an engine that has driven literary studies—as an offspring first of classical study and philology, then of historicism and textual editing, later of New Criticism—and special interest has produced the wonderful revolution in feminist studies, postcolonial studies, and ethnic studies.

Where, let us ask, are theory, criticism, and the study of literature going? I have always doubted that theory was teleologically advancing in a kind of Manifest Destiny from the International Academic Datelines of Paris and New Haven. Why has theory evolved into theology and why do partisans of one or another approach become sects? Is it the power of theory's arguments or, for some acolytes, the importance of *belonging*—and excluding and scapegoating those who do not belong? Theories, including Marxism and deconstruction, are valuable as part of a pluralistic discourse but become oppressive and distorting when they become monolithic paradigms worshiped by monotheistic cults. At times literary studies have suffered from reductive rhetoric that has done intellectual violence to complex texts in the name of various monolithic theories.

I feel like someone who, with a small band of other surviving humanists, has created a little island outpost where we pursued our interests, and perhaps has been grudgingly given a place in the General Assembly—certainly not the Security Council—of theory. While welcoming the destabilizing insights of much recent theory—including the idea that language does not signify absolutely and texts are historically and culturally produced—I am willing to be identified with such quaint ideas as humanism, pluralism, and canonicity, and to use such terms as *ethics* and even *author*. I am for a pluralism of readings, a pluralism of texts, and a pluralism of cultures. Because I assume human agency in writing and reading and believe that there is a space for a non-Marxist version of cultural studies, I am on occasion invited to play the role of *Academic Dissenter* (for some, read: dinosaur) in journals and at conferences.

Within any theory of cultural production, whether of texts or of readers, we need to leave space for the creative intelligence of authors and readers who make choices that have ethical implications. My focus, my concern, is the act of reading specific texts. I have always been wary of extravagant readings that use the text as point of departure for flights of fancy and/or to make a political point. Indeed, for me, extravagant reading is an oxymoron.

As a way of anticipating my approach to *Heart of Darkness,* I provocatively propose two columns:

ingenuous, unsophisticated	rigorous, urbane, or sophisticated
essentialism, idealism	materialism
univocal, monistic	dialogic
positivistic logic and "A" causes "B"	affinities, playfulness
binary thinking	free play of signifiers as revealed to an imaginative, interesting, and powerful reader
conservative	progressive
traditional	avant-garde
close-minded	open-minded
simple, facile, deductively consistent	complex, difficult, disruptive
static	destabilizing
subjective	objective
rational, detached, restrained	passionate, engaged, committed
old-fashioned	enlightened
dogmatic insistence on monolithic truth	belief that some readings are better and truer than others

While the column on the left is usually used to describe humanistic criticism and the column on the right to describe various advanced theories—including deconstruction and Marxism—I suggest that the categories on the right, which are thought to belong to advanced theory, at times more aptly describe humanistic pluralist criticism, and I subversively invite a questioning—a de-deconstruction—of these binary distinctions as they are now often applied. Moreover, I suggest that the best of all criticism understands these supposedly binary concepts in terms of "both/and" not "neither/nor," and that well before deconstruction Kenneth Burke, William Empson, R. P. Blackmur, Dorothy Van Ghent, and M. H. Abrams demonstrated in their works how these supposedly binary concepts cross-fertilize one another, invade each other's borders, and form a continuum.[3]

Gerald Graff calls literary theory "a discourse that treats literature as in some respects a problem and seeks to formulate that problem in general terms."[4] Some recent theory has claimed for itself a position as a master discourse rather than one of many discourses. Let us look for a moment at one of the most brilliant and influential theorists today, Fredric Jameson. When Jameson writes, "[O]nly Marxism can give us an adequate account of the essential *mystery* of the cultural past . . . by arguing its ultimate philosophical and methodological priority over more specialized interpretive codes whose insights are strategically limited as much by their own situational origins as by the narrow or local ways in which they construe or construct their objects of study,"[5] that is an ethical statement. It is also an example of how essentialism finds a home in the house of materialism. And his notion of history as an "absent cause . . . inaccessible to us except in textual forms" is only paying homage to language's need to be understood—hypothetically and within its "as if" metaphoricity—as essential. Graff rightly urges us to "think of literary theory not as a set of systematic principles, necessarily, or a founding philosophy, but simply as an inquiry into assumptions, premises, and legitimate principles and concepts."[6] Yet, all too often the energy and unruliness of a text disappear in the hegemonic claims made by followers of Marx, Lacan, and Foucault.

Jameson believes that if we can locate the master narrative of a particular age,

---

3. I have explored these distinctions in depth in my book *The Case for a Humanistic Poetics*. See also my "Culture, Canonicity and Pluralism: A Humanistic Perspective on Professing English."

4. *Professing English: An Institutional History*, 252.

5. *The Political Unconscious: Narrative as a Socially Symbolic Act*, 21.

6. *Professing English*, 252.

we can get at the political unconscious. For him, "only Marxism can give us an adequate account of the essential *mystery* of the cultural past." He disdains the notion of freedom from the "omnipresence of history and the implacable influence of the social."[7] Is Jameson's claim for Marxism an *ethical* approach toward texts and the variety of lived life? Or is such a reductive and extravagant approach unethical in its distortion of the specificities and differences of human experience? As an Aristotelian and pluralist, I ask why rewrite, resolve, and homogenize the whole rich and random multiple realities of concrete everyday experience into a monolithic story of the political unconscious?

I I

Let me state my credo. I believe that the close reading of texts—both from an authorial and from a resistant perspective—enables us to perceive more clearly; I believe in a continuity between reading texts and reading lives. I believe that the activity of critical thinking—not merely literary criticism—can be taught by the analysis of language. I believe in the place of the aesthetic. I believe that we can enter into imagined worlds and learn from them. Following Aristotle, I believe that the aesthetic, ethical, and political are inextricably linked.

In considering ethical reading, I want to differentiate between an **ethics *of* reading** and an **ethics in reading.** For me, an ethics *of* reading includes acknowledging who we are and what are our biases and interests. An ethics of reading speaks of our reading as if, no matter how brilliant, it were proposing some possibilities rather than reporting God's Holy Word; it means reading from multiple perspectives, or at least empathically entering into the readings of those who are situated differently. For me, an ethics in reading would try to understand what the author was saying to his or her original imagined audience and why, as well as how, the actual polyauditory audience might have responded and for what reasons. An ethics in reading is different from but, in its attention to a value-oriented epistemology, related to an ethics of reading. An ethics in reading implies attention to moral issues generated by the events described within an imagined world. It asks what ethical questions are involved in the act of transforming life into art, and notices such issues as Pound's anti-Semitism

7. *The Political Unconscious,* 19–20.

and the patronizing racism of some American nineteenth- and early twentieth-century writers. What we choose to read and especially what we choose to include on syllabi have an ethical dimension. Thus, I select other Conrad works for my undergraduate lecture course than the unfortunately titled *Nigger of the "Narcissus."*

Why did ethics disappear from the universe of literary studies? Was it in part the disillusionment of the Vietnam War that seemed to give the lie to the view after the Second World War that we could cultivate our minds and control our lives after the defeat of the Nazis and the Japanese? As critics, we once addressed the ethics of reading and the ethics in reading; that in part is what Arnold meant by "high seriousness" and Leavis by such phrases as "tangible realism" and "bracing moralism" and Trilling by "the hum and buzz of implication." All theory is in part disguised autobiography, and the recent emphasis on the meaninglessness of language and on the overwhelming power of history to produce cultural effects without allowing room for explanations that stress creative intelligence, as well as the emphasis on the transformation of the author into author-function, reflects a kind of skepticism about human agency; such skepticism at times approaches a harsh, abrasive ahumanistic cynicism.

Let me continue my credo: literary meaning depends on a trialogue among (1) authorial intention and interest; (2) the formal text produced by the author for a specific historical audience; and (3) the responses of a particular reader in a specific time. Texts mediate and condense anterior worlds and authors' psyches. The condensation is presented by words, words that are a web of signs but that signify something beyond themselves; within a text, words signify differently. Some words and phrases almost summon a visible presence; others are elusive or even barely matter in the terms of representation—as in Joyce's encyclopedic catalogs in "Cyclops." The context of any discourse determines the meaning—or should we say the epistemological and semiological value?—of the word or sentence. And once we use the word *value,* are we not saying that words have an ethical quotient? Human agency—on the part of author, reader, or characters within real or imagined worlds—derives in part from will, from the idiosyncrasies of the human psyche, and, in part, from cultural forces beyond the control of the individual. That is another way of saying that language is constituted and constituting, although it gives subjective human agency to the act of constituting. While we need to be alert to the implications of racist, sexist, and anti-Semitic nuances, we also need to stress reading the words on the page in terms of the demands made by the text's context and form—in particular, by its structure of effects, or what I have called the *doesness* of the text.

If self-awareness and one's relationship to family and community—including one's responsibilities, commitments, and values—is part of the ethical life, then reading contributes to greater self-understanding. Reading complements our experience by enabling us to live lives beyond those we live and to experience emotions that are not ours; it heightens our perspicacity by enabling us to watch figures—tropes, that is, personifications of our fellow humans—who are not ourselves, but are like ourselves. For me, books are written about humans by humans for humans, and elaborate "theories" that ignore narrative and representational aspects of literature in favor of rhetorical, deconstructive, or politically correct readings are unsatisfactory.

Let us welcome the turn to considering the relation between literature and theory but insist with Aristotle on the interrelationship between the political, the aesthetic, and the ethical. In prior academic generations, insulation from politics was mirrored in the supposedly objective and hermetic world of art, and New Criticism (and in more recent times deconstruction) often encouraged the binary opposition between art and life. For me, the intentional fallacy has always been to ignore how art is self-expressive and the affective fallacy has always been to ignore real readers reading. For New Criticism, the text existed in a Platonic world of ideas and was resolved in a unity that provided an aesthetic alternative to the political chaos—the Depression, World War II, the threat of nuclear war, the Vietnam War—that raged outside. Later, at the time of the totalizing vision of Reaganomics and accumulation of ostentatious wealth, texts were reexamined—sometimes by deconstructive picaros—for their rhetorical subtext that undermined unity and order.

Humanists have also been attacked implicitly and explicitly for not opening up the canon or profession on their watch. Yet, notwithstanding resistance from others in their generation, in the 1960s and 1970s it was often liberal humanists espousing free speech, respect for others, the value of listening, tolerance to diversity of ideas, who opened the door to the theorists and pushed for inclusion of diverse perspectives, including feminism and Marxism, and who welcomed women and minorities. But we intellectuals differ from cannibals in that cannibals only eat their enemies while we eat our friends, particularly our elders, our predecessors, and our teachers. For some, committing intellectual matricide and patricide has become a ritual of our profession. At times the younger turn on us elders because we are not as zealous as they in pursuing imagined ancient enemies. Are not we—in our conflicts—like the Torajans of Sulawesi who celebrate funerals by killing a member of a village that contains, as tradition has it, the weakest members of their tribe because, according to oral history, centuries ago that village didn't join the rest of the Torajans in a war against their ancient enemy, the Bugis? Do we not need to remember that all of us literary intellectuals belong to that odd collection of freemasons whose secret rituals consist of reading books, speaking about them to colleagues and students, and writing articles and books about them?

Why have concepts like objective truth, essence, nature, identity, and teleology—once-progressive ideas that insisted on the separation of the aesthetic from the political—become labeled as conservative and reactionary? As Graff remarks: "If one wished, a plausible case could be made for the view that the interpretive *objectionists* are the real heirs of the radical tradition which has sought to secularize and demystify the concept of meaning, and that the deconstructionists are carrying on a rearguard attempt to preserve some element of linguistic mystery from secularization."[8]

How has the evidentiary test for testing our readings changed? Dominick LaCapra has cautioned against overuse of "world-in-a-grain-of-sand anecdotes" as if these anecdotes imply universals; we should be as wary about finding the secret of a text in a few subversive lines. In the name of interesting or extravagant readings, have we strictly differentiated between logical argument and random association? Have we installed the critic/theorist as *vates* and substituted paralogic for logic? As LaCapra writes, "Old historicism sometimes placed a premium on aimless exhaustiveness and contextualization. New historicism often opts for a rather precious play of analogies, anecdotes, and associations."[9]

Graff has commendably argued that those of us who use contemporary theory need to defend the truth claims of our readings. In the act of doing so, do we not need to consider in our arguments issues such as narrative cohesion, agency, aesthetic achievement, and authorial intention? Because, on the whole, feminist and postcolonial readings have drawn upon the texture—I use that word deliberately—of lived experience, they have more frequently met the truth claims test than those extravagant readings that place being "interesting" before respect for what the text does say. The glory of the best of resistant read-

8. "The Pseudo-Politics of Interpretation," 153.
9. "On the Line: Between History and Criticism," 7.

ings—gay, new historical, feminist—is that they often meet the truth test and provide logical, plausible readings based on evidence.

When we enter into an imagined world, we become involved with what Nadine Gordimer has called "the substance of living from which the artist draws his vision," and our criticism must speak to that "substance of living."[10] In Third World and postcolonial literature—and in politically engaged texts like *Night*—this involvement is much more intense. Thus the recent interest in the postcolonial and Third World literature—accelerated by Wole Soyinka's and Derek Wolcott's Nobel Prizes—challenges the tenets of deconstruction. Literature written at the political edge reminds us what literature has always been about: urgency, commitment, tension, and feeling. Indeed, at times have we not transferred those emotions to parochial critical debate rather than to our responses to literature? While it may not be completely irrelevant to talk about gaps, fissures, and enigmas and about the free play of signifiers in the poetry of Wally Serote ("Death Survey") and Don Mattera ("Singing Fools"), we must focus, too, on their status as persecuted blacks in South Africa and the pain and alienation they felt in the face of that persecution before apartheid was abolished. Nadine Gordimer has written—and Joyce might have said the same thing about Ireland—"It is from the daily life of South Africa that there have come the conditions of profound alienation which prevail among South African artists."[11] When discussing politically engaged literature—be it Soyinka, Gordimer, or Wiesel—we need to recuperate historical circumstances and understand the writer's ordering of that history in his imagined world. We need to know not merely what patterns of provisional representation are created by language but the historical, political, and social ground of that representation. We need to be open to hearing the often unsophisticated and unironical voice of pain, angst, and fear.

When we read literature we journey into an imagined land, while at the same time remaining home. Reading is a kind of imaginative traveling; unlike real traveling, it allows us to transport ourselves immediately back "home." Travel is immersive; home is reflective. How we take our imaginative journeys depends on how we are trained to read: what we as readers do with the available data, how we sort it out and make sense of it. Although the text has a kind of stability because it cannot change, our ways of speaking about texts are always somewhat metaphoric.

10. "The Arts in Adversity: Apprentices of Freedom."
11. Ibid.

Aristotle, we recall, inextricably linked the ethical and the aesthetic—seemingly opposites. As Aristotle puts it in *The Poetics,* "Poetry"—by which he means imaginative forms such as tragedy and epic—"tends to express the universal, history the particular. By the universal I mean how a person of a certain type will on occasion speak or act, according to the law of probability or necessity."[12] His very stipulations about what constitutes a good tragedy imply that the artist has an ethical responsibility to his audience to provide a certain kind of action within a set of conventions. What interests Aristotle is what actions reveal about character: "Character is that which reveals moral purpose, showing what kinds of things a man chooses or avoids. . . . Any speech or action that manifests moral purpose of any kind will be expressive of character."[13] And this includes, I propose, any narrative, including narratives about the history of the profession or about a particular theory.

I I I

With the welcome return to mimesis and representation, cultural criticism has opened the door once again to historicizing. Culture is dynamic, and at any given point culture is heteroglossic, a dialogue of diverse thoughts, feelings, goals, and values. According to Isaiah Berlin, "Cultures—the sense of what the world meant to societies, of men's and women's collective sense of themselves in relation to others and the environment, that which affects particular forms of thought, feeling, behavior, action— . . . cultures differ."[14] We need to honor cultural differences and respect the claims of cultural enclaves. Clifford Geertz has written, "The problem of integration of cultural life becomes one of making it possible for people inhabiting different worlds to have a genuine, and reciprocal, impact upon one another."[15] While I respect and welcome other views of culture and understand that civilization has many components, I have been arguing for a cultural criticism that takes seriously the notion of canons, periods, and culture as the best that was thought and created during a period of civilization.

---

12. Aristotle, *Poetics* (1451, chap. 9), trans. S. H. Butcher, 205.
13. Ibid., 207.
14. "Philosophy and Life: An Interview," 50.
15. Quoted from *Local Knowledge: Further Essays in Interpretive Anthropology* (New York: Basic, 1983), 161, in Martin Mueller, "Yellow Stripes and Dead Armadillos," 30.

Let us turn to the concept of canon. Canon, as I have argued, needs to be an evolving concept, a house with many windows and doors, rather than a mausoleum. Within my pluralistic concept of canon there is room for enclaves to establish their own subcanons. I still value the major Western texts—the Homeric epics, the plays of Shakespeare, *Paradise Lost,* the great metaphysical and romantic poems, the masterworks of the novel like *Emma, Wuthering Heights, Jane Eyre, Moby-Dick, Middlemarch, Bleak House, Portrait of a Lady, Lord Jim, Ulysses,* and *To the Lighthouse*—but can we not within a healthy pluralism teach some common canonical texts, while also teaching texts which reflect our interests in burgeoning fields? A curriculum, I suggest, can be something of a smorgasbord, and our courses (and maybe syllabi) need to have room for teachers and students to both define a common cultural heritage and pursue their own interests.

The breakdown into enclaves and tribes—the effect, in part, of the end of the binary cold-war struggle between two superpowers—in the latter part of the twentieth century took the form of curricula battles between people who once thought that they had more in common than they had differences. If we are not careful, the Balkanization of English departments means we will talk to only those in our ethnic neighborhood. Often in a spirit of intolerance, political enclaves seek to *cleanse* the syllabi of objectionable texts—whether the objectionable works be by dead white males or by humanistic theorists. Canonical texts become—as James Clifford wrote of what the West had become for Edward Said—"a play of projections, doublings, idealizations, and rejections of a complex, shifting otherness."[16] The debate about who owns the syllabi and who owns the curricula and canon parallels the debate about who owns the land, whether it be the land of Northern Ireland, Hawaii, Palestine, or Bosnia and Croatia. It is as if cultural stratification were akin to geological stratification. In nineteenth-century American studies, there are black and female and Hispanic and Indian canons and cultural histories that are at once part of and separate from the prevailing hegemonic cultural history. For while the same groups inhabited the same space at the same time, their cultural history is necessarily reflected and refracted, displaced, sublimated, and transposed in different texts.

16. *The Predicament of Culture: Twentieth Century Ethnography, Literature, and Art,* 272.

I V

Let me suggest lines of inquiry to pursue in our reading and teaching of *Heart of Darkness*. Of course, we should regard the questions that follow as only instances of the multiple possibilities of a pluralistic approach. Let us think of these questions as concentric circles of inquiry, circles that vary in their relevance from reading to reading by one reader, from reader to reader, and from passage to passage. Let me point out, too, that my questions stress the inseparability of ethical, aesthetic, political, and contextual issues, and that the order of the questions is not meant to indicate their relative importance.[17]

1. How is *Heart of Darkness* a personal story written out of moral urgency that reflects Conrad's Congo experience and his own epistemological and psychological inquiry at a time of personal crisis in 1898? How can we use the Congo diary and Conrad's letters to relate his life and work? How is Marlow a surrogate for Conrad? If we see Marlow as a fictional surrogate for Conrad, how does such an approach relate to the fiction-making and masques of the late 1890s and the first decade of the twentieth century, as instanced in Wilde's *The Decay of Lying*, Yeats's poems, and Joyce's use of Stephen Dedalus?

2. How is *Heart of Darkness* a voyage of Marlow's self-discovery? Do we need to stress how that self-discovery takes place in a political frame and is a political reawakening? Conrad's narrative enacts the *value* that the Africans and Europeans share a common humanity: the English too were once natives conquered by the Romans, and England too was once one of the dark places of the earth. Moreover, Europeans not only require laws and rules to restrain their atavistic impulses, but they become more monstrous than those they profess to civilize. Finally, terms like *savage* and *barbarian* are arbitrary designations by imperialists who in fact deserve these epithets more than the natives.

3. How is *Heart of Darkness* a political novel concerned with the Belgian King Leopold's rapacious exploitation of the Congo? What attitudes do imperialists take to the natives and why? How is it, as Marxists would contend, a story about the "commodity fetishism" of later capitalism? Is it, as Chinua Achebe has claimed, a racist drama whose images reinforce white stereotypes about the dichotomy of black and white?[18] Is *Heart of Darkness* an imperialistic romance

17. Because of space limitations, my responses need to be limited, but I refer my readers to my article "Teaching *Heart of Darkness:* Towards a Pluralistic Perspective" as well as other discussions in this volume.
18. "An Image of Africa."

about the conquest of Africa? Or is it more accurate to stress how it is an iron-ic inversion, a bathetic reification, of such a genre? Are black and white and light and dark always equated with the polarity of civilization and savagery, good and evil, corrupt and innocent, or is the dialectic of images more subtle than that?

Conrad plays on the clichés and shibboleths of his era when Africa was the "dark continent"—the place of mystery and secrets—and the primitive continent where passions and emotions dominated reason and intellect. He asks us to con-sider whether we can cross cultural boundaries without transgressing them; we then need to ask: in situating himself in response to imperialistic exploitation, is Marlow able to separate himself from colonial domination? And can we as West-erners teach a story like *Heart of Darkness* in a non-Western setting without rein-scribing ourselves as colonialists? When we teach *Heart of Darkness,* are we in the same position as Western museums displaying non-Western art; that is, are we in-vading a different culture with our texts about colonialism? But let us remember that *Heart of Darkness* speaks with passion to the issues of colonialism and em-pire. Whether in Ireland, Malay, or Africa, Western colonialism in the name of civ-ilization despoils the people and the land it touches. *Heart of Darkness* debunks the concept of the white man's burden and shows how the concept of empire is a sham. Conrad chooses to show Kurtz's "Exterminate the Brutes" as a stunning abandonment of the moral pretensions on which imperialism is based. Kurtz's radical transformation exposes his reductive perspective and that of Marlow, King Leopold of Belgium, other Europeans—indeed, all of us who would seek to adopt a stance where one culture views another from an iconoclastic patronizing stance.

4. How is the disrupted narrative, the circumlocutious syntax, the alterna-tion between impressionistic and graphic language indicative of modernism? Should we also not think of *Heart of Darkness* as part of the awareness of mod-ern artists that multiple perspectives are necessary? After all, in 1895, Conrad wrote, "Another man's truth is a dismal lie to me."[19] We need to stress how *Heart of Darkness* takes issue with Victorian assumptions about univocal truth and a divinely ordered world.

Picasso's and Braque's cubist experiments demonstrate how they, too, are trying to achieve multiple perspectives. Conrad was freeing black and white from the traditional morphology of color, just as the fauvists and cubists were freeing traditional ideas of representation from the morphology of color. Con-

---

19. Letter to Edward Noble, November 2, 1895, in *Collected Letters of Joseph Conrad, vol. 1, 1861–1897,* ed. Frederick Karl and Laurence Davies, 253.

rad is also freeing his language from the morphology of representation—as in his use of adjectives for purely affective rather than descriptive reasons. Conrad's use of allegorized rather than nominalistic adjectives such as "subtle" and "unspeakable" invites the frame narrator and Conrad's readers to respond in terms of their own experiences and to validate in their responses that they, too, dream alone. When creating his Congo, Conrad knew Gauguin's 1893 Tahitian journal *Noa Noa* and was influenced by that and perhaps by Gauguin's paintings. Gauguin anticipated Picasso and other modernists in seeing the elemental and magical aspects of primitive lives as well as the passion, simplicity, and naturalness of primitive lives.

5. How does *Heart of Darkness* relate to the intellectual history of modernism? How is Kurtz indicative of the Nietzschean will-to-power that was a major strand of the intellectual fabric of imperialism and fascism? How does Conrad's text relate to his contemporary Freud's probing of the unconscious? How does *Heart of Darkness* speak to the breakdown of moral certainty, the sense that each of us lives in a closed circle, and the consequent fear of solipsism? Conrad feared that each of us is locked in his or her own perceptions and despaired in his letters that even language will not help us reach out to others. Thus, Marlow's fear that "we live, as we dream—alone" is also an idea that recurs throughout the period of early modernism, a period in which humans felt, to quote F. H. Bradley, that "my experience is a closed circle; a circle closed on the outside. . . . In brief . . . the whole world for each is peculiar and private to that soul."[20] That the frame narrator can tell the story shows that Marlow has communicated with someone and offers a partial antidote to the terrifying fear of isolation and silence that haunted Conrad.

6. How is *Heart of Darkness* a comment on the idea of social Darwinism that mankind was evolving into something better and better? *Heart of Darkness* refutes the position that history was evolving historically upward. Recall Conrad's famous letter about the world as a knitting machine, where the ironic trope of the world as a machine is a rebuttal to Christianity: "It knits us in and it knits us out. It has knitted time, space, pain, death, corruption, despair and all the illusions—and nothing matters. I'll admit however that to look at the remorseless process is sometimes amusing."[21] Conrad uses this elaborate ironic trope to speak to the late Victorian belief that the industrial revolution is part of an up-

20. *Appearance and Reality: A Metaphysical Essay*, 346.
21. Letter to R. B. Cunninghame Graham, December 20, 1897, in *Collected Letters*, ed. Karl and Davies, 425.

wardly evolving teleology; this belief is really a kind of social Darwinism. According to Conrad, humanity would like to believe in a providentially ordered world vertically descending from a benevolent God; that is, to believe in an embroidered world. But, Conrad believed, we actually inhabit a temporally defined horizontal dimension within an amoral, indifferent universe—or what in the above passage Conrad calls "the remorseless process."

7. How would a pluralistic approach address the meaning of "The horror! The horror!" as a part of an evolving agon that generates a structure of affects? Let us look at "The horror! The horror!" in the context of what precedes. That Kurtz has achieved a "moral victory" may very well be a necessary illusion for Marlow. But did Kurtz pronounce a verdict on his reversion to primitivism and achieve the "supreme moment of complete knowledge" (149)?[22] Or is this what Marlow desperately wants to believe? Coming from a man who "could get himself to believe anything," how credible is Marlow's interpretation that "The horror! The horror!" is "an affirmation, a moral victory paid for by innumerable defeats, by abominable terrors, by abominable satisfactions" (151)? When Kurtz had enigmatically muttered, "Live rightly, die, die . . . ," Marlow had wondered, "Was he rehearsing some speech in his sleep, or was it a fragment of a phrase from some newspaper article?" (148). Marlow had just remarked that Kurtz's voice "survived his strength to hide in the magnificent folds of eloquence the barren darkness of his heart" (147). If Kurtz had kicked himself loose of the earth, how can Kurtz pronounce a verdict on his ignominious return to civilization or an exclamation elicited from a vision of his own imminent death? For the reader—the reader responding to the inextricable relationship between the ethical and the aesthetic in Conrad's text—Kurtz remains a symbol of how the human ego can expand infinitely to the point where it tries to will its own apotheosis.

8. In what ways does *Heart of Darkness* reveal overt and covert sexist attitudes? Is *Heart of Darkness* a sexist document? Patrick Brantlinger writes, "The voices that come from the heart of darkness are almost exclusively white and male, as usual in imperialist texts."[23] In a situation where opportunities for heterosexuality are limited, what does *Heart of Darkness* say about male bonding among the whites and about miscegenation? Are we offended that one of Kurtz's supposedly "abominable practices" is the taking of a savage mistress? If we understand Marlow's patronizing attitude toward women as naive and simple, can

---

22. Page numbers in parentheses refer to the Kent edition of *Heart of Darkness*.
23. *Rule of Darkness: British Literature and Imperialism, 1830–1914,* 271.

we not use the text to show the difference between authorial and resistant readings, between how texts are read when they are written and how they are read now? Does the lie to the Intended reveal Marlow's sexism? Is Conrad aware of Marlow's sexual stereotyping, even if he means the lie to the Intended to be a crucial moment of self-definition for Marlow? We need to examine the assumptions about women that dominate this final episode, and to align them with the passage in which he tells us that the women are always "out of touch with truth." But, of course, the tale dramatizes that all of us live in a world of our own, and none of us is in a position to patronize the other, be it natives, women, or others who go to the Congo armed with ideals.

9. How is *Heart of Darkness* a heteroglossic text embodying diverse modes of discourse? Marlow's recurring nightmare begins not only to compete with his effort to use language discursively and mimetically but also to establish a separate, more powerful telling. The narrative includes the semiotics of a primitive culture: nonverbal gestures of the savage mistress and, yes, the Intended; the beating of the drums, the shrill cry of the sorrowing savages; and the development of Kurtz into Marlow's own symbol of moral darkness and atavistic reversion. This more inclusive tale, not so much told as performed by Marlow as he strains for the signs and symbols that will make his experience intelligible, transcends his more conventional discourse. Conrad shows that these instinctive and passionate outbursts, taking the form of gestures, chants, and litany, represent a tradition, a core of experience, that civilized man has debased.

V

Finally, why do we continue to teach and read Conrad? Does the concept of canon have value? Is it not the urgent questions—and, yes, their relevance to us and to our students' *minds*—that *Heart of Darkness* elicits that give it value today? We need a criticism that, as Martha Nussbaum has put it, "talks of human lives and choices as if they matter to us all. . . . [Literature] . . . speaks about us, about our lives and choices and emotions, about our social existence and the totality of our connections. As Aristotle observed, it is deep and conducive to our inquiry about how to live, because it does not simply (as history does) record that this event happened; it searches for patterns of possibility—of choice, and circumstance, and the interaction between choice and circumstance—that turn up in human lives with such a persistence that they must be regarded as *our* possibilities."[24] A study of modernist culture and the colonial Congo, Conrad's *Heart of Darkness* also speaks to our culture and raises urgent issues for us. Is that not why we read it, even as we consign some former canonical texts to the margins? Because it is an urgent political drama, because it raises questions of racial and sexual identity, and because it is a wonderful story that probes our identity with our human antecedents, *Heart of Darkness* lives for us as surely as Kurtz lives for Marlow, and Marlow lives for the narrator.

What does Marlow's reading of Kurtz teach us about our reading of texts and lives? As an allegory of reading, *Heart of Darkness* resists easy simplifications and one-dimensional readings, resists attempts to explain in either/or terms. Even as *Heart of Darkness* remains a text that raises questions about the possibility of meaning, it suggests the plenitude of meaning. Just as Marlow gradually moves from seeing a drama of values to living a drama of character, so as readers do we. Like him, we make the journey from spectator to participant. Are we not trying to make sense of Marlow as he is trying to make sense of Kurtz? And are we not also trying to make sense of the frame narrator who is trying to make sense of Marlow making sense of Kurtz? Does not the tale's emphasis on choosing a sign for our systems of meaning call attention to the arbitrary nature of choosing a framing sign and make us aware of the need for multiple perspectives? Do we not learn how one invests with value something not seen or known in preference to the ugly reality that confronts us? Is not Conrad's ironic parable about belief itself, including the Christian belief in whose name much of imperialism was carried on? Thus, in essence, the tale urges us toward a pluralistic perspective. Finally, one-dimensional readings bend to the need for a pluralistic reading that takes account of Marlow's disillusionment and his magnetic attraction to Kurtz as the nightmare of his choice. For Conrad has turned a story about a present journey to Africa into a journey through Europe's past as well as into each human being's primitive psyche. Our students remind us that narrative, story, and response in human and ethical terms triumph over excessively ideological readings. Our students remind us, too, of the need to link hermeneutics and rhetoricity; for them, "bits of absurd sentences" of their reading—to use Marlow's words to describe what he hears from the manager and the manager's uncle and tries to *read* in terms of his experience—need to be understood in terms of our most fundamental text: the story of our own lives.

---

24. "Perceptive Equilibrium: Literary Theory and Ethical Theory," in *The Future of Literary Theory*, ed. Ralph Cohen, 61.

VI

I conclude with a scene from the Book of Daniel when the Babylonian king Belshazzar is feasting and drinking from sacred vessels that his father Nebuchadnezzar had plundered from the Holy Jewish Temple in Jerusalem; suddenly a hand unattached to a body appears and writes mysterious words on the wall: "Mene, Mene, Tekel, Upharsin." But neither Belshazzar nor his followers can understand the words, which seem to be written in an unknown tongue. Desperate to know what has been written, Belshazzar summons Daniel, who has a reputation for wisdom. Daniel can read the words, which are in an early Semitic language, Aramaic, from which Hebrew is derived. Literally, Daniel explains, the words mean "numbered, numbered, weighed, and divided." But Daniel offers an ethical interpretation, foretelling the destruction of Belshazzar and his kingdom. Daniel's story of reading is a prophecy: "God hath numbered thy [Belshazzar's] kingdom, and brought it to an end; thou art weighed in the balances, and found wanting. Thy kingdom is divided, and given to the Medes and the Persians." In offering this interpretation, Daniel acts as a literary critic with an ethical bent and tells Belshazzar a story of reading.

Let us use the mysterious words that appear to Belshazzar and that require an interpretation as a parable of what readers must do. While Daniel's prophecy comes true, is it because Daniel knows and speaks God's will or because he is lucky? In any case, because most of us do not read texts with a sense that God has blessed our readings, we must draw upon our own intelligence, ethics, imagination, perspicacity, and experience. Whenever we read texts—or life experiences—we are a little bit like Daniel. Snippets of texts require that they be read, and yet they always remain partially understood or at least open to diverse interpretations. Texts—and our life experiences—cry out for understanding even as they resist our understanding. Since we cannot call upon Daniel, we have to be our own Daniel and do the work ourselves. To be sure, there are commentators and teachers—and theorists—who would be our Daniel, and we should make use of them. But, finally, we must interpret our words and experiences according to our own perspectives and believe in our intelligence, imagination, and ethics. Occasionally, we have works like Joyce's *Ulysses* or *Finnegans Wake* or difficult poems like Wallace Stevens's *Notes Toward a Supreme Fiction* (or, for some of us, an organic chemistry textbook) that seem to require the presence of an external Daniel; but even these reveal their mysteries to an experienced reader. Words that we read may have never before appeared to us in the context in which we see them now; even if we have read them before, rereading puts them in a new context, for we have inevitably changed. As for Belshazzar, for us words may have no prior significance other than their own manifestation; or, more likely, they may refer to something with which we are familiar. But they must always be understood anew and brought within the ken of our experience and values.

The Influence of Gauguin on
HEART OF DARKNESS

My approach to establishing the dialogue between literature and the visual arts includes the study of sources and influences, of intertextual relationships by which one art form illuminates the other, and of cultural configurations that develop from diverse artistic and historical phenomena. In this essay I want to use Conrad's reading of Gauguin's *Noa Noa* as a way of raising issues about race, gender, sexuality, colonialism, and nativity in *Heart of Darkness* (1898). Conrad, I shall suggest, probably knew Gauguin's journal, *Noa Noa*—based on his visit to Tahiti from 1891 to 1893—and probably wrote *Heart of Darkness* with that journal and Gauguin's Tahitian paintings in mind. When Conrad read *Noa Noa*—Noa Noa means "fragrance"—he would have been reminded of his 1890 journey into the Congo and his own even more sketchy Congo diary. I shall consider how Conrad supplemented his own journey to the Congo with Gauguin's texts and paintings.

Gauguin's process of disillusionment with European culture and his reversion to savagery as described in his 1897 version of *Noa Noa* formed a model for Conrad's depiction of his character Kurtz. Conrad uses Kurtz's reversion to savagery as a model for examining how African and so-called primitive material is inscribed in Western work. By pursuing the response of both figures to primitivism, sexuality, and wilderness, I raise larger issues about how Western modernism confronts and demonstrates *difference* and *other*.

Gauguin, and later Picasso and Fernand Léger, discovered the primitive at a time of growing *negrophilie*. As James Clifford puts it:

> Picasso, Léger, Apollinaire, and many others came to recognize the elemental, "magical" power of African sculptures in a period of growing *negrophilie*, a context that would see the irruption onto the European scene of other evocative black figures: the jazzman, the boxer (Al Brown), the

Originally published in my *Reconfiguring Modernism: Explorations in the Relationship between Modern Art and Modern Literature* (1997).

sauvage Josephine Baker. . . . The discovery of things "nègré" by the European avant-garde was mediated by an imaginary America, a land of noble
savages simultaneously standing for the past and future humanity—a perfect affinity of primitive and modern.[1]

Not only did Gauguin anticipate Picasso and Léger in his Tahitian paintings, but
in Conrad's *Heart of Darkness* and "An Outpost of Progress" (1897) we see early claims for the nobility of the primitive and for the perception of the innocent
impulses of the black Africans. It is the Westerners, not the savages, who have
the heart of darkness. Anticipating Conrad, Gauguin was interested in the *fris-
son* between Western European and other cultures. On his Tahitian journeys, he
brought along photographs of European paintings as well as of the Dionysian
sculptures in the Parthenon and the sensual sculptures of Borobudur.

In Gauguin's paintings we see multiple uses of non-Western material; to be
sure, we see the kinds of distortions that we find in Polynesian sculptures. Perhaps the bold expressive lines as well as the negative space derive from Japanese
prints. Gauguin clearly influenced Picasso's primitive masks in *Les Demoiselles
d'Avignon* (1907). The three-dimensionality of Picasso's *Two Nudes* (1906), *The
Portrait of Gertrude Stein* (1906), and *Les Demoiselles d'Avignon* owes something
to African sculpture. So does the simplification of forms, particularly facial features, and the disfigured faces. Matisse's *Two Negresses* (1908) drew upon Gauguin's fascination with the primitive. Matisse's only sculpture of more than one
figure, *Two Negresses* is an example of the African influence; as Jack Flam puts
it, "The anatomical articulation of the two figures owes a good deal to African
sculpture, especially in the relation between the buttocks and torsos and in the
breasts."[2] Based on a photograph of two Tuareg women, the work overflows
with sensuality.

As Griselda Pollack notes, Gauguin

> is usually perceived as having revolutionized Western art by rejecting the
> etiolated civilization of Europe and its cities by seeking to reconnect with
> basic human sensation, impulses and feelings in a rural paradise. . . . Per-
> sonal liberation through an unfettered sexuality and aesthetic refreshment
> through an appropriate and exploitative multi-culturalism—what the

1. *The Predicament of Culture: Twentieth Century Ethnography, Literature, and Art,* 197–98.
2. Jack Flam, *Matisse: The Man and His Art, 1869–1918,* 238.

modernizing European termed "primitivism"—are part and parcel of this nineteenth century myth of the tropical journey.[3]

Pierre Loti and Eugène Delacroix are sources for Gauguin's eroticism, but so was the nineteenth-century Romantic myth of a Golden Age. As Nicholas Wadley notes, "The nineteenth-century European view of the primitive life contained a strong sense of rejuvenation, of return to the unspoilt infancy of the human race. Gauguin shared this general view, but it also took on a more personal meaning for him: he constantly associated his mature escape from Europe with his own roots, his exotic ancestry, his childhood in Peru and so on."[4] And didn't Conrad as a Slav see in himself something of that primitivism in response to the decadent West? Isn't that one reason he was drawn to the primitive simplicity of the Bugi Malays?

Gauguin left France for the last time in 1895. In his second Tahitian period, 1895 to 1903, he painted far more mythic works such as *Where Do We Come From? What Are We? Where Are We Going?* (1897), his last painting before his 1897 suicide attempt. In this period he used the photographs from Borobudur. In *Te arii vahine* (*The Noble Woman;* 1896), an important influence is, according to Richard Brettell, "the reclining figure of a monk (*biksu*) from the high-relief frieze on the second corridor of Borobudur." While we have no proof that Gauguin saw this frieze in the Exposition Universelle of 1889, "the physiognomy of the head, the swollen proportions of the limbs, the softening of the contours, and the exaggeration of the feet that characterize Gauguin's nude" are more evident in the Borobudur figures than in any Western sources.[5] While the scene is from early Buddhist tales called *The Awadenas* and *The Jatakas,* Gauguin also wanted to place his painting within the Western tradition. Manet's *Olympia* is an important influence on Gauguin's South Pacific nudes of the 1890s, including *Manao tupapau* (1892) and *Te arii vahine.* Not only had Gauguin copied *Olympia* in Paris, but he also brought with him to Tahiti a photograph of the original.

Conrad was almost certainly indebted to *Noa Noa,* which was published in 1897 in the avant-garde journal *La Revue Blanche;* this version contained the original 1893 draft plus some new material by Gauguin's collaborator, the

---

3. Griselda Pollack, *Avant-Garde Gambits, 1888–1893: Gender and the Color of Art History,* 8.
4. Nicholas Wadley, ed., *Noa Noa: Gauguin's Tahiti,* 130. Page numbers in parentheses refer to this edition of *Noa Noa.*
5. *The Art of Paul Gauguin,* 399.

poet Charles Morice. Conrad surely would have heard of, if not seen, the Tahitian paintings. My quotations are from the 1893 draft published in Nicholas Wadley's 1985 edition because that draft is untouched by Morice and gives us the best idea of the discontinuity, spontaneity, improvisation, and fragmentariness of Gauguin's literary imagination. As a narrative formed by his visual imagination, Gauguin's text of *Noa Noa*, like his paintings, follows a modernist tendency to equate the autobiographical with the universal. He thought of his writings as dreamscapes. *Noa Noa* is also influenced by Voltaire's *Candide,* a text Gauguin admired.

Gauguin read his 1893 draft in Paris salons when he returned from his first trip to Tahiti. His appearances were the equivalent of contemporary talk television, except the audiences were smaller. Given that the Maori, his subjects—often idealized into paradigms—had an oral culture and their history survived in oral renditions, Gauguin wanted to render his narrative orally; his illustrations speak of a desire to render a culture that used visual language. He created a public persona, a figure of fascination who had returned from an exotic experience. Until 1895 Conrad was in close correspondence with Marguerite Poradowska, a distant relative whom he called his aunt, a cultured woman to whom he felt very close; she maintained an apartment in Paris, and she would probably have known of, if not attended, Gauguin's readings and known his 1892 Tahitian paintings.

While *Noa Noa* also may have influenced Conrad's Malay novels and short stories—*Almayer's Folly* (1895), *An Outcast of the Islands* (1896), "Karain: A Memory" (1897), "The Lagoon" (1896), and surely *Lord Jim,* which was published after the first version of *Noa Noa* appeared—my focus is on *Heart of Darkness.* To Conrad, fascinated by his own travels to exotic places, Gauguin must have been a kind of French Gulliver. Gauguin's escape to Tahiti parallels Jim's retreat to Patusan and his escape from the Western ethical framework after he fails on the *Patna* and no longer has a place in the maritime world. For Conrad, Jim's desire to eschew Home Service and to join the *Patna* in the first place is an indication of his flawed character. But Jim's Crusoeism is really the other side of his inability to meet the ethics and standards of the British Merchant Marine—to escape Home Service—as when he threw in his lot with decadent Europeans who savored the distinction of being white and were willing to serve "Chinamen, Arabs, half-castes."

At the outset, let me make clear that I am reading *Noa Noa* as a narrative that often reveals what it means to conceal. Gauguin's narrative is a kind of semi-

perceptive construct that is often evasive and contradictory. As if he were discovering the natural man within him, Gauguin speaks with pride about how
each day he became a little more savage and primitive:

> Every day gets better for me. . . . my neighbours . . . regard me almost as
> one of themselves, my naked feet, from daily contact with the rock, have got
> used to the ground, my body, almost always naked, no longer fears the sun;
> civilization leaves me bit by bit and I begin to think simply. . . . and I func-
> tion in an animal way, freely . . . every morning the sun rises serene for me
> as for everyone, I become carefree and calm and loving. (24–25)

(Soon, except for a loincloth, he is not wearing clothes.) In a note accompanying this page, he wrote of "The purity of thought associated with the sight of
naked bodies and the relaxed behavior between the two sexes" (74).

Gauguin wanted to preserve the naïveté of his narrator even while preserving in the voice his own disdain for the rottenness of Europe. Perhaps he had
imagined in their putative collaboration that Charles Morice's voice would be
the sophisticated written part, but, as we can see when we read the collaborated
version, the better and more perspicacious written part is Gauguin's. It is worth
noting that the Tahiti Gauguin imagined no longer existed, and that fact is a
source of the narrator's occasional anger. Most of what Gauguin knows about
Tahitian legend and myth comes from J. A. Moerenhout's two-volume *Voyages
aux Iles du Grand Ocean* (1837). The text for Gauguin's notebook *L'Ancien
Culte Mahorie* comes from Moerenhout, although he invented the fiction that
Tehamana, his thirteen-year-old *vahine,* taught him about Maori lore.

Yet, reading *Noa Noa,* we realize that Gauguin himself—far more than he acknowledges—oscillated between seeing himself as a Parisian and seeing himself as a born-again native. Ironically, Gauguin sees himself in the role of the
inferior and overcivilized European. That, while in Tahiti, he actively corre-
sponded with friends in France may have reinforced his sense that it was easier
to cast off his clothes than his European identity. Anticipating Conrad, Gauguin
used the journey to a primitive culture as an opportunity to ask central philosophic questions, as Gauguin does in the painting *Where Do We Come From?
What Are We? Where Are We Going?* As Wadley writes of the painting, "The questions of its title are all posed in the visual form of an opposition. Its extremes
are the depressed introversion and self-awareness of the thinking European on
the one hand and on the other the unaffected and irresponsible innocence of

the primitive being, who lives, loves, sings and sleeps" (124). Put another way, the painting dramatizes the epistemological journey Conrad's Marlow takes as he sifts through his experience in *Heart of Darkness*.

Gauguin's Tahitian paintings depend on a dialogue between East and West, between primitive art and the tradition of painting he knew. Gauguin's women have a fuller emotional life than his myth of Paradise would suggest. As Wadley remarks, "Gauguin's women have a brooding, inturned quality somewhat at odds with descriptions of the lethargic but carefree, loving children of a native paradise" (128). Beginning with the first one, they are basically whores—as young as thirteen; as Gauguin acknowledges, "I well knew that all her [Titi, his first mistress] mercenary love was composed merely of things that, in our European eyes, make a whore, but to one observer there was more than this. Such eyes and such a mouth could not lie" (14). In *Te arii vahine*, the Tahitian woman is a mysterious seductress, confident in her body; the black dog on the ground suggests animality, sexuality, and mortality. Conrad's mysterious, sexual native women—Kurtz's savage mistress, Jewel (a half-caste), and Aissa in *Almayer's Folly*—may owe something to Gauguin's Tahitian women, especially those from the first Tahitian phase. Except for his permissive sexual behavior, Gauguin's conversion to savagery was far less pronounced than that of Conrad's Kurtz.

Not only was Gauguin influenced by Egyptian, Assyrian, and Far Eastern sculpture that he had seen in the Louvre, but so, too, was Picasso. Anticipating Picasso, Gauguin used art to exorcise not only evil but also fear of aging and death. He believed that hostile forces are all around us. His reaching back to the primitive anticipates not only Conrad but also D. H. Lawrence's use of Indian myth in *The Plumed Serpent* and Egyptian myth in "The Man Who Died," and E. M. Forster's use of the caves in *A Passage to India*.

The occasion of Gauguin's voyage between 1891 and 1893 was his appointment to an official mission with no real duties. Indeed, we might recall how Marlow got his appointment through his aunt's intervention. Like Conrad, Gauguin begins by describing the voyage out, his first sighting of the landscape, and the corrupting influence of Europeans; when he describes the indifference of the French, we think of Marlow's disillusionment at the outer station. On the very first page of his journal Gauguin writes, "Having only just arrived, rather disappointed as I was by things being so far from what I had longed for and (this was the point) imagined, disgusted as I was by all this European triviality, I was in some ways blind" (12–13). And the theme of awakening insight is important here, as it is in *Heart of Darkness*. When Gauguin paints, "it was a portrait resembling what my eyes veiled by my heart perceived" (20). The first of the Tahitian paintings is *Vahine no te Tia* (*Woman with a Flower;* 1891). Gauguin sees the painting of a woman as a kind of seduction: "I realized that in my painter's scrutiny there was a sort of tacit demand for surrender, surrender for ever without any chance to withdraw, a perspicacious probing of what was within. . . . All her features had a raphaelesque harmony in their meeting curves, while her mouth, modelled by a sculptor, spoke all the tongues of speech and of the kiss, of joy and of suffering" (20). He inverts the expected meaning of what he calls "civilized people" and "savages" by showing us that the civilized French influence had undermined the savage innocence that he had expected and *imagined* existing before the arrival of the French colonialists. He finds that the savages are the Europeans and the civilized are actually the savages.

Just as Marlow turns toward an alternative to the cynicism and greed of the manager and the manager's uncle, so in *Noa Noa* does Gauguin: "Shall I manage to recover any trace of that past, so remote and so mysterious? and the present had nothing worthwhile to say to me. To get back to the ancient hearth, revive the fire in the midst of all these ashes" (13). He wants "To leave Papeete as quickly as I could, to get away from the European centre. I had a sort of vague presentiment that, by living wholly in the bush with natives of Tahiti, I would manage with patience to overcome these people's mistrust, and that I would Know" (Gauguin capitalizes "Know" for emphasis; 14). Anticipating Conrad, he sees his voyage as one backward in time to the antecedents of civilization. When he goes inland, he does not know how to gather food: "So there I was, a civilized man, for the time being definitely inferior to the savage" (20).

Gauguin's text fiercely attacks the Western illusions of progress and civilization. Like Conrad, Gauguin stresses how Western culture has imported not only sickness—syphilis in particular (from other sources, we know that Gauguin himself seems not to have been exempt from trading in this export)—but also alcoholism and moral decadence. Yet his experience contains many paradoxes. What he experienced was poverty, hunger, ill health, antagonism, and isolation; indeed, after a year he wanted to be repatriated, but it took two more years to get back to France.

Gauguin was fascinated with the uncorrupted innocence and sexuality of the Tahitians. In stressing the magnitude and purity of their emotions, whether anger, jealousy, or passion, he is an important source not only for Conrad but also for Lawrence, who believed that civilization corrupted the passions and feelings and reduced them to parodies of themselves. In *No te aha oe riri* (*Why*

Are You Angry? 1896), the profiled standing woman at the right suggests the fig-ure in Georges Seurat's *Sunday Afternoon on the Island of La Grand Jatte* (1894–1896); as Griselda Pollack notes, Seurat's satire of upper-class pretensions and manners is striking: "Seurat's painting not only differed critically from the sun-filled gentility and simulated spontaneity of Renoir's *Luncheon of the Boating Party* but made it seem fanciful, romanticized and hopelessly out of date."[6] Here we see Tahitians at leisure, but the title and the expression of the standing woman, who seems—in relation to the sitting figure on the right who is look-ing away—angry and accusatory in her stance of modesty and quiet but righ-teous indignation, make us aware of how Gauguin is transforming and ironiz-ing Western perspectives and assumptions. But as Brettell has noted, Gauguin hedges his bets: "The figures have a quality of classic ease, innocence, and grace that would have been immediately acceptable to a French bourgeois public ac-customed to nudes from the Salon."[7]

In *No te aha oe riri* the roosters to the right of the standing women imply male sexuality. They are a metonymy for the subject of female tension—that is, hormonal males—and as such are a comic version of the signified that is miss-ing from the human drama; the hens standing in between the standing clothed woman and the front-facing bare-breasted woman stress this parabolic aspect of the painting. The figures in *Two Tahitian Women* (1891) recall the way Manet's nudes—say in *Déjeuner sur l'herbe* (1863) or *Olympia*—confront the viewer. The red mash of papaya and mango stresses Gauguin's emphasis on col-or for its own sake, free of the morphology of representational codes. In this re-gard Gauguin anticipates Matisse and the other fauvists.

I I

Let us imagine Conrad's response to his reading of *Noa Noa*. Perhaps hearing about Gauguin's oral rendition, would he not have asked himself—thinking of his Congo and Malay experience—what if the European had be-come so disgusted with his fellow Europeans that he began, like Gauguin, to em-pathize with the primitive culture and then, like Gauguin at times, what if he lacked the moral and emotional tools to cope and became not only a sensualist but also a misanthrope and a cynic, and later a megalomaniac and a solipsist,

6. Pollack, *Avant-Garde Gambits*, 29.
7. *Art of Paul Gauguin*, 424.

namely a Kurtz? In *Heart of Darkness* Conrad responds to Gauguin's complex perspectives in *Noa Noa:* (1) Tahiti is Paradise—or rather it was before Western corruption; (2) Gauguin's speaker has discovered the *fragrance* of innocence within himself; (3) but he has also discovered a savage and atavistic potential when stripped of civilization. He understands that Gauguin has discovered not only an innocent primitive but also darkness within himself as a savage who enjoys a certain amount of violent behavior, including rape. Isn't Kurtz a perverse and ironic version of Gauguin's idea that reversion to primitive life can bring about rejuvenation from decadent Western influence? Like Gauguin, Kurtz has a mixed and complex heritage. Kurtz has a German name, but his mother is half English and his father half French: "All Europe contributed to the making of Kurtz" (117).[8] Gauguin romanticized about Inca blood in his veins. In Conrad the savages have been Europeanized by Westerners, even while Kurtz has become a self-proclaimed savage, a fate that Marlow resists in part because of his dedication to task, specifically repairing the steamboat to go down the Congo. In *Noa Noa* Gauguin wants to dramatize himself as a European turned savage, but the self-dramatization, as Conrad would have seen, is more complex; in *Heart of Darkness* when Kurtz reverts to savagery, he becomes a demonic figure.

What Cleo McNelly wrote of Conrad is also true of Gauguin: "For Conrad (and for Baudelaire and Lévi-Strauss as well) home represents civilisation, but also order, constraint, sterility, pain and ennui, while native culture . . . represents nature, chaos, fecundity, power and joy." It is the complex view of native life that gives both *Noa Noa* and the far richer narrative of Conrad much of their power. As Edward Said has noted in *Culture and Imperialism:* "Never the wholly incorporated and fully acculturated Englishman, Conrad therefore preserved an ironic distance in each of his works."[9] *Noa Noa* and Gauguin's Tahitian paintings resist the imperialistic discourse that stresses the superiority of the white man, but they do not propose their alternative—Tahitian paradise— as simply as it had once been thought. Yet by recognizing an alternative to materialism and acquisitiveness, by responding to passion, romance (or his version of it), intuition, imagination, and, yes, the essence or *fragrance* of experience, Gauguin does imply ways of resisting imperialism and finding interior and later external space for native cultures. And, as I mentioned in the previous essay, Conrad goes a step further, for *Heart of Darkness* speaks directly to

8. Page numbers in parentheses refer to the Kent edition of *Heart of Darkness.*
9. Cleo McNelly, "Natives, Women, and Claude Lévi-Strauss: A Reading of *Tristes Tropiques* as Myth," 25.

the issues of colonialism and empire, to the corrupting influence of European culture on African customs and civilization. Conrad plays on the clichés and shibboleths of his era when Africa was the "dark continent"—the place of mystery and secrets—and the primitive continent where passions and emotions dominated reason and intellect. He asks us to consider whether we can cross cultural boundaries without transgressing them, for in situating himself in response to imperialistic exploitation, is Marlow able to separate himself from colonial domination?

I want to take partial issue with Said's view that "Marlow and Kurtz are also creatures of their time and cannot take the next step, which would be to recognize that what they saw, disablingly and disparagingly, as a non-European 'darkness' was in fact a non-European world *resisting* imperialism so as one day to regain sovereignty and independence, and not, as Conrad reductively says, to reestablish the darkness."[10] Whether in Malay or in Africa, for Conrad, Western colonialism in the name of civilization despoils the people and the land it touches. As Marlow puts it, "We were wanderers on prehistoric earth, on an earth that wore the aspect of an unknown planet. We could have fancied ourselves the first of men taking possession of an accursed inheritance, to be subdued at the cost of profound anguish and of excessive toil" (95). Yet Conrad understands that the natives are part of a common humanity: "They howled and leaped, and spun, and made horrid faces; but what thrilled you was just the thought of their humanity—like yours—the thought of your remote kinship with this wild and passionate uproar. . . . The mind of man is capable of anything—because everything is in it, all the past as well as all the future" (96). Conrad wants to propose the possibility of human continuity, even as he suggests that perhaps civilization corrupts native energy. *Heart of Darkness* debunks the concept of the white man's burden and shows how the concept of empire is a sham. It is the narrator, not Marlow, who speaks of "The dreams of men, the seed of commonwealths, the germs of empires" (47). Marlow speaks about European newspaper articles that made ethical claims for the trade mission, articles that spoke of "weaning those ignorant millions from their horrid ways" (59). In *Heart of Darkness,* Western man is imaged as the idiosyncratic Brussels doctor who measures crania, the cynical manager and his more cynical uncle, the chief accountant of the outer station, and, of course, Kurtz. Isn't imperialism figured as the pail with the hole in the bottom with which one of the white men at the central

10. *Culture and Imperialism,* 30.

station tries to put out fires? Supposed emissaries of light, like Kurtz, become forces of exploitation.

Our multicultural perspective needs mention Conrad's use of Asian and Eastern contexts to comment on European behavior. A traveler who becomes transformed into a scathing critic of Western pretensions, Marlow is aligned by Conrad with the East: "He had sunken cheeks, a yellow complexion, a straight back, an ascetic aspect, and, with his arms dropped, the palms of hands outwards, resembled an idol" (46). A moment later the first narrator remarks on Marlow's lotus posture and contemplative demeanor: "[L]ifting one arm from the elbow, the palm of the hand outwards, so that, with his legs folded before him, he had the pose of a Buddha preaching in European clothes and without a lotus flower" (50). Marlow had returned from "six years in the East," the time presumably when *Lord Jim* took place. His familiarity with the East extends to Noh plays and puppet theater: the place-names in Africa, given by Europeans, "seemed to belong to some sordid farce acted in front of a sinister back-cloth" (61); perhaps such names as "Central Station" and "Inner Station" speak to the Japanese propensity to allegorize experience.

Let us return to *Noa Noa,* which is far from a panegyric of Tahitian life, and let us recall that Gauguin's paintings present a more complicated vision of Tahitian life than often has been supposed. For within Gauguin's written and visual paradisiacal lyric of Tahiti, too, is a strong overtone of discovering the forbidden, the atavistic, and the dimly acknowledged darker self. Readers of *Noa Noa* will recall that Gauguin's speaker's main pleasures seem to be sexual license and sexual variety, even with adolescents as young as thirteen, the age of his child bride; at times it seems like the hormonal appeal is central to his embrace of Tahiti. The original draft manuscript of 1893 says little about Tahitian life, culture, setting, and values. *Noa Noa* is in the genre of a journal—like the anonymous Victorian text *My Secret Life*—in which the author discovers sexual freedom.

Like Kurtz, Gauguin left a European woman—he a wife, Kurtz the Intended—behind and took a savage mistress; in fact, Gauguin took several. In *Heart of Darkness,* the savage mistress becomes a metonymy for the atavistic and primitive, indeed, for Africa itself. For Gauguin, Tahiti represented *difference*—difference from the so-called civilized world he had known—and *other.* He loved the spontaneous sexuality and unself-conscious nudity of the Tahitians. Like Conrad's Marlow, Gauguin's narrative voice tries to convey a mysterious dream, a world beyond his comprehension. We might recall that the hypnotic effect of Kurtz's voice has a kinship with the incantations of the savages rather than with the syntactical patterns of ordinary discourse. Kurtz's world takes shape from forbidden dreams of being worshiped and from libidinous needs that brook no restraint. In transforming his imaginative world into reality, Kurtz "had kicked himself loose of the earth. . . . He had kicked the very earth to pieces" (144).

Let us call attention to some aspects of our reading of *Heart of Darkness* that bear upon our current argument. After Marlow remembers having read Kurtz's report to the International Society for the Suppression of Savage Customs and hearing Kurtz's eloquence, Marlow's telling radically changes. His narrative becomes more inclusive of the gestures of the savage mistress and the Intended, the beating of the drums, the shrill cry of the sorrowing savages, and the development of Kurtz into Marlow's own symbol of moral darkness and atavistic reversion. Marlow's recurring nightmare begins not only to compete with his effort to use language discursively and mimetically but also to establish a separate, more powerful telling. This more inclusive tale, not so much told as revealed by Marlow as he strains for the signs and symbols that will make his experience intelligible, transcends his more conventional discourse. Conrad shows that these instinctive and passionate outbursts—taking the form of gestures, chants, and litany—represent a tradition, a core of experience, that civilized man had debased. In a brilliant surrealistic touch, Conrad makes Marlow's consciousness an echo chamber for the haunting sounds of his "culminating" experience. After recalling that Kurtz "was little more than a voice," Marlow finds that the past rushes in to disrupt the present effort to give shape and meaning to his narrative: "And I heard him—it—this voice—other voices—all of them were so little more than voices—and the memory of that time itself lingers around me, impalpable, *like* a dying vibration of one immense jabber, silly, atrocious, sordid, savage, or simply mean, without any kind of sense. Voices, voices—even the girl herself—now—" (115, emphasis added). The temporary breakdown of Marlow's syntax in the passage dramatizes the resistance of his experience to ordinary discourse, even as the simile comparing Kurtz's voice to an "immense jabber" reveals the challenge of his nightmare to language.

For Gauguin, there is a world beyond utilitarianism, materialism, and empiricism. Just like Kurtz, Gauguin is attracted to a native woman, but he is also a pedophile who has sex with young pubescent women, eventually marrying a thirteen-year-old. We should be skeptical about the claims by Gauguin's defenders that a thirteen-year-old Maori is really an adult. As Pollack writes, "the bourgeois European's fascination with what he desires but cannot have is recouped by projection onto an infantalized and primitivized woman. She is made a sign of a culture which is distanced and subdued, put in its place like a native child—wild, primitive, superstitious, but desirable."[11] As his letters and *Noa Noa* make clear, Gauguin, like Conrad, creates from his own experience. He transforms his perceptions of innocent sexuality into a spectacle. Most unpleasantly, Gauguin's concept of sexual freedom from civilization's constraints includes violent fantasies. Indeed, he speaks of the desire to rape women: "I saw plenty of calm-eyed young women, I wanted them to be willing to be taken without a word: taken brutally. In a way a longing to rape" (23).

Tahiti awakened atavistic and forbidden impulses in Gauguin; he not only speaks of the desire to take women by force but also acknowledges homoerotic impulses. The diarist of *Noa Noa* reveals his presumably latent homoerotic impulses when he goes inland from Papeete. Gauguin writes of his powerful attraction to a young male who was "faultlessly handsome" and "who wants to know a lot of things about love in Europe, questions which often embarrassed me" (25). One day he and the young male go up a mountain to get some rosewood for Gauguin's sculptures; Gauguin writes: "From all this youth, from this perfect harmony with the nature which surrounded us, there emanated a beauty, a fragrance (*noa noa*) that enchanted my artist soul. From this friendship so well cemented by the mutual attraction between simple and composite, love took power to blossom in me" (25). Gauguin was fascinated with what he called the "androgynous nature of the savage"; to him the Maori men and women had much more in common physically with each other than Westerners do. We don't know what occurs, but it is characteristic of Gauguin to break off when he approaches the moment of sexual union. His next words reveal how his European values shadow his supposed liberation from conventions: "And we were only . . . the two of us—I had a sort of presentiment of crime, the desire for the unknown, the awakening of evil—Then weariness of the male role, having always to be strong, protective; shoulders that are a heavy load. To be for a minute the weak being who loves and obeys" (25). It seems as if he were the passive figure in sexual intercourse between males. It is probably, but not certainly, only a fantasy experience, for Gauguin continues, "He had not understood. I alone carried the burden of an evil thought, a whole civilization had been before me in

11. Pollack, *Avant-Garde Gambits*, 68.

evil and had educated me" (28). Is this elision not an example of the hermeneutics of evasion, of narrative displacement?

In the past decade there has been a recognition of the importance of male bonding in Conrad and the realization that we need to examine what is going on between males. As Robert Ducharme has argued, male bonding in the Malay culture may well have included "explicit sexual behavior"; "[I]n warrior cultures, such bonds supercede all other attachments, including those to wives."[12] The homoeroticism of the warrior cults among the Bugi in Malaya gives us a way of understanding the commitment between Jim and Dain Waris. Marlow's attraction to Kurtz is not homosexual, but does it have an aspect of homoerotic fantasy at a time of great stress and the absence of available and culturally sanctioned—read *white*—women? As Conrad knew and hints on occasion, homosexual acts and homoerotic feelings were more common on ships long absent from port or among men in remote outposts without women. Is it not possible Kurtz's lack of restraint in "the gratification of his various lusts" includes homosexuality? Do the "abominable practices" of which Marlow speaks include that kind of male bonding? Does it explain in part the odd behavior of the Russian harlequin figure and his ties to the charismatic Kurtz, who, he says, "has enlarged my mind" (125)? Does it explain Marlow's temptation to go ashore for "a howl and a dance"?

Does Gauguin, we might ask, equate violence and license with freedom? Often his words have a more aggressive edge, as when he speaks in violent terms of how he wields an ax to chop down trees: "Savages both of us, we attacked with the axe a magnificent tree. . . . I struck furiously and, my hands covered with blood, hacked away with the pleasure of sating one's brutality and of destroying something" (28). Is this deforestation, we might ask, any more politically correct than the ivory trade's inexcusable depopulation of elephants? Gauguin believed that he had left behind everything that was artificial and conventional and had escaped the disease of civilization to become one with nature. But much of the text and some of his Tahitian paintings reveal more complex emotions. For example, in Gauguin's *Two Nudes on a Tahitian Beach* (1891/1894), the women eye each other warily and with tension, as if bound by some hidden emotion of anger or jealousy or a secret they share. They stare hostilely at each other. Is the woman on the left covering her breast out of sexual embarrassment, as if she were defending herself against a sexual accusation—whether it be spo-

---

12. Robert Ducharme, "The Power of Culture in *Lord Jim*," 19.

ken or unspoken—or is she provocatively answering the accusation by fondling herself? Is the painting unfinished to heighten the mysterious chasm between the two woman and to leave the text indeterminate, or did Gauguin simply fail to complete it? As we look at the painting, it is as if the savage mistress of *Heart of Darkness* and a native companion were standing on the shore of the Congo after Kurtz has departed with Marlow. Gauguin's two women could even be passionately attracted to one another. Perhaps the complexity of feeling hints at the *effects* of the colonial presence, most of which is ostentatiously absent from Gauguin's first Tahitian phase. Gauguin takes the expected symbolism of the dog representing obedience and implies that human life need obey the laws and rhythms of nature, but in the women's mysterious attraction—the passion and repulsion—he also suggests that we cannot control our emotional life or give it the direction we wish. It is the shared *knowing* between the two women that is both attractive and frightening.

III

Gauguin, like Conrad, was fascinated by nightmares, dreamscapes, and the unconscious. Marlow speaks of Kurtz as the nightmare of his choice. In *Noa Noa,* Gauguin wrote: "[T]he night is loud with demons, evil spirits, and the spirit of the dead. Also there are tupapaus, with pale lips and phosphorescent eyes who loom in nightmares over the beds of young girls."[13] Gauguin frequently included the *tupapaus*—spirits of the dead—in paintings. A painting like *Manao tupapau* (*Spirit of the Dead Watching;* 1892) speaks to the Tahitian belief in the life beyond the natural world. Gauguin was fascinated by pagan forms of devotion. (We recall parenthetically how in *Lord Jim* the two Malay steersmen aboard the *Patna* are sustained by the belief that the white men are ghosts who will return as mysteriously as they left.) In *Heart of Darkness,* as we have seen, Conrad's Marlow learns about intuition, instinct, ritual, chants, and spectral forms of knowledge.

Manao tupapau is also an ironic version of Manet's *Olympia*, which Gauguin had copied before leaving Paris. He was married to the thirteen-year-old who is his model and subject. In an early draft of *Noa Noa,* Gauguin makes clear that he based the painting on seeing the girl in the picture in the position depicted

13. Brettell, *Art of Paul Gauguin*, 281.

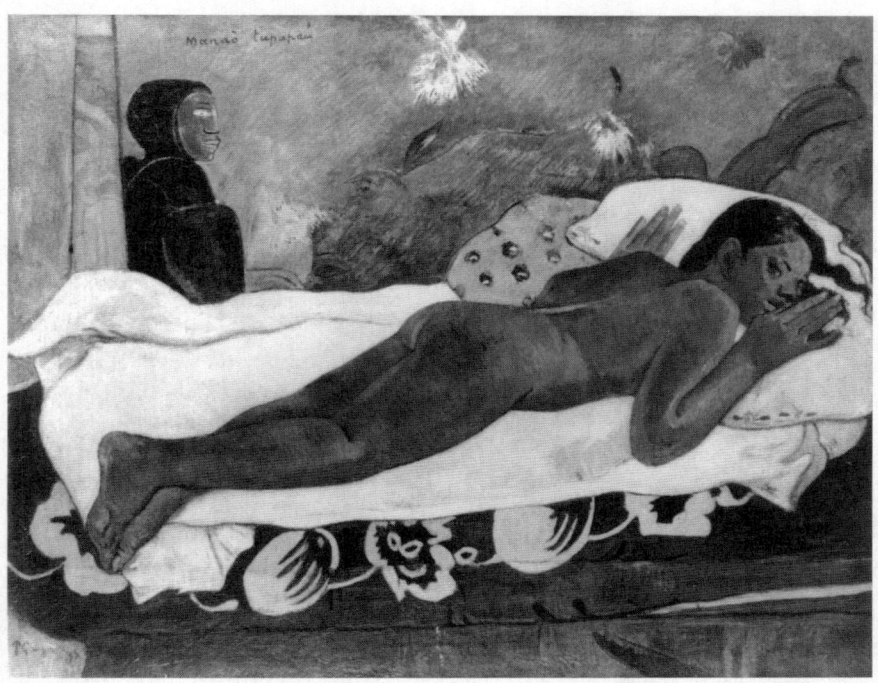

Paul Gauguin, *Manao tupapu* (*Spirit of the Dead Watching*), 1892. Alfred-Knox Art Gallery, Buffalo, New York. A. Conger Goodyear Collection, 1965.

and with an expression of dread. It is not clear from the painting whether the girl thinks of the ghost, or whether the ghost voyeuristically watching the girl creates the kind of complex perspective that would have appealed to Conrad; this complexity is framed by another perspective, the painter's, who reinscribes both possibilities without resolving them. Like Conrad, Gauguin is in the position of trying to convey a mysterious dream, an experience beyond his comprehension. The yellows and violets and the *hoti* flowers, as Bretell notes, "represent the [supposed] phosphorescent emanations of the spirits"[14] and suggest Marlow's ties to unseen devils; they also show Gauguin's dependence on form and color.

We note similarities between *Olympia* and Gauguin's *Manoa tupapau* in the juxtaposition of white and black. Discussing the similarities between the two

14. Ibid.

paintings, Pollack writes, "the massive bed across the plane of the painting on which is spread a naked body served up on a sheet of dazzling white linen, set off by a patterned background. In both there are expressive hand gestures, and the composition is based on a contrast between a supine nude and a clothed but upright figure." But in Gauguin's painting the maid becomes the spirit of death. Rather vatically and without any supporting argument, Pollack comments, "the shift is possible only through a signifying chain in Eurocentric discourse which slides from Blackness to Darkness and Death." In Manet we have two working-class women, maid and courtesan, black and white. Both paintings assume the gazing of a third party: "a viewer for the scene is invoked by the direction of the gaze of the woman on the bed."[15]

Gauguin's fascination with *tupapaus* recalls Marlow's fascination with spirits hovering over the land in *Lord Jim,* but perhaps more to our concern it recalls Kurtz's "taking a high seat among the devils of the land," and Marlow's commitment to Kurtz as "the nightmare of his choice." We recall Marlow's discussion of the various devils that haunt his imagination in *Heart of Darkness:* the ironic flabby devils of Western man and the incomprehensible devils and spirits of African life. After Kurtz's death, he says, "I remained to dream the nightmare out to the end" (150). While we cannot be sure, Conrad might well have known of Gauguin's paintings, including those with dreamscapes, nightmares, and diabolical themes.

That both Conrad and Gauguin see art as a kind of mystical and spiritual experience derives in part from the aestheticism of the 1890s. Like Marlow, Gauguin, too, thought of his narration as a dream: he described his writings as "without sequence, like dreams, like all life, made of fragments."[16] Marlow tells his audience, "It seems to me I am trying to tell you a dream" (82). The free association of Gauguin's narrative parallels the "segue" technique of Maori oral tradition and may be one source of Marlow's orally driven, complex reminiscence of his journey of self-discovery to the Congo. Marlow describes what he sees in a series of compelling images that can be thought of as cinematic or photographic but resemble more the heightened and distorted images of postimpressionist painting and the particular images of Gauguin. Such images arc the visual correlative of Conrad's adjectival rhetoric. Conrad may have been influenced by Gauguin or simply responded to the same desire to render memory

15. Pollack, *Avant-Garde Gambits,* 21, 23, 25.
16. Brettell, *Art of Paul Gauguin,* 145.

visually and performatively through speaking voices—Marlow's and that of the frame narrator.

I V

Kurtz's savage mistress might have been taken from Conrad's memory of a Gauguin painting or from his imaginative reading of *Noa Noa:*

> And from right to left along the lighted shore moved a wild and gorgeous apparition of a woman. . . . She was savage and superb, wild-eyed and magnificent; there was something ominous and stately in her deliberate progress. And in the hush that had fallen suddenly upon the whole sorrowful land, the immense wilderness, the colossal body of the fecund and mysterious life seemed to look at her, pensive, as though it had been looking at the image of its own tenebrous and passionate soul. . . . Suddenly she opened her bared arms and threw them up rigid above her head, as though in an uncontrollable desire to touch the sky, and at the same time the swift shadows darted out on the earth, swept around on the river, gathering the steamer into a shadowy embrace. A formidable silence hung over the scene. (*Heart of Darkness*, 135–36)

The similarity to Gauguin's images can be seen in the visual tableaux. Illustrating the ravages of imperialism, Conrad's visual images include the French gunboat firing into the bush, black men chained together, and the aimless blasting of the outer station. We see the grim images of starving Africans that have intermittently invaded Western consciousness:

> Brought from all the recesses of the coast in all the legality of time contracts, lost in uncongenial surroundings, fed on unfamiliar food, they sickened, became inefficient, and were then allowed to crawl away and rest. . . . The black bones reclined at full length with one shoulder against the tree, and slowly the eyelids rose and the sunken eyes looked up at me, enormous and vacant, a kind of blind, white flicker in the depths of the orbs, which died out slowly. (66)

It is as if Conrad were imagining a Hieronymus Bosch or a macabre James Ensor.

A crucial link between Gauguin and Conrad is that *Heart of Darkness* also contains a painting, namely Kurtz's painting of his Intended, which Marlow finds with Kurtz and expects to give back to the Intended: "I had taken him for a painter who wrote for the papers, or else for a journalist who could paint" (153–54). He had first seen the Intended's portrait at the Central Station: "Then I noticed a small sketch in oils, on a panel, representing a woman, draped and blindfolded, carrying a lighted torch. The background was somber—almost black. The movement of the woman was stately, and the effect of the torchlight on the face was sinister" (79). In its late-Victorian—perhaps Pre-Raphaelite—mode of painting, the portrait idealizes and allegorizes her: "She struck me as beautiful—I mean she had a beautiful expression. I know that the sunlight can be made to lie, too, yet one felt that no manipulation of light and pose could have conveyed the delicate shade of truthfulness upon those features. She seemed ready to listen without mental reservation, without suspicion, without a thought for herself" (154–55). Thus *Heart of Darkness* creates a dialectic between the European ethos and the African one, between the assumptions of an art that emphasizes truth to nature and one that renders diverse perspectives, interiority of subject, and the painter's imagination. The grotesque image is almost Surrealistic; Conrad has Marlow's visual depictions of the native women, the jungle, and Kurtz comment on the aesthetic assumptions of the staid and conventional portrait, just as Kurtz's moral devolution ("Exterminate all the brutes") and reversion to savagery have commented on the civilized moral assumptions.

The idealized portrait of the Intended influences Marlow's behavior in the final scene. What is striking is the difference between the conventional and stereotypical late Victorian portrait and the modernity and metaphoricity of Marlow's visual imagination. But can we be sure that Marlow can be trusted as a perceiver here? By depicting women in graphic visual terms, as if they were paintings on which to gaze—from the Manet-like depiction of the knitting women in Brussels ("Two women, one fat and the other slim, sat on straw-bottomed chairs, knitting black wool" [55]) to the savage mistress to the allegorized Pre-Raphaelite Intended—isn't Marlow revealing something about himself? Isn't he too a kind of painter? Marlow's visual memory of Kurtz is the kind of illuminating distortion that we associate with modernism: "He looked at least seven feet long. His covering had fallen off, and his body emerged from it pitiful and appalling as from a winding sheet. I could see the cage of his ribs all astir, the bones of his arm waving" (134). The figure of Kurtz occupies the entire canvas. Conrad anticipates the Surrealistic distortions of Ernst and Dalí and the powerful images of *Guernica*. Conveying elaborate ritual patterns, the image of Kurtz might be an African statue embodying spiritual insight and demonic transcendence. More important, Conrad's visual images are free from the mid-nineteenth century's morphology of representation and give the experience the form and perspective—even the lines and color—of postimpressionism.

Marlow's images reflect the movement in late-nineteenth- and early-twentieth-century painting away from realism to illuminating distortion, to the grotesque, and to the abstract. His experience in the Congo is, among other things, about the challenge to his visual expectations, particularly to his sight. Notice the *metaphoricity* with which Marlow's imagination transforms what he sees: "I came upon a boiler wallowing in the grass, then found a path leading up the hill. It turned aside for the boulders, and also for an undersized railway truck lying there on its back with its wheels in the air. One was off. The thing looked as dead as the carcass of some animal" (63). Or, note how the postimpressionist perspective—with its stress on light and shadow—of Marlow's response to the natives mixes foreground and background and focuses on sharply drawn physical shapes: "Black shapes crouched, lay, sat between the trees leaning against the trunks, clinging to the earth, half coming out, half effaced within the dim light, in all the attitudes of pain, abandonment, and despair" (66). Like Gauguin's paintings, these passages reveal as much as they conceal and depend on the perceiver's gaze to recompose them into significance.

V

A final word: As westerners, we might ask, How can we teach a story like *Heart of Darkness* with its non-Western setting without reinscribing ourselves as colonialists? When we teach *Heart of Darkness,* are we in the same position as Western museums displaying non-Western art, that is, are we invading a different culture with our texts about colonialism? But not so fast. Conrad was avant-garde for his time in acknowledging that, on occasion, Africans were more controlled and ethically advanced than Westerners; he, like Gauguin, knew that African cultural practices—chants, dance, drumming—were alien to Western concepts of display, that African art was religious in function and linked daily experience to abstract beliefs, and that African art was cultural practice, used performatively in funerals, weddings, and initiation rites. While Western history is preserved as literature, isn't Maori oral tradition preserved as memory and artistic objects? Memory, as Conrad and Gauguin stress in their oral narratives, is personal, selective, amorphous, and emotionally charged, while Western history is more objective, verified, and sorted out. Memory and history are intertwined not only in nonwhite cultures, but even—as Conrad understood—in Western culture. Has not Conrad's perspective seemed to have found confirmation in postmodern theory and the history and criticism it shapes?

Reading LORD JIM

I shall argue that the experience of reading *Lord Jim* enacts a dialogue between the major ideologies of reading on the late-twentieth-century critical mind-scape—deconstruction and what I call humanistic formalism—and that *Lord Jim* privileges the reading of humanistic formalism, which urges an absolute judgment on Jim's behavior and an organic and coherent text, over the decon-structive reading, which raises questions about the possibility of formal unity, explanations of behavior, and standards of judgment. Ultimately, *Lord Jim* af-firms the possibility of significance and values, and refuses to endorse the rela-tivity of Marlow or the solipsism of Stein.

Since J. Hillis Miller is perhaps the most influential of the deconstructionists working in prose fiction, I would like to take a moment to look at his argument about *Lord Jim*. In his chapter on *Lord Jim* in *Fiction and Repetition,* Miller has proposed that the repetition—the structural and thematic doubling that dom-inates the language and form of *Lord Jim*—implies that Jim's behavior cannot be explained. By contrast, I shall contend that Jim's behavior can be judged. *Lord Jim* proposes—and Conrad expects the reader to perceive—a hierarchy of ex-planations. But to see the hierarchy, one has to understand that the omniscient narrator proposes an absolute judgment, just as surely as Marlow proposes a rel-ative one based on his complex and often sympathetic understanding of Jim. When Miller contends that *Lord Jim* lacks the reliable narrator of Victorian fic-tion, he is misreading the first four chapters. Miller argues that *Lord Jim* "reveals itself to be a work which raises questions rather than answering them. . . . The indeterminacy lies in the multiplicity of possible incompatible explanations given by the novel and the lack of evidence justifying a choice of one over the others."[1] By contrast, I shall be arguing that *Lord Jim* in its complex and eccen-tric way answers the questions it raises.

Originally published in *The Transformation of the English Novel, 1890–1930: Studies in Hardy, Conrad, Joyce, Lawrence, Forster, and Woolf* (1989).
1. *Fiction and Repetition: Seven English Novels,* 39–40.

Our first critical task is to recall that *Lord Jim* has three separate tellings: first, the omniscient narrator's presentation of Jim in the first four chapters; on occasion this voice returns to remind us of his presence; second, Marlow's long monologue from chapters 5 through 35; and third, Marlow's response to Jim's demise on Patusan, which takes the form of an epistle received by one of the listeners to his monologue.

Let us recall Conrad's ironic trope for the cosmos of a knitting machine (from the 1897 letter to Cunninghame Graham that I quoted in the first essay) that indifferently knits a "remorseless process." According to Conrad, we recall, humankind would like to believe in a providentially ordered world vertically descending from a benevolent God—that is, to believe in an embroidered world. But we actually inhabit a temporally defined horizontal dimension within an amoral, indifferent universe—or what Conrad calls "the remorseless process."[2]

In *Lord Jim,* in particular, Conrad dramatizes that humans always judge one another in terms of their own psychic and moral needs at the time that they are making judgments. Put another way, we recall that Conrad believes that "another man's truth is a dismal lie to me."[3] But—and here I shall iterate a major point in my first chapter, but one for which *Lord Jim* is a paradigmatic example in the Conrad oeuvre—notwithstanding the fallibility of all judgments, we must strive to make objective judgments and to sustain values and ideals, even if we know that we will always fall short of them. Thus when Conrad writes that all is illusion, he means that all we can do is make working arrangements with the cosmos, and that there are no absolute values derived from an external source. But he does not mean that all values are equal. Similarly, merely because we cannot discover an absolute, final, original reading, it does not follow that all readings are equal. Rather, as readers, even while acknowledging that our readings are a function of our limitations, we must strive to establish judgments and values within complex texts. By affirming the value of the search for meaning in the lives of his characters within his imagined world, Conrad is rhetorically enacting the value of this search in our reading of texts.

The process of reading *Lord Jim* involves the reader in the remorseless process of responding to different judgments of Jim's behavior. First, there is the judgment of the omniscient narrator that precedes not only our meeting Marlow but also our learning what happens on the *Patna.* Does the reader ever forget

2. In *Collected Letters of Joseph Conrad, vol. 1, 1861–1897,* ed. Frederick Karl and Laurence Davies, 425.
3. In ibid., 253.

the original rigorous judgment established by the omniscient narrator in the first three chapters, a judgment that is based on adherence to absolute standards? Does not that judgment accompany the reader as he wends his way through Marlow's narrative of his own efforts to find some terms with which to understand Jim's terrible failure on the *Patna* when Jim, along with the rest of the white officers, abandons the native crew and passengers? And, of course, the reader must sort out the significance of Stein's oracular but hazy pronouncements. No sooner do we hear Marlow's judgment delivered in his long monologue after knowing that Jim has succeeded on Patusan and, at least in Marlow's eyes, justified Marlow's confidence in him, than we are confronted with Marlow's final, inconclusive judgment after Jim has failed; this judgment is halfway between the rigorous one of the absolute narrator and the empathetic one that had informed Marlow's telling.

Let me conclude my introduction by outlining the program for the rest of this essay. In my next four sections I shall focus respectively on the function of the omniscient narrator in the novel's opening chapters; on Marlow's complex response to Jim; on the role of Stein, that odd figure who inhabits the middle of the novel; and on the implications of the ending for shaping our final response to the novel. Finally, in the last section I shall offer suggestions for reading *Lord Jim* that have implications for reading other novels.

I. THE FUNCTION OF THE OMNISCIENT NARRATOR

Prior to Marlow's first words in chapter 5, the omniscient narrator in the opening chapters judges Jim by fixed standards and shows him wanting. Without any ambiguity, Conrad uses this narrator to show us that Jim's jump from the *Patna* is a characteristic one rather than—as Jim would like to believe and as Marlow is at times tempted to accept—a gratuitous action that just happened to an unfortunate young man.

Lost in his fantasies of heroism, Jim fails to respond to an emergency on the training ship. Because Jim has not internalized the proper responses, when he is faced with an actual chance to take part in a rescue he becomes physically and morally paralyzed: "He stood still. It seemed to him he was whirled around" (5).[4]

---

4. Page numbers in parentheses refer to the Norton Critical edition of *Lord Jim*, ed. Thomas Moser.

But he rationalizes that he had not really failed: "The gale had ministered to a heroism as spurious as its own pretence of terror. . . . [A] lower achievement had served the turn. He had enlarged his knowledge more than those who had done the work. When all men flinched, then—he felt sure—he alone would know how to deal with the spurious menace of wind and seas" (7). The strength and resilience of Jim's imagination enable him to forget his failure, and to transfer—in the phrases "the pretence of terror" and "the spurious menace"—the *pretense* of his courage and the *spurious* quality of his fantasies to the physical events that revealed his pretense. We should note that, at this point before he succumbs to the temptation of the exhortation to "Jump," Jim is a kind of magician with language—a poet—who can arbitrarily rearrange words as he sees fit.

Jim's second failure is when, while serving as first mate, he loses his nerve. The omniscient narrator tells us that until then Jim had never been tested by "those events of the sea that show in the light of day the inner worth of a man, the edge of his temper, and the fibre of his stuff; that reveal the quality of his resistance and the secret truth of his pretences, not only to others, but also to himself" (7). Notice how the narrator ironically applies to Jim the term "pretence"—the very word Jim had used to describe the gale on the training ship. When the storm strikes, Jim is disabled: "[He] spent many days stretched on his back, dazed, battered, hopeless, and tormented as if at the bottom of an abyss of unrest. . . . He lay there battened down in the midst of a small devastation, and felt secretly glad he had not to go on deck. . . . [He felt] a despairing desire to escape at any cost" (8). The "abyss of unrest" looks forward to the abyss or "everlasting deep hole" (68) into which Jim jumps, while the word "secretly" not only scathingly echoes and exposes the secret truth of *Jim's* pretenses, but also reinforces our sense of the immense schism between the man Jim would be and the man he is. With bitter irony and without any interrupting transition, the omniscient narrator concludes the above paragraph: "Then fine weather returned, and [Jim] thought no more about it" (8). In the "despairing desire to escape at any cost," do we not sense a foreshadowing of Jim's suicide at the novel's end? Like Jukes in Conrad's 1902 novella "Typhoon," Jim has an imaginative ability to think of *what might possibly happen* that leads him through corridors of terrible fantasies and finally to a nervous exhaustion indistinguishable from catatonia. Didn't Conrad himself, the seaman who would be an author, fear that what the omniscient narrator calls "Imagination, the enemy of men, the father of all terror" would prey upon his own capacity for action (8)?

Conrad's narrative coding continues to create a concatenation of episodes that judges Jim's moral dereliction and psychological incapacity. Each episode iterates the prior one's indictment, even while it adds another piece of evidence to the charge that Jim has not internalized the fixed moral standards of the merchant marine—the code stipulating honor, fidelity, courage, and a highly developed sense of responsibility—on which civilized life in the colonies depends. Thus Jim, after he recovers from his leg injury, throws in his lot with those who eschew the "home service" of the merchant marine for easier employment:

> They loved short passages, good deck-chairs, large native crews, and the distinction of being white. . . . They talked everlastingly of turns of luck . . . and in all they said—in their actions, in their looks, in their persons— could be detected the soft spot, the place of decay, the determination to lounge safely through existence. (9)

As in the above passage, it is characteristic of Conrad to introduce parallel phrases with recurring words; within a sentence these phrases often increase in intensity as they move to an explosive conclusion; thus in the first of the above sentences, Conrad's appositional phrases move from the rather neutral descriptive phrases to the morally intense and scathing indictment (in the climactic phrase "the distinction of being white") of those who believe they are privileged on racial grounds. While Jim assumes that he will not be tarnished by the company of the kind of men who choose to work on boats like the *Patna,* the ironic narrator places Jim among these men with soft spots and places of decay. Conrad's adjectives here do not so much describe an internal condition as they participate in a structure of effects to give the reader a sense of Jim's moral flaw. We cannot visualize a soft spot or a place of decay any more than we can see an "*invisible* halt" in Jim's gait.

The fourth episode or vignette that inexorably illustrates that, contrary to Jim's contention, his jump was a characteristic rather than a gratuitous action is his behavior on board the *Patna;* as on the training ship his mind is wooed from his duty to the "human cargo" of pilgrims by fantasies of accomplishment: "[H]is thoughts would be full of valorous deeds: he loved these dreams and the success of his imaginary achievements. They were the best part of his life, its secret truth, its hidden reality" (13). That the words "achievement" and "secret" echo prior passages documenting his flawed nature shows how Jim is iterating his past as he will throughout his life. Repeating the term "secret"—which has, as Stephen

Marcus has shown in *The Other Victorians,* a sexual connotation (as in *My Secret Life*)—underlines how Jim has separated himself from reality and has paradoxically created *in his actions*—as opposed to his dreams—a self that has no social role to play; Conrad thus gives the nuance of narcissism to Jim's self-indulgent fantasies. Living in the world of his fictions rather than in the world of actual duties and responsibilities, Jim is a hopelessly divided self unfit for his tasks.

Cumulatively, these four vignettes stand as an absolute judgment of Jim, a judgment based on applying the rigorous standards of the merchant marine, which, Conrad believed, were the essential underpinnings to life at sea and to colonial life in primitive areas. Even as Marlow becomes an apologist for Jim, even as he uses Jim's case to look into his own case and the moral nature of all men, these vignettes retain their validity and accompany our reading, just as surely as Jim's past experience accompanies him after he abandons ship and wanders from place to place trying to catch up with his irrevocably lost self.

Conrad uses the omniscient narrator to establish that, contrary to Jim's argument to Marlow, Jim's jump was not something that could have happened to anyone but was, rather, the inevitable result of a character flaw. The omniscient narrator conducts his trial—performs Jim's trial for the reader—before the actual trial at which Marlow meets Jim. By beginning the novel with an omniscient voice that clinically and ironically shows that Jim's jump is characteristic of a morally flawed person, Conrad gives the reader a standard—a moral barometer—from which he cannot escape. Just as Jim feels imprisoned by a "serried circle of facts" after he has jumped and must explain what happened to the human community and, in particular, to a tribunal of his peers, Conrad has created in the remarkable opening chapters a narrative code that uses "a serried circle of facts" to indict Jim and imprison him. Conrad thus prevents the reader from fully joining Marlow's subsequent apologia for Jim. Moreover, by scrupulously alerting the reader to Jim's process of rationalization and self-delusion, Conrad rhetorically prepares the reader to judge Marlow's myopia when he, Marlow, begins to rationalize both his own responses to Jim and, increasingly, his own behavior.

II. MARLOW'S ALL-TOO-HUMAN JUDGMENT

Originally, Marlow wanted to judge Jim by absolute standards. Marlow would have liked to read Jim as if he, Marlow, were the omniscient narrator, and, indeed, for a brief moment, Conrad teases us into thinking that we have been listening to Marlow—or at least an omniscient double of Marlow—all along. In the first moments of his monologue about Jim, Marlow aligns Jim with beetles, criminals, alloyed metal, and "men with soft spots, with hard spots, with hidden plague spots" as if he were going to continue the narrator's indictment (21).

But the self-dramatizing Marlow soon reveals that he is vulnerable to those who, like Jim, claim extenuating circumstances because Marlow does not sufficiently believe in himself to uphold absolute values. Marlow cannot, as Stein will advise, shut his eyes and see himself as a fine fellow, a saint. He must face the ambiguity of living in a relative world that lacks anterior concepts of order. Because of his own needs, he begins to read Jim as Jim would like him to. In Marlow's evolving sympathy with Jim as "one of us," in Marlow's taking up a position as Jim's apologist, in his gnawing and disturbing suspicion that he may not be able to claim a superior moral position because anyone might do what Jim did, Marlow begins to abandon the credo of the merchant marine and British imperialism and increasingly allows Jim to become a standard by which he, Marlow, measures himself. But the omniscient narrator has taught us not to be a Jim-reader of Jim, and when Marlow becomes a Jim-reader of Jim, we back off from accepting Marlow's authority as a reader of himself. In Marlow's world, once he loses his beliefs in fixed standards, there are no sources or origins and everything exists—as the replicating text indicates—as a variation of the other; such infinite variation makes judgments difficult.

As Marlow becomes an apologist for Jim, the reader is expected to adopt a stance of judgment toward Marlow—is expected to see that Marlow, too, is a fallible human being who is different in degree but not in kind from Jim. On three occasions Conrad undercuts Marlow's pretensions to moral authority: first, during Jim's trial, when Marlow offers Jim Brierly's plan to evade the trial and escape the rituals of civilized judgment (93); second, when Marlow goes to Stein because he wishes to "dispose" of Jim, in part to avoid his bizarre fear of having Jim—in the role of a common vagrant—confront him in London; and, finally, when Marlow, during his visit to Patusan, loses control in his interview with Jewel for no reason other than his own need to assure himself that he is better than Jim at a time when Marlow's ability to make moral distinctions is threatened: "I felt the sort of rage one feels during a hard tussle . . . 'You want to know [why the world does not want him]?' I asked in a fury. 'Yes!' she cried. 'Because he is not good enough,' I said brutally" (194). Marlow's self-indulgent indiscretion—what purpose is served by telling Jewel that Jim is not good enough?—strikingly contrasts with the climax of *Heart of Darkness*. There, we recall, when an embittered and disillusioned Marlow returns to Europe, he is, although he hates a lie, willing to lie to the Intended and to let her think that Kurtz's last words were her name in order that she have the sustaining illusion of Kurtz's undying devotion.

The novel questions the possibility of absolute standards in other ways. That Brierly, the precociously successful young captain who seems to have achieved everything that Jim dreams of, and who seems to be the very man most suitable to judge Jim, kills himself after serving on the tribunal at Jim's trial structurally illustrates the impossibility of one man judging another. Who could have had better personal and professional credentials to judge Jim than Brierly, whose career trajectory was the exact opposite of Jim's? Yet, looking into Jim's case, Brierly begins to look into his own and begins to believe that what one person does any person can do. Does not Brierly's radical empathy become a warning to the reader of what could happen to Marlow if he allows the distance between himself and Jim to close? (We recall "The Secret Sharer," where the captain irrationally identifies with the escaped murderer Leggatt, with whom he has very little in common and whose values are diametrically opposed to his own.) Isn't Conrad using Brierly's strong misreading of Jim's life to issue a rhetorical warning to the reader to strive for distance and judgment and to avoid the radical empathy that leads to flagrant misreading? Within the text, we are being told to attend to the rhetoric of the text and not to create our own text. To recall my subtitle: "Reading Texts, Reading Lives."

Throughout the novel, the omniscient narrator's judgment coexists with Marlow's inevitably human, somewhat sentimental, and finally flawed perspective.[5] Even when we as readers participate in Marlow's search for explanations, even when we are moved by his efforts to make sense of Jim's behavior and his, Marlow's, own life, the original, objective judgment of Jim remains engraved on our minds. While Marlow's judgment is wavering, relative, and unsure of its ground, the omniscient narrator's judgment is absolute and refers to anterior standards. To read *Lord Jim* properly, one must hold in mind these contradictory perspectives.

Do not the absolute judgment of the omniscient narrator and the relative,

---

5. I discuss Marlow's shortcomings in greater detail in my *Conrad: "Almayer's Folly" to "Under Western Eyes."* See my *Lord Jim* chapter, pp. 76–97.

human judgment of Marlow revolve around one another as we read *Lord Jim?* As humans with our doubts and anxieties, with the memories of our failures, and fears about our shortcomings, we are prone to the kind of humane, and, yes, on occasion, sentimental sympathy and radical empathy with which Marlow responds to Jim. In current terms, it is tempting to say that these judgments deconstruct one another so that neither becomes privileged. Indeed, Marlow's reading of Jim can be taken as a model for intratextual reading based on contiguous relations within a text, while the omniscient narrator's reading depends on a belief in anterior standards. The paradox is that here it is the humanistic reading that is deconstructing the novel's—and the reader's—quest for unity.

But while Marlow enacts the moment of irreconcilable impasse or *aporia* of modernism, Conrad, I am arguing, does not. For, as we have seen, Conrad's omniscient voice stands in judgment of Jim's behavior and of Marlow's understandable efforts as one of us—lonely, doubting humans in a confusing world that Conrad thought of as a "remorseless process"—to explain Jim's behavior. Conrad expects the reader to understand that Marlow's confidence in absolute values has been undermined by his own experience, and that we readers must, like judges, sift through the data as objectively as possible, even while recognizing that, like Brierly and Marlow, we are all prone to skewed judgments based on our own needs. But while the novel tempts us to be a Jim-reader of Jim, or a Brierly-reader or a Stein-reader, and even more urgently to be a Marlow-reader—who at times is a Jim-reader, a Brierly-reader, and a Stein-reader—it finally insists on our being an omniscient reader and as unforgiving and unyielding in our judgments as the omniscient narrator.

The taut organic unity of the novel in which every part echoes every other part and in which every word rings with resonance is the significant form for establishing a world dense with meaning and judgment. It is the form—including the relationship between the romantic second part in unexplored Malaysian islands and the realistic first part within the colonized East where western maritime values have gained a foothold, between the part dominated by the *Patna* and the part dominated by Patusan—that enables Conrad to reclaim the subject, center the meaning, and reject *aporia*. Does not even such a small matter as the name "Patusan" being an anagram of the letters of *Patna* plus "us" remind the reader of the community commitment that Jim lacked on board the ship? Does not the novel's doubling call attention to the almost reflexive nature and organic form of Conrad's fictive world?

III. THE FUNCTION OF STEIN

The oracular Stein makes a claim for omniscience, or, rather, Marlow, in search of a telos or ultimate meaning, seeks to apotheosize Stein. By placing Stein in the center of the novel, by endowing his life with heroic proportions that make him an image of what Jim would like to be, by giving him a history that in many ways echoes that of Jim (excluding, of course, jumping ship), and, finally, by giving him the ambiguous speech of an oracle figure, Conrad arouses the reader's expectations that Stein may solve the novel's moral issues.

Let us look briefly at Stein's argument. Stein proposes that man must existentially commit himself to one's ideals as a means of dealing with the "destructive element." Shouldn't we think of that element as the necessary result of an indifferent, amoral cosmos that Conrad conceived in terms of a machine that insisted on knitting rather than embroidering? Because Jim has not internalized his dreams, because they do not support his ego-ideals, he cannot sustain his dreams. Man has a need to fulfil anterior ideals and at the same time has baser impulses that may result in cowardice and mediocrity. But if one shuts one's eyes to reality and embraces one's dreams, then one has a chance of sustaining oneself in the destructive element or remorseless process:

> [Man] wants to be a saint, and he wants to be a devil—and every time he shuts his eyes—he sees himself as a very fine fellow—so fine as he can never be. . . . In a dream . . . and because you not always can keep your eyes shut there comes the real trouble—the heart pain—the world pain. I tell you, my friend, it is not good for you to find you cannot make your dream come true, for the reason that you not strong enough are, or not clever enough. *Ja!* . . . And all the time you are such a fine fellow, too! (130)

In an ironic reversal of Jim's jump that occurs when Jim abandons his dreams and sees that he will certainly drown, dreaming—closing one's eyes and living one's dreams and illusions—is equated by Stein with falling into the sea: "A man that is born falls into a dream like a man who falls into the sea. If he tries to climb out into the air as inexperienced people endeavor to do, he drowns— *nicht war?* . . . No! I tell you! The way is to the destructive element submit yourself, and with the exertions of your hands and feet in the water make the deep, deep sea keep you up" (130). Climbing into the air is a metaphor for failing to keep oneself afloat in one's dreams; if one does climb into the air, then one opens one's eyes to one's own limitations and sees the world as it is—as a destructive element. The way to survive, according to Stein, is "To follow the dream, and again to follow the dream—and so—*ewig—usque ad finem"*—which translates "perpetual until the end" (131). When Jim opens his eyes on the *Patna* to the real danger, he abandons his dream of heroism and the merchant marine credo that insists that he stick to the ship under all circumstances. When he lets the scoundrel Gentleman Brown insinuate a kinship with him, he abandons his position as the political and ethical leader of the Patusan community. In both cases, his self-image is not strong enough to stand up to his collision with circumstances in the not-I world that represent the destructive element or remorseless process.

Something more of an 1890s figure than is usually noticed, Stein understands the nature of masques and fictions; he knows the value of adhering existentially to one's dream or values as a way of making sense of a meaningless world. But has it sufficiently been stressed how Stein is preaching a form of solipsism and that he says nothing at all about the failure of Jim to sustain traditional community values? Critics have mistakenly privileged Stein's remarks because they have failed to notice that Conrad no sooner raises expectations that Stein might be a Wisdom Figure than he deflates those expectations. For one thing, what he says in his broken English is rather ambiguous. For another, no sooner does he deliver his advice than his pretensions to sphinxian wisdom are undermined; Marlow notices that Stein loses his poise and confidence: "The hand that had been pointing at my breast [like a pistol] fell. . . . The light had destroyed the assurance which had inspired him in the distant shadows" (130). And, finally, that Stein is depicted by Marlow in the novel's last paragraph as aging and ineffectual shows us not only that he has not found any absolute knowledge, but also that he may not even retain faith in the credo that he has articulated in the above passage. The Stein episode teaches that there can be no one center of meaning in texts or in life. Just as neither Stein nor Jim can be the key to meaning for Marlow, so Marlow cannot be the source of meaning for his listeners; and, for us readers, no one character or scene can be privileged over the others.

Of course, discrediting Stein as a Prospero figure does not invalidate the human search for meaning; nor does the absence of ultimate meaning suggest that there cannot be hierarchies of relative meaning. The reader is expected to understand Stein's advice as another working arrangement that individual humans make with the cosmos. Even Marlow does not arrive at formulations that would replace Stein's, for ultimately Conrad does not believe in static philosophic formulations.

IV. THE ENDING OF *LORD JIM*

Jim's betrayal of his followers in Patusan derives from his inability to believe in his own triumph—or, put another way, to read the text he himself wrote about the hero who makes good on his second chance. He alone does not believe in his triumph and believes that his accomplishments are apocryphal. (Doesn't he say at the height of his triumph: "If you ask them who is brave—who is true—who is just—who is it they would trust with their lives?—they would say, Tuan Jim. And yet they can never know the *real, real, truth*" [185, emphasis added]?) Because Jim does not believe in his own redemption, words cannot be part of what Marlow calls "the sheltering conception of light and order which is our refuge"—a conception that, as Marlow puts it, protects us from "a view of the world that seemed to wear a vast and dismal aspect of disorder" (190); do we not hear in these words an echo of Stein's destructive element? Once Jim responded to the word *Jump* on board the Patna, he had leapt into an abyss where belief in the innocence of language as an ordering principle in a fundamentally hostile world is no longer possible. Like a voice from within insidiously suggesting to Jim that he *belongs* to Jim as part of his imprisoning fate, Gentleman Brown convinces Jim that they are moral and emotional brothers and that Jim must provide him a safe departure. But Brown and his murderous band betray Jim's trust and slay Jim's followers. In Marlow's words, "[Jim] had retreated from one world, for a small matter of an impulsive jump, and now the other, the work of his own hands, had fallen in ruins upon his own head" (248).

In the imagined world of *Lord Jim,* Conrad—that non-Derridean—gives voice and speaking precedence over writing. For Marlow, who has used spoken language to summon almost magically what is past and to put his back to the future, who has used telling to re-create himself, the written word is a kind of deferral of the immediacy of spoken language and an indication that he is giving up his inquiry into himself. Thus the written language of the epistolary section becomes itself a metaphor for the moral weariness and resignation he feels and a recognition of mortality and defeat. Now Marlow too seems to have lost faith in language. Marlow's valedictory passage defers meaning and leaves him without that presence or epistemological counter which Jim had provided for Marlow's quest for moral and spiritual meaning:

> And that's the end. He passes away under a cloud, inscrutable at heart, forgotten, unforgiven, and excessively romantic. . . . For it may very well be

that in the short moment of his last proud and unflinching glance, he had beheld the face of that opportunity which, like an Eastern bride, had come veiled to his side.

But we can see him, an obscure conqueror of fame, tearing himself out of the arms of a jealous love at the sign, at the call of his exalted egoism. He goes away from a living woman to celebrate his pitiless wedding with a shadowy ideal of conduct. Is he satisfied—quite, now, I wonder? We ought to know. He is one of us—and have I not stood up once, like an evoked ghost, to answer for his eternal constancy? Was I so very wrong after all? Now, he is no more, there are days when the reality of his existence comes to me with an immense, with an overwhelming force; and yet upon my honour there are moments, too, when he passes from my eyes like a disembodied spirit astray amongst the passions of this earth, ready to surrender himself faithfully to the claim of his own world of shades. (253)

Does Marlow forgive him? Note how Marlow sometimes forgets Jim, while in *Heart of Darkness* he never could forget Kurtz, who haunts his memory. When he describes Jim in such terms as "under a cloud, inscrutable at heart, forgotten, unforgiven and excessively romantic," Marlow is describing his *response* to Jim, rather than Jim. (As readers of *Heart of Darkness* recall, this is not unusual in Conrad, where such adjectives as "abominable" or "unbounded" are used more to create a structure of effects for the reader than to describe an objective situation within the imagined world.) But these nonreferential adjectives enact how, since the omniscient narrator turned over the narration to Marlow, he has moved from reflection to self-immersion. Perhaps Marlow's final judgment (especially "unforgiven") is a step toward reasserting the rigorous code from which he had departed. While Marlow withholds judgment—"I affirm nothing" (206)—does he not send his packet to a listener whose views are close not only to those of the omniscient voice, but also to those Marlow had held when he first met Jim? For the privileged recipient is chosen because he believed in the imperialistic dream that the white Europeans are emissaries of enlightenment "in whose name are established the order, the morality of an ethical progress" (206).

Surely, we readers moving outside the linguistic circle of Marlow and Stein understand that the cloud, like the invisible halt of Jim's gait and his spot of decay, is a metaphor for Jim's moral blemish; we cannot see Jim clearly because, for Marlow, his morally ambiguous behavior places him in the shadows of Marlow's imagination. And do not the above adjectives call attention finally to Jim's moral emptiness and raise questions about whether Jim is still worth the effort? Marlow understands that Jim is still wooed by his fantasies; Jim leaves behind the reality of the woman who loves him, and to whom he has human ties, for a romantic ideal of honor. Isn't Marlow's final stance, as much as Stein's aging, a reassertion of the impossibility of permanently suspending time and of creating an imaginative world? But this impossibility paradoxically gives the omniscient narrator's positivistic judgments validity.

Poignantly, in allowing Doramin to shoot him, Jim chooses the masculine world of physical action, represented by the pistol (recall how he had entered Patusan "with an unloaded revolver in his lap"), over the alternative, more feminine world of values, represented by the talismanic friendship ring given to him by Stein—the ring that he gave to his messenger, "Tamb Itam, to give to Dain Waris as a sign that his messenger's words should be trusted" (149). Just as his achievements in the native black world can never be as real to Jim as the failures in the white home world, feminine values—romantic love and personal ties—cannot be as real to him as the world of male heroism. Jim can love Jewel in his romance world of "knight and maiden," but not in the relative world of partial failures and relative successes (189). By choosing to face the male pistol, Jim, in fact, ironically closes the eternal circle implied by the feminine ring. After Doramin shoots Jim:

> People remarked that the ring which he had dropped on his lap fell and rolled against the foot of the white man, and that poor Jim glanced down at the talisman that had opened for him the door of fame, love and success within the wall of forests fringed with white foam, within the coast that under the western sun looks very like the stronghold of the night. (252–53)

Is not Jim's suicide—along with Jim's jump from the *Patna* and his trusting of Gentleman Brown—a third betrayal? Do not the moral absolutism and breakdown of distance that propel him to suicide repeat Brierly's suicide? In Conrad's moral universe a man's character is his fate, and Jim has not fundamentally changed. But this does not invalidate meaning. Indeed, what happens is that Jim accepts the verdict of the omniscient narrator, the verdict that had judged Jim's jump from the *Patna* not as a gratuitous act but as part of a concatenation of events that revealed Jim's flawed character. More than Marlow, Jim had continued to judge himself according to absolute standards from which he had departed—the very standards articulated by the omniscient narrator at the beginning of the novel. Doesn't Jim's internalizing of these judgments make the circular ring an appropriate image for the form of the novel? In retrieving the original standards by which he had failed, Jim most certainly weds himself to what Marlow calls "a shadowy ideal of conduct" (253). But that shadowy ideal is in fact the credo of the novel that is articulated by the omniscient narrator in the opening chapters.

In the ending, then, we see not an abandonment of values but a reassertion of the original values articulated by the omniscient narrator. To be sure, individual voices—whether Stein's, Brierly's, or Marlow's—are unable to establish authority. In Marlow's and the novel's last paragraph, Stein is reduced to speaking vacuously of "preparing to leave" and seems to lack both the imaginative and rhetorical energy of his prior appearance. Marlow no longer imposes his all-too-human order on his experiences (258). Jim dies "with his hand over his lips," an emblem—or a statue—of his estrangement from language. Conrad himself will no longer rely on Marlow as a surrogate for his epistemological quests; he moves on to other voices and techniques, returning in *Chance* (1912) to a Marlow who resembles the earlier Marlow more in name than in intellect or the ability to make subtle moral discriminations. But the words of the novel and, in particular, of the omniscient narrator survive to communicate their judgments to the reader.

V. SUGGESTIONS FOR READING *LORD JIM*

Like any complex work, *Lord Jim* teaches us how to read itself. We should think of our experience—our process—of reading it as the reader's odyssey. We should be aware of what the novel does to us as we read it and how its disrupted chronology and multiple modes of narration establish an unusually complex relationship between text and reader. In my view the principal interest of *Lord Jim*'s chronological disruptions, its multiple perspectives, its structural doubling, and its stylistic idiosyncrasies should be how they shape a reading of the novel. Just as Marlow is engaged in a moral odyssey as he repeats the journeys of Jim's physical odyssey, so the reader takes part in an odyssey of judgment in which she or he is presented with an abundance of evidence and opinions. The reader must establish a perspective for both Marlow and Jim that survives and transcends the novel's plethora of judgments, its wealth of detail, and its protean transformations of characters. Conrad's use of adjectives—in, for example, the passage we examined from the ending—as a kind of subjective correlative for which the reader must fill in the space between signifier and signified is a kind of linguistic model for the necessary corrective judgment that the reader must provide. In Conrad, style is inseparable from what it *does* to the events and characters it describes and what it *does* to the reader as he negotiates his journey through the novel to his final destination, the novel's end. Since Conrad's focus always returns to the characters and their meaning, we should assume that the effects of his language upon the reader—what we might think of as the *doesness* of the text as opposed to the *isness*—were never far from his mind.

The odyssean reader must wend his way through a variety of experiences, but these experiences can best be understood in terms of *Lord Jim*'s major formal principle. This formal principle urges the reader to see *Lord Jim* as a completely organic and integrated novel in which one can conceive in every part some aspect of the meaning and harmony of the whole.[6] In his book *Gödel, Escher, Bach,* Douglas Hofstadter describes the graph of a mathematical function INT[eger](x), every section of which is a replica of the whole. Since every individual part of each section is also a replica of the whole, the graph consists of an infinite number of copies of itself. Thus INT[eger](x) becomes an apt metaphor for a humanistic reading of *Lord Jim,* because it expresses the humanistic idea that within the specific narrative about a few characters can be perceived universal truths or at least important evidence of what a culture values. Another model for organic unity is the genetic code which determines the macrostructure of an organism, but which is contained in every separate part of the organism.

Opposed to this totalizing perspective is the formal principle that insists that, as Geoffrey H. Hartman puts it, "literary language displays a polysemy, or an excess of the signifier over the signified."[7] While, for the most part, *Lord Jim* insists that its readers interpret every detail in terms of larger patterns, one must acknowledge a secondary and subordinate story of reading *Lord Jim.* At times, the novel's focus on isolated moments of life and ingenious linguistic pyrotechnics may temporarily deflect the reader from stories of reading that propose organic unity. At some points in our reading experience, the text seems to be questioning the reader's quest for meaning with troubling data, as in the pas-

---

6. *Gödel, Escher, Bach: An Eternal Golden Braid.*
7. "The Culture of Criticism," 386.

sage where Stein's oracular stature is undermined or when Marlow loses control. On occasion, focusing on the quirky and idiosyncratic aspects in human behavior, *Lord Jim* does immerse the reader in the nominalistic world of the lives of a few characters; furthermore, by presenting Jim through Marlow's explanatory and apologetic lens, Conrad does raise the possibility that some of the novel's implications cannot be resolved.

Throughout *Lord Jim,* Conrad is aware that the possibility of meaninglessness is inseparable from the probability of significance. By constantly proposing, testing, and discarding multiple explanations for Jim's behavior and by presenting Marlow as an evolving self-dramatizing character, Conrad urges us toward such a complex response. He wants us to read profanely and to experience the agony of Jim's demise through Marlow's puzzled eyes; he wants us to entertain the possibility that *Lord Jim* is not merely inconclusive, but that it is skeptical about discovering significance from the plethora of details within his novel—and, by implication, as skeptical of our own efforts to come to terms with crucial events in our own lives.

But ultimately the narrative form of *Lord Jim* privileges the original judgment—the prologue narrated by an omniscient voice preceding Conrad's elaborate orchestration of the multiple but limited and self-interested perspectives of the novel. And Conrad reintegrates those moments of seeming *aporia* into his pattern of moral significance. By doing so, he establishes a hierarchy of meanings in which the relative, marginal, or deconstructive reading is subordinated to the novel's moral judgment as revealed by the novel's organic form.

The dialectic between the two modes of reading—the formally coherent humanistic one and the skeptical deconstructive one—is crucial to the experience of reading not only *Lord Jim* but many modern (and postmodern) novels. While nineteenth-century novels are more likely to use the omniscient speaker and to propose a unified artistic and moral vision, modern novels as diverse as *Ulysses* and Umberto Eco's *The Name of the Rose* characteristically carry seeds of their own self-doubt about the possibility of meaning and coherence. For the sake of intellectual housekeeping, it would be neater either to give the two modes of reading *Lord Jim*—the one that insists on moving from immersion to interpretive reflection and to acts of construing, the other that stresses immersion in the text for its own sake—equal importance, or to claim that the linguistic reading deconstructs the humanistic one. But it is more accurate to say that for the most part *Lord Jim* invites the first mode of reading, the traditional humanistic mode of reading that stresses unity of form and content, rather than the latter, deconstructionist mode of reading that questions meaning, coherence, and significance. Put another way, in *Lord Jim* the humanistic reading is dominant and the deconstructive reading is subordinate. Although Marlow's empathetic involvement, Brierly's fallibility, and Stein's obscurantism challenge and ironically undermine our desire for order, Conrad depends upon the reader's expectations of coherence and unity—what Wallace Stevens in "The Idea of Order at Key West" calls our "rage for order." For, finally, Conrad wants us to read *Lord Jim* as a sacred text—as his own embroidery—in which every episode signifies and in which the words on the page represent the possibility for unity and wholeness in the modern world.

Conrad's Quarrel with Politics in
NOSTROMO

For Conrad, contentment was found in alternatives to ideology, politics, and material interests, in a small viable self-created space of the mind in which one insulates oneself as best one can from the hurt of politics. Conrad's boyhood experiences under totalitarianism led him to believe in the importance of the private realm and to believe, like Hannah Arendt, that in the private realm people can find some respite from politics and might find in their personal lives freedom and the possibility of intimacy, friendship, trust, and spontaneity. Conrad understood that authoritarian politics could deprive humans of their private lives, their imagination, their very reason for living. Among other things, "The Secret Sharer" is a story of friendship, and *Heart of Darkness* is about various kinds of loneliness and isolation.

Writing enabled Conrad to define his values and his character. He used his narrators and dramatic personae to objectify his feelings and values. Marlow is a surrogate through whom Conrad works out his own epistemological problems. Marlow's search for values echoes Conrad's. Understanding the meaning of several novels, most notably *The Nigger of the "Narcissus"* and *The Rescue,* depends on understanding the way Conrad's emotional life becomes embodied in the text. In *Nostromo* the suicidal despair of Decoud reflects a mood that Conrad had known many times in his novel-writing years. Even such an objective work as "The Secret Sharer" becomes more meaningful once we recognize that it has an autobiographical element. At the outset of his voyage, the captain not only relives emotions Conrad once felt during his first command but also reflects the uncertainty and anxiety that Conrad experienced at the time he wrote the story.

Conrad's pessimism and nihilism have been overemphasized, while his humanism has been neglected. As readers, we feel Conrad's living presence within his fiction. Frequently, he is expressing his deep sympathy for suffering hu-

Originally published in *College English* 59.5 (September 1997): 548–68.

manity. At other times, he is struggling to discover the appropriate form with which to render his concern and values. Surely his dramatization of diverse perspectives derives from his profound need to understand humanity. For all his personal agony, Conrad recognized both the grandeur and the pathos of human life. From his Polish heritage he claimed: "An impartial view of humanity in all its degrees of splendour and misery together with a special regard for the rights of the unprivileged of this earth, not on any mystic ground but on the ground of simple fellowship and honourable reciprocity of services" (*Personal Record,* ix).[1] He conceived of his art as homage to mankind: "An imaginative and exact rendering of authentic memories may serve worthily that spirit of piety towards all things human which sanctions the conceptions of a writer of tales, and the emotions of the man reviewing his own experience" (*Personal Record,* 25). Yet, throughout his career, Conrad's humanism conflicted with his skepticism. In his works he showed how the urge to self-fulfillment often interfered with a person's moral responsibilities to his fellows. As Aileen Kelly wrote of Tolstoy, "Those of his characters who devote themselves to deliberate and reasoned altruism, whether in their personal relations or in social action, are shown as both impotent in their efforts to divide the ocean of good and evil and sterile in their inner lives."[2] Gould, Jim, and Peter Ivanovitch of *Under Western Eyes* are in this category. But a more reflective and modest group, including Marlow, Monygham, and the language teacher in *Under Western Eyes,* redeem themselves by an instinctive commitment to ideals, values, and other persons.

Conrad understood, as Steven Marcus wrote in a different context, that "It is when the super-ego sanctions us to act freely and punitively in the name of some of humanity's highest ideals—whether it be the Deity, or the Nation, or Democracy, or Revolution, or Science itself—that the greatest horrors of human aggressiveness, violence and destruction are unleashed."[3] *Nostromo* shows that history is composed of personal dramas, acted out not in service to political ideals—no matter what the actor espouses as his motive—but in response to dimly understood needs that are transferred by rationalization into public rhetoric. Conrad often sympathized with idealists who sought change through politics even while he dramatized not only the futility of political action but its dehumanizing quality. He had to convince himself that turning his back on his

---

1. Page numbers in parentheses refer to the Kent edition of Conrad's works.
2. "Tolstoy in Doubt," 23.
3. Review of *Obedience to Authority,* by Stanley Milgram, 3.

country and, in particular, his father's revolutionary heritage was a proper decision. The political novels were a means by which Conrad could atone for his neglect of political involvement, and exonerate himself at the same time, by showing the ultimate futility of a life based on preserving or reforming society. Through such diverse characters as the Professor in *The Secret Agent,* the Monteros, Haldin in *Under Western Eyes,* and even the respectable Don José and Charles Gould, Conrad implies that those who are zealously committed to political ideas sacrifice their potential for personal growth. In *Nostromo, The Secret Agent,* and *Under Western Eyes,* too, characters whose active lives revolve around either upholding the status quo or destroying it have sacrificed their humanity to a ritualistic hunt in which values and ideals are subsumed by the chase and in which each character is bathetically both hunter and prey.

Nostromo is a sublimated act of self-justification on Conrad's part. Conrad was deeply troubled over accusations that he had abandoned Poland. He suspected his motives for settling in England and turning his back upon his country and his family heritage. Once he left the sea and became a writer, the justification that Poland lacked the facilities for his chosen career was difficult to sustain. It may be that *Nostromo* also reflects Conrad's subconscious resentment of a father who neglected family for politics and ultimately left him an orphan, after inflicting exile, disgrace, and economic hardship upon his family. If *Nostromo* was subconsciously written to atone for Conrad's having turned his back on his father's tradition, it is hardly surprising that the catalytic act that generates the novel's plot and the decisive act in the history of Costaguana is Gould's return to the land of his father's defeat for the purpose of reviving the mine. By denying the possibility of change through politics, Conrad convinced himself of the rectitude of his own decision to desert Poland, to which his father had made a complete political commitment. Given his father's zealotry and Conrad's consciousness of it, it is hardly too much to say that politics becomes a paternal abstraction to which Conrad owes atonement, palliation, and self-justification. The means of palliation are his political novels. *Nostromo* justifies the choice of personal fulfillment over political involvement because it shows politics as a maelstrom that destroys those it touches and shows, more importantly, that one inevitably surrenders a crucial part of one's personality when one commits oneself to ideology.

Conrad understood that history is composed of individuals often seeking to fulfill their own private needs and to find a space in which to live and love. History is, as we once again recall one of Conrad's most chilling letters, a remorseless process that is indifferent to our aspirations and—note the facetious use of a domestic image—knits us in and out:

> There is a—let us say—a machine. It evolved itself (I am severely scientific) out of a chaos of scraps of iron and behold!—it knits. I am horrified at the horrible work and stand appalled. I feel it ought to embroider—but it goes on knitting. You come and say: "this is all right: it's only a question of the right kind of oil. Let us use this—for instance—celestial oil and the machine shall embroider a most beautiful design in purple and gold". Will it? Alas no. You cannot by any special lubrication make embroidery with a knitting machine. And the most withering thought is that the infamous thing has made itself; made itself without thought, without conscience, without foresight, without eyes, without heart. It is a tragic accident—and it has happened. You can't interfere with it. The last drop of bitterness is in the suspicion that you can't even smash it. In virtue of that truth one and immortal which lurks in the force that made it spring into existence it is what it is—and it is indestructible![4]

This famous image of a universe created by an indifferent knitting machine is an ironic comment on the pretensions of industrial machinery to wear the mantle of human progress. Yet within Conrad's morally neutral universe, humans can for a time create their own islands of satisfaction and meaning. Conrad's values have often been explained in terms of his sea ethos, to the exclusion of his other concerns. To be sure, fidelity, courage, responsibility to one's fellows, and dedication to the task for its own sake are crucial values. But Conrad also dramatizes how creative action, family relationships, and passionate love enable people to escape the psychological imprisonment of fears, doubts, obsessions, compulsions, and fixations. Perhaps because Conrad was an orphan and an émigré, the importance of restoring personal and family ties is a major theme throughout his career, a central motif of the political novels, and the cornerstone of his values. As he came to respect the English tradition of manners, particularly in his later work, he emphasized such private virtues as consideration for others, tact, sensitivity, flexibility, and tenderness. Conrad's belief in the efficacy of fiction underlines his humanism. The 1897 preface to *The Nigger of the "Narcissus"* stresses the ability of fiction to make a man see with more clarity, insight, and understanding. A decade later in *A Personal Record*—note the ti-

4. Letter of December 20, 1897, in *Collected Letters of Joseph Conrad, vol. 1, 1861–1897*, ed. Frederick Karl and Laurence Davies, 425.

tle—he contended: "And what is a novel if not a conviction of our fellow-men's existence strong enough to take upon itself a form of imagined life clearer than reality and whose accumulated verisimilitude of selected episodes puts to shame the pride of documentary history?" (15).

No one, Conrad knew, can subtract oneself from the intricately woven historical labyrinth. Like Yeats in "No Second Troy," he understood how politics was corrupted by private needs masquerading as public purpose. Conrad's skepticism about politics was shared by his contemporaries. Not only did Joyce, Lawrence, and Woolf stress the possibilities of reviving family as an alternative to history and politics, but so did Matisse and Picasso, both of whose own obsessive interest in form, epitomized by cubism and fauvism, is something of a retreat from history. As much as we might wish to politicize modernism, modernism is often about the possibility of art in the face of inchoate and uncontrollable history. Conrad was a powerful critic of all ideology, and his agon in *Nostromo*—and elsewhere—enacts that and places him within the tradition of what we might call aesthetic high modernism.

Conrad's friendships with diverse and idiosyncratic political and social thinkers such as R. B. Cunninghame Graham, H. G. Wells, and George Bernard Shaw show that he put personal relationships before political ideology. His concern for the working class derives not from political theory but from his experience as a seaman and from his imaginative response to the miseries of others. Conrad's humanism informs his political vision. In his political writings, it is the abstractions upholding private virtues that carry conviction. He wrote in "Autocracy and War" (1905) that it was to "our sympathetic imagination" that we must "look for the ultimate triumph of concord and justice" (*Notes on Life and Letters,* 84). In this essay the paramount values threatened by Russian autocracy are "dignity," "truth," "rectitude," and "all that is faithful in human nature" (99). Thus, Russia is "a yawning chasm open between East and West; a bottomless abyss that has swallowed up every hope of mercy, every aspiration towards personal dignity, towards freedom, towards knowledge, every ennobling desire of the heart, every redeeming whisper of conscience" (100).

Ideological readings of *Nostromo* and indeed of Conrad's other two political novels often depend on overreading "Autocracy and War," where Conrad uncharacteristically affirms a belief in the evolution of both nations and mankind:

> The true greatness of a State . . . is a matter of logical growth, of faith and
> courage. Its inspiration springs from the constructive instinct of the peo-

ple, governed by the strong hand of a collective conscience and voiced in
the wisdom and counsel of men who seldom reap the reward of gratitude. . . .
    A revolution is a short cut in the rational development of national needs
in response to the growth of world-wide ideals. (91, 101)

In that essay, Conrad proposes abstract ideals rather than political theory, shibboleths rather than working programs; for example, he writes: "The common
ground of concord, good faith and justice is not sufficient to establish an action
upon; since the conscience of but very few men amongst us, and of no single
Western nation as yet, will brook the restraint of abstract ideas as against the
fascination of material advantage" (111).

    Despite Conrad's conservatism, I find little evidence to support Avrom
Fleishman's thesis that Conrad regards the state as "a source, perhaps the only
source, of the values by and for which [individuals] live." Nor do I believe Conrad emphasizes "the primacy of the community, which gives individual life its
possibility and its value."[5] Perhaps on board ship the community must take
precedence over the individual in moments of crises, but Conrad's political fiction argues for the *primacy* of the individual and perceives social organizations
as necessary evils. In all his work—to play on the phrase "one of us" in *Lord
Jim*—Conrad is concerned with the dialogue between the *one* individual and
the *us* of community, but he always understands that the community is an ag-
gregation of "ones."

    Indeed, Fredric Jameson's influential explication acknowledges the disjunc-
tion between the individual act and the historical process, but he explains the
disjunction in terms of how history inevitably "steals" individual agons:

> [The] central act, the heroic expedition of Decoud and Nostromo, which
> ought to have grounded their status as heroes, as ultimate legendary forms
> of the individual subject, is appropriated by collective history, in which it
> also exists, but in a very different way, as the founding of institutions. In
> classical Sartrean language, we can say that the historical act of Decoud and
> Nostromo has been alienated and stolen from them even before they
> achieve it; or in more Hegelian terminology, their action can be character-
> ized as that of structurally ephemeral mediation. . . . Decoud's and Nos-
> tromo's is the moment of the action of the individual subject, but one
> which is at once reabsorbed by the very stability and transindividuality of

5. Fleishman, *Conrad's Politics: Community and Anarchy in the Fiction of Joseph Conrad,* 57, 56.

the institutions it is necessary to found. History uses their individual passions and values as its unwitting instruments for the construction of a new institutional space in which they fail to recognize themselves or their actions and from which they can only, either slowly or violently, be effaced, remnants of another age—not, this time, the myth of origins and the golden age of the giants, but rather the moment of the mediatory transition to another social form, a form as degraded, as transindividual, as non-narratable, as the one that preceded it, although in its own quite different way.[6]

Jameson's argument is a paradigm of an approach to *Nostromo* and Conrad's other political novels that prevailed in the last decade or so, an approach that displaces history's dialectical process onto the major agons of characters—or vice versa. I do not believe readers respond to anthropomorphized "history" as an antagonist and doubt—as Conrad would doubt—that we should assign to history the responsibility for human infirmities, private motives, individual fixations and compulsions.

Before turning to my own reading, I want to give readers some sense of the focus of recent Conrad scholarship. I will cite passages from discussions of *Nostromo* representative of critical and theoretical discussions of the Conrad canon. One could cite many fine pieces that discuss *Nostromo* in terms of "the very making of history," as Pamela H. Demory puts it; for her, Conrad's novel is about "the problem of the relationship between history and the past, between historical narrative and history, between, in effect, historiography as signifier and event as signified. . . . [*Nostromo*] critiques both the traditional nineteenth-century notion of history and the nineteenth-century realistic novel." For Daniel Visser, another critic who wishes to argue in terms of Marxist dialectics, "the *decisive* political import of *Nostromo* is found in the insights generated into the social and economic significance of the mine, which in turn operates as a powerful synecdoche for the broader material and social transformation of Sulaco under impact of international capital."[7]

By contrast, I am arguing that Conrad's political novels belie the sweeping and vague rhetoric of both "Autocracy and War" and the above passage from Jameson, and reduce these comments to fustian. In the political novels Conrad is disillusioned with materialism and imagines that "industrialism and commercialism" may foster wars between democracies. Like Dostoevsky, Conrad

6. *The Political Unconscious: Narrative as a Socially Symbolic Act,* 278–99.
7. Demory, "*Nostromo*: Making History," 317; Visser, "Crowns and Politics in *Nostromo,*" 12.

disavows the "Crystal Palace," the Victorian symbol of science and progress: "The dreams sanguine humanitarians raised almost to ecstasy about the year 'fifty of the last century by the moving sight of the Crystal Palace—crammed full with that variegated rubbish which it seems to be the bizarre fate of humanity to produce for the benefit of a few employers of labour—have vanished as quickly as they had arisen" (*Notes on Life and Letters,* 106). In such a mechanistic, amoral world—also described in the aforementioned "knitting machine" letter—Conrad understands the necessity for political and social organization. While he dissects flaws in various systems, states, and communities, he does not propose alternative programs. But he does insist on preserving the freedom of individuals to live their own lives as long as they do not pose a physical threat to others. What totalitarianism encourages is failure of responsibility, shallowness, thoughtlessness, and remoteness from personal ties and commitments.

Two important relatively recent readings address the relationship between aesthetic and political issues. Elizabeth Langland in her excellent *Society in the Novel* argues from a neo-Aristotelian perspective that *Nostromo* is a novel in which "the writer makes society the protagonist":

> To say that society is protagonist is not to claim that society is a character or has an ego analogous to that of an individual; rather it is to state that society, a set of principles or social ideals, functions in the narrative in the same way a human hero would. We are made to care about the fate of a set of principles, a society, whose movement from instability to stability compels the focus and our interest, determines the novel's unity, and resolves the series of artistic expectations established in the work. . . .
>
> The individuals who are principal agents by which a positive social order is to be realized may take on rather complex definition as long as the result of their complexity increases our understanding of how their personal strengths and limitations will complicate or hasten the resolution of society's instabilities. Usually, the identities of these principal agents are very clear. In fact, they often tend toward highly representative types whose personalities remain relatively static throughout the novel. Their significance resides in the fact that they embody those positive social principles being challenged or seeking realization.[8]

But, I shall argue, Conrad's interest is at least divided between a grammar of *motives* and a grammar of *political cause and effect*. In *Coercion to Speak,* Aaron Fo-

8. *Society in the Novel,* 148–50.

gel uses a Bakhtinian approach to makes this point: "[I]f we want to understand the dialogical forces of *Nostromo*, both in its own form and in relation to other writings, we have to point toward the special poetics of this ironic project, which led Conrad to reject . . . the historical novel's dialectic of inclusion, and to insist upon the falsity of any historical 'dialectic' that disguises or ignores the reality of the coercive dialogic." I would want to stress that Conrad believes politics and history are and must be *conversations* in which diverse perspectives take part, rather than axioms deriving from ideology. In his *Challenge of Bewilderment*, Paul Armstrong argues, "*Nostromo* is not so much a realistic presentation of a given historical situation as a paradigm of political processes—a model through which Conrad explores the ontology of the social world." Conrad's history within his imagined ontology, Armstrong argues persuasively, is created from retrospective views after the ramifications of actions are known. But Armstrong's approach, while interesting on the narratology of time, pushes the characters' psyches and motives too far from the center of attention.[9]

I I

Criticism that insists upon discussing *Nostromo* from a predominantly political perspective often seems to confuse the novel's subject matter with its values. An earlier version of the view I am refuting is in Eloise Knapp Hay's learned *The Political Novels of Joseph Conrad:* (1) "Everything illustrates the author's theory of history"; (2) "Evil . . . is exterior and is not, even, moral."[10] When Conrad created imagined worlds with a political and historical dimension, as he did most notably in the three consecutive novels generally classified as political—*Nostromo* (1904), *The Secret Agent* (1907), and *Under Western Eyes* (1911)—he was concerned less with political theory than with the cost of politics in terms of disruption of family ties, of personal relationships, and, ultimately, of personal growth. To be sure, Conrad was fascinated by political doctrines, movements, and ideals. But he despaired that political activity could make a difference in a world he regarded as a "remorseless process." He sadly realized that political activity fails because most men are selfish; those who are not selfish are victims of their own obsession, and thus are incapable of sustained

9. Fogel, *Coercion to Speak: Conrad's Poetics of Dialogue,* 96; Armstrong, *The Challenge of Bewilderment: Understanding and Representation in James, Conrad, and Ford,* 155.
    10. *The Political Novels of Joseph Conrad,* 175, 183.

activity on behalf of the community. I shall not deny that Conrad considers how, why, and for what values men organize themselves into various communities, parties, factions, and interest groups. But I shall argue that Conrad indicts political activity as both suspect in its causes and pernicious in its effects. In his view, Costaguana's oscillation between revolution and autocracy, between secession and federation, has little to do with the question of what political system governs best. Even at the close, when Gould's vision for the mine is fulfilled and Sulaco flourishes, the conditions for the next revolutionary uprising are growing, like poisonous mushrooms, in the discontented hearts of Captain Fidanza and his comrade, the malevolent "blood-thirsty" photographer.

With deep regret, Conrad came to believe that political activity was a threat to the traditional paradigms on which civilization depends: intimate relationships, family relations between parents and children as well as among siblings, and other personal relationships—between all those who seek to understand and to be understood, to love and to be loved. Thus, in the political novels, Conrad posits interpersonal relationships and family ties as *alternative* values to political doctrines, while he demonstrates that humankind can be destroyed when the individual allows political abstractions to subsume the private self. In *Nostromo*, even when high-minded characters espouse ideals, political principles are thinly veiled disguises for the desire to control the enormous treasure of the San Tomé mine. Because of their own obsessions and moral weaknesses, the Goulds, Decoud, Antonia, Nostromo, and even the Viola family are engulfed by politics created by the insistent demands of materialism. *Nostromo* is the story of people who, while seeking to define their own lives in bold and heroic terms, become entrapped by the circumstances that they seek to control and the political activity in which they engage.

The disrupted chronology, the rapidly shifting focus, and the ominous instability of the ending dramatize a world that has lost its moral center, a world in which, as Yeats puts it in "The Second Coming," "the best lack all conviction, while the worst / Are full of passionate intensity." The form is a correlative to a narrative about a civilization that lacks a moral center. Like *Dubliners, Nostromo* is really a series of episodes in the moral history of a nation; Costaguana and Sulaco are metaphors for a nation and a major city under siege. Despite the hectic activity—the political machinations, the riots and uprisings, the marches and retreats—the novel moves toward climactic moments when the major characters are isolated and must discover the essential self that has survived the public self. The scenes in which Mrs. Gould gradually and incompletely awakens to her loneliness, Gould to his position as an adventurer, and Nostromo to the awareness that he has been manipulated by those who do not care for him, are all the more effective because they are in stark contrast to the rapid and confusing external events. Decoud's excruciating discovery of his moral emptiness and his subsequent suicide are rhetorically and structurally climactic because each of the major characters has already discovered an inner self distinct from the position society defines for him or her. No matter what illusion or abstraction a character is committed to—whether it be Viola's republicanism, Monygham's devotion, Gould's idealism, or Nostromo's "good name"—each major character returns to a position in which he or she is alone, stripped of public self, and exposed to the vicissitudes of an indifferent cosmos. At first, each major character is depicted as part of the social and political order of Sulaco; only then is he or she examined in his or her private facet and shown to be serving not community values but dimly understood psychic needs and unacknowledged obsessions. In other words, Conrad reveals that each of the major characters—even idealists like the Goulds upon whom civilization depends— has given him- or herself to serving, at the behest of psychic needs, an external political or economic entity and, in doing so, has sacrificed his or her own possibilities for love, friendship, and self-development.

I I I

What follows illustrates how a humanistic critic responds, from a formalist perspective, to the narrative thematics of a text with political and historical implications. *Nostromo* is a series of personal agons. By contrast, Jameson argues,

> *Nostromo* is a dialectical intensification and transformation of the narra
> tive apparatus of *Lord Jim*, and it is well, in conclusion, having shown all
> the things which Conrad preferred not to see, to show what he could see in
> a demanding and ambitious effort of the social and historical imagination.
> The point is less a matter of Conrad's personal development between 1900
> and 1904 than it is a demonstration of structural transformations, and the
> way in which analogous materials are utterly metamorphosed when they
> are wrenched from the realm and categories of the individual subject to the
> new perspective of those of collective destiny.[11]

11. *Political Unconscious,* 269.

Passion and love are victims of history's duplicities. If we first consider the Goulds, we shall see that *Nostromo* stresses how fanatic commitment to economic goals and concomitant political action can destroy the relationship between man and wife. Moreover, we shall see how Gould's public self derives from private needs and psychological causes that he neither understands nor acknowledges. Gould's plan to revive the mine shows how a man gives the *names* of ideals to his psychic needs and libidinous impulses. He has an irrational need to revive the mine, to perform a ritualistic act of slaying the dragon that slew his father. An infantile but understandable anger at the death of his absent but revered father and the shock to his own identity now that he has no father figure to sustain him are causes of his willful disobedience to his father's wish that he not return to Costaguana. Gould defines his goals to his wife in terms of moral abstractions in which he *must* believe:

> I pin my faith to material interests. Only let the material interests once get
> a firm footing, and they are bound to impose the conditions on which they
> alone can continue to exist. (84)

But this speech, filled with non sequiturs and with wishes posing as logic, shows how Gould seeks to transform his own subjective needs into a viable political theory. As he once idealized his father, he now idealizes his own motives. Yet Conrad is not without sympathy for those such as Gould, or even the subservient Tekla and the fanatic Haldin in *Under Western Eyes,* all of whom believe that political action can make a difference. As Decoud understands, Gould "could not believe his own motives if he did not make them first a part of some fairy tale" (215). Gould's irrational and subconscious needs to assuage his conscience because of his absence while his father was victimized, and to revenge himself on the forces that he consciously blames for the death of his father, have entrapped him into compulsive behavior that prevents him from fulfilling his wife sexually or emotionally.

Mrs. Gould, as an orphan, responds to Gould because he is an authoritarian Victorian father figure who provides resolution and direction to her life. Living a drab life with a nearly destitute and eccentric aunt, she is psychologically ready to be "inspired by an idealistic view of success" (67) that professes to be interested in the mine because it will create the appropriate conditions for "law, good faith, order, security" (84). She lacks the will to oppose Gould's indomitable ego because she needs to apotheosize him. She believes his abstract parables because they give her "a fascinating vision of herself" as a companion in heroic activi-ties (65). She is attracted to his "unsentimentalism" and, as the narrator notes facetiously, "that very quietude of mind which she had *erected in her thought* for a sign of perfect competency in the business of living" (50; emphasis added).

Gould's libidinous energies are engaged by the mine instead of by his rela-tionship to his wife. The first silver that the mine produces is described in terms that suggest a demonic birth: "[Mrs. Gould] laid her unmercenary hands, with an eagerness that made them tremble, upon the first [spongy lump] turned out still warm from the mould; and by her imaginative estimate of its power she en-dowed that lump of metal with a justificative conception, as though it were not a mere fact, but something far-reaching and impalpable, like the true expres-sion of an emotion or the emergence of a principle" (107). Mrs. Gould is mid-wife to silver rather than mother to children. Just as the uncorrupted waterfall is transformed into a silver-fall, Gould's sexual substance becomes a stream of silver and his offspring a lump of silver: "[Mrs. Gould] heard with a thrill of thankful emotion the first wagon load of ore rattle down the then only shoot; she had stood by her husband's side perfectly silent, and gone cold all over with excitement . . . when the first battery . . . was put in motion for the first time" (107). She has sublimated her sexual needs and has tacitly permitted the pro-duction of the silver to become her husband's homage to her and to substitute for intercourse. As a result, she is not only childless but lonely and sexually frus-trated. Potentially tender moments climax not with intimacy but with Gould's return to the mine at night. For the spongy lump grows into a wall that divides her from her husband.

Mrs. Gould's solitude and personal deprivation are progressive conditions, evolving and intensifying as a direct response to the success of the mine and the growth of Gould's public identity as "Señor Administrador" and "King of Sula-co." It is almost as if by a process of grotesque metamorphosis Gould was turned into "the mysterious weight of a taciturn force" (203). Part of Gould's tragedy is that his position as "King of Sulaco" and his concomitant identification with the mine have transformed him into an extension of the inanimate world. Be-cause he has *become* synonymous with the mine, it is ironically appropriate that he uses silence as a means of communicating its power and force: "Behind [his silences] there was the great San Tomé mine, the head and font of the material interests, so strong that it depended on no man's good-will" (203). Because Gould's libidinous needs are fulfilled through the "flow" of the mine, he plans to respond to a challenge to his position by destroying it. For all his high-minded ideals, Gould's real interest is in dominating and controlling the mine. His fantasies of playing what he calls "my last card" and "send[ing] half Sulaco, into the air if I liked" reveal him as a rogue, a "hustler" and megalomaniac on the model of Kurtz (67, 204, 206). The self-controlled and repressed Gould may at first glance seem Kurtz's opposite, but Gould's subordination of ends to means is a repressed and respectable version of Kurtz's reversion to savagery. Both are imperialists who espouse the highest ideals, but their actions undermine the stability and morality of the indigenous culture that they expect to civilize. Yet Conrad is grimly sympathetic to Gould, while he regards Kurtz as a man who lacks "restraint in the gratification of his various lusts." Just as Kurtz turns from his Intended, once he has made his political, materialistic, and sexual conquests, Charles Gould turns from his wife to the mine when she is no longer required to fulfill his ego. (The reader understands that she is really the first external entity that he has conquered and dominated.)

Mrs. Gould is an important figure in my argument, and she is a figure that recent criticism has pushed to the margins. She embodies an English tradition of manners and morals for which Conrad's respect grew throughout his career. She represents the possibility of family, but that possibility is undermined by the grotesque birth of the mine instead of a human conception within her womb. She is life-giver and victim, castrated by material interests. Like Woolf's Mrs. Ramsay, she radiates personal warmth, generosity, and hospitality and so creates an alternative to political turmoil and materialistic greed. Even while repressing her own sexuality, she provides warmth, understanding, and sympathy not only to her husband, Monygham, and the Viola family but also to Decoud, Sir John, and finally Nostromo himself. After five chapters in which cultivated behavior and civilized discourse between two individuals have been ostentatiously absent, she is presented without irony as a woman "guided by an alert perception of values. She was highly gifted in the art of human intercourse, which consists in delicate shades of self-forgetfulness and in the suggestion of universal comprehension" (46). By circumstances rather than choice, she dedicates herself to perpetuating Agape rather than Eros. Conrad understands that Mrs. Gould's character is partially determined by the frustrations of her marriage. The repeated juxtaposition of her with the statue of the Madonna on the staircase and the image of her as a good fairy emphasize the connection between her asexuality and her position as a viable alternative to her husband's values. After her return from Europe, her sexless and loveless marriage is stressed by the icon of Madonna and Child, which "seemed to welcome her with an aspect of pitying tenderness" (505), and by the emphasis on the fecundity of Basilio and Leonardo. The doctor's failure to develop his interest in her beyond worshipful devotion anticipates the narrator's poignant summary, a summary that almost seems an epitaph for a woman whose life has been all but completed: Mrs. Gould is "wealthy beyond great dreams of wealth, considered, loved, respected, honoured, and as solitary as any human being had ever been, perhaps, on this earth" (555). Although Mrs. Gould's public role as the "first lady of Sulaco" remains unchanged, "the silver threads" beneath her "fair hair" indicate metaphorically how she, too—like Nostromo and her husband—has become a slave of the mine (555).

Notwithstanding her role in resurrecting Dr. Monygham, her dignity, harmony, and warmth are ineffectual. Nor does her social position fulfill her. As Mrs. Gould gradually becomes aware of the mine's gruesome effects upon her husband and turns toward Dr. Monygham for some crumbs of human relationship, her own feeling of solitude increases. When Gould announces that he will openly support the plan of separation, Mrs. Gould is no longer concerned with participating in his imaginative world. Although it is the narrator who makes the harsh judgment about Gould's sanity, she intuitively knows more than she can acknowledge to herself: "Mrs. Gould watched his abstraction with dread. It was a domestic and frightful phenomenon that darkened and chilled the house for her like a thunder-cloud passing over the sun. A man haunted by a fixed idea is insane" (379). Before Dr. Monygham leaves Mrs. Gould in the scene in which both fail to seize the opportunity of passionate love because of their acceptance of social conventions, the narrator notes that Mrs. Gould's "immobility" and "grace" give "her seated figure the charm of art, of an attitude caught and interpreted forever" (520). The narrator emphasizes that Monygham is sexually attracted to her. But both repress their sexual needs in a peculiar psychodrama in which Monygham's libido finds an outlet in "an augmented grimness of speech" (513). Her entirely uncharacteristic "smile of gentle malice" shows Conrad's awareness of libidinous, but sublimated, needs; yet her passion in this interview remains repressed as she contents herself with discussing the sexual activities of others.

Mrs. Gould's response to Antonia's loss of Decoud reflects her own plight. While Mrs. Gould is consciously empathizing with a woman whose deprivation seems an alternative to her fulfillment, she subconsciously sees Antonia's life as a version of her own, just as surely as Brierly (and, to a lesser extent, Marlow) judges himself when he is asked to judge Jim's case. But Mrs. Gould's complex

defenses will not allow her to look too deeply into her own case: "'What would
I have done if Charley had been drowned while we were engaged?' she exclaimed
mentally, with horror. Her heart turned to ice, while her cheeks flamed up as if
scorched by the blaze of a funeral pyre consuming all her earthly affections"
(379). Ironically, the funeral pyre consumes the values that Mrs. Gould represents and that are defeated by materialism and political machinations. Mrs.
Gould's final meditation on her husband dramatizes her continued need to believe in his sanctimonious abstractions, despite her knowledge that something
has gone egregiously wrong in the behavior of the man she apotheosized. Always idealizing and sentimentalizing like her husband (whom *she* now has difficulty thinking of except in his public position as "Señor Administrador"), she
needs to place his behavior in the context of a comfortable theory: "There was
something inherent in the necessities of successful action which carried with it
the moral degradation of the idea" (521). (Since the entire paragraph is her
meditation, this speech should not, as some critics have argued, be thought of
as Conrad's message.) Yet, in a moment of poignant honesty and profound cynicism, she acknowledges her isolation and the deterioration of her hopes and
dreams when she tells Giselle: "I have been loved, too" (561).

I V

Nostromo—our man—is captured by history and made a cog in its knitting machine; almost mechanistically he recoils and makes his own life, but his
rebellion is defined purely by money. Nostromo, the man garbed in silver trappings, is the offspring of the mine. Virtually anonymous, with only the vaguest
claims to a personal past or national identity, he is metaphorically the spongy
lump of silver metamorphosed into a fully grown adult. Nostromo is the child
of materialism and imperialism; he is created by Mitchell and Gould as a human instrument who can be depended upon to place the interests of those he
serves before his own. That he belongs to the imperialists and their political interests is implied by the title that has been conferred upon him by those he
serves: Nostromo, "our man." Such a name deprives him of a personal identity
in the eyes of those he serves. When he flippantly promises the chief engineer
that he will "take care" of Sir John "as if [he] were his father" (43), he acknowledges the patrimony of materialism and concomitantly neglects his own need
for human relationships. He is an example of how totalitarian government

turns the victims into the victimizers. Nostromo represses his private self to become a material instrument of the mine.

Nostromo's relation to the cargadores and natives parallels Gould's relation to the aristocrats. Both men are motivated by intense vanity arising from their need to compensate for a disrupted family. Both rely on taciturnity and detachment to maintain their positions, and both are treated almost like royalty by obsequious followers because of the power they are perceived to hold. When Nostromo gradually drifts into bondage to the treasure, he becomes Gould's double. The terms on which he rebels only establish the dominance of the paternity of material interests. He wants to overthrow the flourishing regime he helped to establish. He supports a socialist party which seeks to undermine the authority figures whom he allowed to become his political fathers in place of Viola; he wants to assuage his guilt for betraying the trust of the people, specifically the cargadores, even though Sulaco's prosperity has clearly brought tangible benefits to the people. His rightful name, Fidanza, is an ironic suggestion of *fidanza*, the Italian word for "confidence," the quality for which he is recognized by others but which in its most profound sense he lacks, and of the Latin root, *fidelitas*, or loyalty, the value he has implicitly renounced.

The most important facts shaping Nostromo's prior life are that he is an orphan and that he had been exploited by an abusive uncle. But he has found in the Violas a surrogate family to whom he is deeply attached. The Violas address him by his rightful name, offer him a home, and treat him as a replacement for the son they had lost. Amid the political turmoil that follows Don Ribiera's overthrow, he makes his first appearance "protecting his own," the Violas (16). He allows Teresa to berate him as a mother would a son because he instinctively realizes that she is concerned with his welfare, concerned lest he become the chattel of the English.

That he places great value on his relationship with his surrogate mother is emphasized by the guilt he feels for refusing to get the dying Teresa a priest. His is the response of a man to whom family claims are of great importance. He takes his failure to fulfill her request hardly less seriously than Jim takes his jump from the *Patna* or Razumov takes his betrayal of Haldin. Because at this point he desperately needs to have her love and understanding, Nostromo calls Teresa "mother" and offers explanations that contrast with his usual taciturnity. With Teresa he has a strange love-hate intimacy which at times is almost Oedipal in its passionate intensity. Just as Gould needs to atone for his father's death, so Nostromo must atone for a "burden of sacrilegious guilt" (420) which makes

him believe that he has prevented the salvation of Teresa's eternal soul by placing his duty to the mine ahead of his duty to his surrogate mother. As soon as
he is on the lighter, he begins to fret about not fulfilling her wishes, even though
he tries to rationalize that, with Father Corbelán away, no priest would have
come. He is obsessed with his refusal, and as Jim does to Marlow, he speaks lo-
quaciously to Decoud because he seeks to justify himself *to himself* and also to
establish a personal tie to Decoud. Explaining to Decoud why he did not kill
Hirsch, Nostromo shows how his primitive superego acknowledges and seeks
fraternal ties: "I could not do it. Not after I had seen you holding up the can to
his lips, as though he were your brother" (284). As the perspicacious Decoud
notices, Nostromo's loquacity is a subconscious symptom of his lost self-re-
spect: "The usual characteristic quietness of the man was gone. It was not equal
to the situation as he conceived it. Something deeper, something unsuspected
by everyone had come to the surface" (282).

Edward Said recognizes in this episode Conrad's personal engagement in his
text:

> The authentic ring of this scene derives, I think, from Conrad's obsessive
> notions about himself. The two adventurers are the double strain in Con-
> rad's life which . . . he had come to believe made him a "*homo duplex.*" The
> atmosphere of deadly peril in which the two men find themselves uncon-
> genial partners represents the nightmare world that Conrad inhabited as
> he worked on his fiction. The analogies between Conrad and the two men
> extend even into the past histories of Nostromo and Decoud. The Genoese
> adventurer is a sailor whose desertion of his ship is kept rather noticeably
> in the background; throughout his career Conrad was fascinated with the
> idea of desertion. . . . Nostromo is a thoroughgoing man of action who has
> successfully moved his profession from sea to land; if this is still Conrad
> talking about one of the two men he was, Nostromo is an idealization of
> the sailor-turned-landlubber that Conrad himself had become.

I might note that while Said's focus in *Beginnings: Intention and Method* is on
showing how "each piece of fiction . . . excludes a larger truth than it contains,
even though it is the novelist's task to make his readers see active relationships
among various orders of reality or truth both inside and outside the text,"[12]
mine is on presenting a specific response to the evolving narrative structure in

---

12. *Beginnings: Intention and Method,* 130, 100.

Nostromo, and on showing how that structure shapes the reader's response to the novel's human drama.

Nostromo's personal life is given short shrift by critics focusing on historical process. Critics perceive Nostromo, like Gould, in terms of an illicit sexual relationship to the material world. He has anthropomorphized the treasure into a beloved object. The narrator renders his bondage to the silver in psychosexual language that obliquely suggests Nostromo's need (not unlike the doctor's) to abase himself. Nostromo cannot simply carry off Giselle because "The slave of the San Tomé silver felt the weight as of chains upon his limbs, a pressure as of a cold hand upon his lips" (539). When Giselle asks what stands between her and him, he answers "a treasure" (540). The silver has become an invisible wall that divides the two lovers. The parallel to the Goulds is evident. Because Nostromo is submissive to the silver, it is all the more important to him that he choose a woman who will allow him to be dominant. If he could tell Giselle his secret, he feels that he could break the spell of the treasure that holds him in bondage and win his release. But his psyche *requires* the libidinal bondage to the silver. Ultimately, this perverse bondage causes his death. Because he is wedded to the silver, because "he had welded that vein of silver into his life" (526), Nostromo chooses the very kind of light-headed woman that he formerly patronized. He is sexually attracted to Giselle Viola because with her he can compensate for his bondage to the silver by being the dominant authoritative figure that he cannot be for Linda, the older Viola daughter to whom he is officially betrothed. While Linda "pronounces [his] name with her mother's intonation," which makes Nostromo experience "a gloom as of the grave," Nostromo thinks of Giselle as a "child" to whom he can minister (532). (At one point with Giselle he becomes "gentle and caressing, like a woman to the grief of a child" [538].)

Nostromo's death derives from the conflict between materialism and an older tradition in which the family's honor is a paramount value and in which courtship must take place under the auspices of the father's approval. While the mine has created conditions in which Nostromo cannot fulfill his positions as betrothed and as adopted son, the reason for his failure is that, as Marlow says of Jim, he is not good enough, that is, he is psychically and morally flawed. Politically, Nostromo is not a man of principle but a tabula rasa until educated by materialism. Had he not been in bondage to the silver, he might in his role of adopted son have already taken his place beside Viola, defending the family honor against unwanted intruders. Instead, Nostromo is the intruder who threatens that honor and who is shot by Viola in the dark. After Viola's shot separates him from his surrogate father and his beloved, he turns desperately to Mrs. Gould as a replacement for Teresa; she becomes for him a mother figure to whom he turns to make a dying confession and thus undo Teresa's curse.

To refute the reliance of Jameson and others I have cited on the abstraction "history," let us turn to the narrator as character, for he is the proponent of family values. As the novel progresses, the narrator evolves; his detachment, rationality, scrupulous fairness, and reluctance to probe into psychosexual problems or to meditate upon psychic motives gradually find expression in a voice in whose balance decorum, and restraint the Edwardian reader would have had confidence. He observes Edwardian literary and social amenities by sidestepping sexual matters, involved psychological analyses, and prolonged interior monologues. The efficacy of the novel's satire of imperialism and materialism depends upon the narrator conveying an alternative to zeal, intemperance, and self-delusion. The speaker's restraint contrasts with Gould's seething turbulence, Decoud's bitter irony deriving in part from his own self-loathing, Mitchell's complacency, and Monygham's obliqueness.

Because Conrad creates a voice concerned with the moral and psychological lives of his characters, the novel's texture does not support a view that the novel is fundamentally mythic. For example, the narrator's bathetic rendering of Monygham's psychosexual difficulties hardly supports Dorothy Van Ghent's reading that Monygham's past corresponds to the "phase" of "self-knowledge" within the heroic ideal: "The doctor, with a lifting up of his upper lip, as though he were longing to bite, bowed stiffly in his chair. With the utter absorption of a man to whom love came late, not as the most splendid of illusions, but like an enlightening and priceless misfortune, the sight of that woman . . . suggested ideas of adoration, of kissing the hem of her robe" (513).[13] (Although thirty years old, Claire Rosenfield's *Paradise of Snakes* contains a provocative and still brilliantly original mythopoeic reading.)

Conrad's narrator undermines the heroic pretensions of his characters and disabuses the reader of the notion that materialism has its heroes. My argument here specifically takes issue with Royal Roussel's phenomenological reading in which he interestingly contends that "The anonymity of the narrator [of *Nostromo*] is thus the deliberately chosen stance of a consciousness which has abandoned the adventure and, with it, any hope for a positive self."[14] By using leg-

---

13. Van Ghent, introduction to *Nostromo*, xvi.
14. *The Metaphysics of Darkness: A Study in the Unity and Development of Conrad's Fiction*, 113.

endary material such as a quest for treasure and by including isolated acts of courage by those who are potential heroes, Conrad raises expectations of heroic behavior. But he deflates them as he gradually reveals the limitations and ineffectuality of his potential heroes: Gould, the "King of Sulaco"; Nostromo, the Adamic man; and Mrs. Gould, whose innocence and moral purity suggest the Madonna.

The speaker does not use bitter, scathing irony to separate himself from a world to which he adheres. He is not, like the narrator of *The Secret Agent*, a man who, as I have argued elsewhere, uses verbal aggression as an outlet for his frustration at being unable to change the world he describes. With his vast knowledge of Costaguana's history and geography and his familiarity with the characters, the narrator speaks both as historian and as journalist. The very care with which the narrator makes distinctions, in contrast to the glib use of abstractions by those political paternalists who seek to disguise their motives in moral bromides (Gould, Sir John, Holroyd, Mitchell), is itself an important statement about the narrator's values.

The narrator avoids the kind of intense psychological analysis of the turn-of-the-century Marlow tales and "The Secret Sharer" because Conrad wants gradually to display the private characters beneath the public rhetoric and social amenities and to show that the characters have fundamentally different identities from the ones that they originally imagined themselves to have. *Heart of Darkness* and *Lord Jim* are predicated on dramatizing the process of Marlow discovering the subtleties of another character, and *Nostromo* bears some important vestiges of Conrad's interest in the epistemological problem of how we can possibly understand and empathize with another person. He places the reader in the position Marlow once occupied. The narrator creates the moral context in which the reader makes his or her judgments; for example, take his extended metaphor of wealth as a poisoned sword that turns upon its bearer: "More dangerous to the wielder, too, this weapon of wealth, double-edged with the cupidity and misery of mankind, steeped in all the voices of self-indulgence as in a concoction of poisonous roots, tainting the very cause for which it is drawn, always ready to turn awkwardly in the hand" (365). At the point where the characters come closest to self-discovery, the narrator sympathetically renders their plights, but he does not draw conclusions or propose alternative abstractions to the ones that have been discredited by the characters' actions. The reader must do that for him- or herself.

Our inquiry into *Nostromo* may suggest the difficulty of subordinating the *novel*—as in *unique*—story of individuals to ideology. It may be that, like Conrad, we respond to the psyches of fellow humans—their compulsions, fixations, needs, and quirks—and that the political and socioeconomic unconscious dims as a compelling factor in our reading because (like our sense of the zeitgeist in which we live) that unconscious lies within cracks and crevices and must be naturalized and domesticated within our discourse as comprehensible socioeconomic cause and effect. I am not denying the political unconscious, but rather wish to reclaim a place for the personal, the grammar of motive and manners, and behavioral cause and effect. Do not Marlow and Kurtz, Marlow and Jim, the Captain and Leggatt, Decoud and Nostromo *live* in our memories and feelings rather than find places in our ideological constructions?

V

The search for a restored family is an underlying motif in Conrad's fiction. An orphan since childhood, an expatriate living in an adopted country with a tradition of strong family ties, a man who did not become a husband or father until middle age, Conrad was preoccupied with the value and meaning of traditional family ties and figurative variations of them within interpersonal relationships.

As I have argued elsewhere, most notably in *The Transformation of the English Novel, 1890–1930: Studies in Hardy, Conrad, Joyce, Lawrence, Forster, and Woolf,* Lawrence, Woolf, and Joyce also are preoccupied with revivifying family paradigms, particularly in their major works *The Rainbow, To the Lighthouse,* and *Ulysses.* Lawrence, Woolf, and Joyce were immersed in the British novel and a cultural tradition that stresses the value of close family ties. Likewise, Conrad's personal history and psychic needs made him deeply concerned with revivifying personal and family relationships. Conrad, Lawrence, Woolf, and Joyce focus on the family as the basic unit of civilization during a time when political ideology and religious belief seemed ineffectual to them. From Richardson (*Clarissa*) and Fielding (*Tom Jones*) through Dickens (*Bleak House*) and Hardy (*Jude the Obscure*), the British novel is preoccupied with family paradigms: the relationship between fathers and sons, the plight of disowned children and orphans, and the quest for intimate friendships. A recurring pattern is that of a homeless or a rejected child desperately searching for either a father or a heterosexual partner who would compensate for the sense of loneliness caused by the loss of parents. That the British novel remains a fundamentally private genre concerned with a grammar of motives and with nuances of private relationships undoubtedly has to do with its middle-class roots.

Conrad's fiction abounds with homeless young men from disrupted families searching for putative fathers and brothers as well as for compatible women to relieve the pangs of isolation and excruciating loneliness. Within the shipboard community in the early sea tales, including "Youth," *The Nigger of the "Narcissus,"* "Typhoon," and "The End of the Tether," the captain is a patriarchal figure with whom younger men have a complex father-son relationship. In the sea tales, the shipboard community with its defined responsibilities and camaraderie becomes an important surrogate for those men who either lack family ties or, because of their profession, must of necessity turn from them while on ship. Conrad's conception of the shipboard community as an extended family in which each man's place within the hierarchy defines his duties and responsibilities provides an important alternative to the political anarchy in *Nostromo*. *The Mirror and the Sea* (1906) was begun while he was still writing *Nostromo*, and it may be that his eulogy of the sea contains as much of his political philosophy as does the oft-cited "Autocracy and War" (1905). Conrad perceived the love a man has for a ship in terms of analogies to family and passionate love; the men who sail a ship "learn to know [her] with an intimacy surpassing the intimacy of man with man, to love with a love nearly as great as that of man for woman, and often as blind in its infatuated disregard of defects" (58). Conrad's vision of idyllic shipboard life affirms the values of family and personal relations, while placing commitment to community on other than materialist terms. It is to these values that we must juxtapose the compulsive quest for wealth and power in *Nostromo*. Put another way, the political unconscious of *Nostromo* is that politics—often wearing the mantle of materialism—corrodes (or should we say tarnishes?) like silver itself.

Abroad as Metaphor

CONRAD'S IMAGINATIVE TRANSFORMATION OF SPACE

Abroad for Conrad, of course, was England, the country that provided a home and a language with which to write. Conrad was in exile, an expatriate from his native Poland, and during the formative years of his adulthood he was a wanderer. Yet it is not an exaggeration to say that his most important journeys took place in his own mind. Some of his most graphically depicted places—Costaguana, the imagined country of *Nostromo* (1904), and the cosmopolitan Russia of *Under Western Eyes* (1911)—are places he never visited, but Russia, which he regarded as the dreaded enemy to Poland's independence, haunted his imagination. That a *place* could be a source of alienation, marginality, and exclusion derived from his having been born in a section of Poland under Russian rule and having, in his early childhood, accompanied his father and mother into an exile imposed because of his father's radical political activity in Warsaw. Not until late in his life, if ever, did Conrad quite think of himself as settled in an appropriate place, and that sense of himself as wanderer, as not belonging even in England, preyed upon his psyche.

I want to use as my point of departure Wallace Stevens's poem "Mrs. Alfred Uruguay," a poem in which he imagines an elegantly dressed woman undergoing a traditional quest up a mountain that allegorically represents the real. As she makes her way up the mountain on a donkey without companions, she is passed by a lone, poorly dressed man on a horse descending hurriedly from the mountain of the real to the imagined land where experience is reshaped:

> Who was it passed her there on a horse all will,
> What figure of capable imagination?
> Whose horse clattered on the road on which she rose.
> . . . .

Originally published in *The Ends of the Earth*, ed. Simon Gatrell (London: Ashfield Press, 1992), 173–86.

The villages slept as the capable man went down,
Time swished on the village clocks and dreams were alive,
The enormous gongs gave edges to their sounds,
As the rider, no chevalere and poorly dressed,
Impatient of the bells and midnight forms,
Rode over the picket rocks, rode down the road,
And, capable, created in his mind,
Eventual victor, out of the martyrs' bones,
The ultimate elegance: the imagined land.[1]

Is not the man of capable imagination an apt metaphor for Conrad, the man in exile, who negotiates between the reality of his own life and his powerful imagination?

This essay will define how, in Conrad, setting negotiates between the anterior reality in which the author lived and found the ingredients for his experience and the imagined world that results from what Stevens called "the capable imagination." The process of creating setting, or setting-making, may be thought of as a verb to show how the writer moves between the two poles of anterior reality and the fictive world. Let us consider the nature of setting. Setting is the physical place where the action and plot of an imagined world take place. But is it not also the imaginative place where the desires, hopes, and plans of writers contend with their doubts, anxieties, and frustrations? Setting is a seam where author and reader meet. Setting not only reflects the action, character, thematic issues, and linguistic patterns of a novel, but also takes its definition from them.

Like language, setting is constituted and constituting; it reflects not only the historical conditions of the imagined world, but also those of the real world in which the author has lived. It is one of the more determinate codes that authors create for readers, and yet, no matter how precise and graphic the description, setting always leaves cracks and crevices for the reader's imagination. Mikhail Bakhtin's concept of *chronotype* reminds us of the inseparability of space and time: "Time, as it were, thickens, takes on flesh, becomes artistically visible; likewise, space becomes charged and responsive to the movements of time, plot, and history."[2] Novels rescue time from oblivion by giving it the shape of space; they enable us to realize events in tangible readings. The read-

---

1. *Poems by Wallace Stevens,* selected by Samuel French Morse, 102.
2. *The Dialogic Imagination,* ed. Michael Holquist, trans. Caryl Emerson and Michael Holquist, 84.

er recalls setting as a *paysage moralisé,* a mindscape engraved with the events that transpired.

While no amount of precision and nominalism can exclude a reader from creating, as Stevens does when looking at the setting of Key West, "ghostlier demarcations" and "keener sounds," the precision and detail of setting are means by which the author controls and limits the reader. Yet the reader participates in limiting, defining, and clarifying space; as he reads, he goes "abroad" from the text. Setting is perhaps the most likely element to reflect anterior reality because of the authors' investment in the places of their lives and in their narratives of their memories. For Conrad, setting often played a crucial Oedipal role, for it represented the visionary gleam that he was forever deprived of. As we shall see, Conrad's settings are less accurate reflections of the places he had seen than illuminating distortions and metaphors for central themes. Abroad, then, in this essay is less an actual place than a trope created by Conrad's imagination and a process by which the imagination travels to a world elsewhere. In Conrad's work, it is both the fictional other that Conrad seeks and the creative place that both confirms and questions his feeling of exile and marginality.

I I

Conrad's life in the British Merchant Marine and his travels to the East played an important role in his fiction. Since he had actually sailed on a ship named the *Narcissus* in 1884, he could draw upon romantic memories of a successfully completed voyage at a time when his creative impulses were stifled by doubts.[3] Conrad also fused stories he had heard—such as the source story for the tale of James Wait—with his own journeys. Prior to writing *The Nigger of the "Narcissus"* (1897), Conrad sought an appropriate plot structure and point of view with which to organize his subject matter. Imagining the voyage of the *Narcissus* as a structural principle, he overcame writing paralysis. After he had committed himself completely to literature ("Only literature remains to me as a means of existence"), he was bogged down with the early version of "The Rescuer." Agonizing about his inability to make progress on "The Rescuer," he wrote to Edward Garnett: "Now I've got all my people together I don't know what to do with them. The progressive episodes of the story *will* not emerge from the

3. See Jocelyn Baines, *Joseph Conrad: A Critical Biography,* 75–77.

chaos of my sensations. I feel nothing clearly."[4] The imagined voyage of the *Narcissus* became at once the material for a plot to examine ethical and political questions of fundamental importance to Conrad and a private metaphor for the process of creating significance. Frustrated with his inability to write, Conrad found in the voyage of the *Narcissus* an imaginative escape to the space and time of past successes.

"Youth" (1898), too, is a story that transforms the ingredients of a former sea voyage—in this case, Conrad's position as a second mate on the *Palestine* in 1881–1882. Based on his command of the *Otago* in 1888—Conrad's only command—*The Shadow-Line* (1916) explores the difference between merely practicing skills and providing leadership to a community.[5] In contrast, the seemingly similar "The Secret Sharer" (1910), which is also based in part on Conrad's first command and in part on what he had learned of an 1880 incident aboard the *Cutty Sark,* emphasized the captain-narrator's personal psychological development, rather than his ability to occupy a position in terms of standards established by maritime tradition. By fulfilling the moral requirements of a clearly defined position, the captain-narrator fulfills himself; he overcomes ennui, anxiety, and anomie and merges his psychological life with the demands of the external world. Thus the sea voyage—with its clearly defined beginning and ending, its movement through time toward a destination, its separation from other experiences, and its explicit requirements that must be fulfilled by the crewmen and officers—provided a correlative *within Conrad's own experience and imagination* for the kind of significant plot he sought.

I I I

Conrad visited the Malay Archipelago while sailing as first mate on the steamer *Vidar* (1887–1888). Conrad's first two novels, *Almayer's Folly* (1895) and *An Outcast of the Islands* (1896), reflect his 1895–1896 state of mind and

4. Letters of March 23/24 and June 19, 1896, in *Collected Letters of Joseph Conrad, vol. 1, 1861–1897*, ed. Frederick Karl and Laurence Davies, 267, 288. "The Rescuer" later became *The Rescue.* The best biographical source is Zazislaw Nadjer's *Joseph Conrad: A Chronicle.*

5. Conrad had written in Richard Curie's copy of the novel, "This story had been in my mind for some years. Originally I used to think of it under the name of *First Command.* When I managed in the second year of war to concentrate my mind sufficiently to begin working I turned to this subject as the easiest. But in consequence of my changed mental attitude to it, it became *The Shadow-Line*" (Curle, *The Last Twelve Years of Joseph Conrad* [London, 1928]; quoted in Frederick R. Karl, *Joseph Conrad: The Three Lives: A Biography,* 770).

reveal his values.[6] In these early novels Conrad tests and refines themes and techniques that he will use in his subsequent fiction. In what will become characteristic of Conrad's early works, he uses material for his fiction from his own adventures. He not only draws upon his Malay experience but also bases the title character of his first novel on a man he actually knew. While these two novels seem to be about remote events, they actually dramatize his central concerns.

Sambir, the setting for *Almayer's Folly* and *An Outcast of the Islands,* is the first of Conrad's distorted and intensified settings. Like the Congo in *Heart of Darkness* (1899) and Patusan in *Lord Jim* (1900), Sambir becomes a metaphor for actions that occur there. It is also a projection of Conrad's state of mind as it appears in his 1894–1896 letters: exhaustion and ennui alternate with spasmodic energy.[7] Conrad's narrator is in the process of creating a myth out of Sambir, but the process is never quite completed. Like Hardy's Egdon Heath, Sambir is an inchoate form that can be controlled neither by man's endeavors nor by his imagination. The demonic energy that seethes within the forests is a catalyst for the perverse sexuality of the white people and their subsequent moral deterioration. With its "mud soft and black, hiding fever, rottenness, and evil under its level and glazed surface," Sambir refutes the Romantic myth that beyond civilization lie idyllic cultures in a state of innocence (325–26). Sambir's river, the Pantai, is a prototype for the Congo; the atavistic influence it casts upon white men, drawing out long repressed and atrophied libidinous energies, anticipates the Congo's effect on Kurtz. Sambir's primordial jungle comments on the illusion shared by Dain and Nina, as well as by Willems and Aissa, that passionate love can transform the world. Sambir's tropical setting seems to be dominated by the processes of death and destruction, and the jungle's uncontrollable fecundity moves toward chaos rather than toward order. The dominance of the Pantai and the forest implies that Conrad's cosmos is as indifferent to man's aspirations as the cosmos of his contemporary Hardy, whose *Jude the Obscure* was published in 1895.

Had Conrad not gone on to write *Heart of Darkness,* we might be more attentive to the extent to which Sambir embodied Conrad's nightmare of various kinds of moral degeneracy and how it is for him a grim Dantesque vision of

6. Although written first, *Almayer's Folly* takes place twenty years after *An Outcast of the Islands.* Conrad completed *Almayer's Folly* in 1894 and *An Outcast of the Islands* in 1895; the dates in parentheses are publication dates. Page numbers in parentheses refer to the Kent edition of Conrad's works.

7. See *Collected Letters,* ed. Karl and Davies. For example, John A. Lee and Paul J. Sturm, eds., *Letters of Joseph Conrad to Marguerite Poradowska, 1890–1920,* 63, 82, 86, 88.

damnation. Upon the anarchical and primordial Sambir, man seeks to impose his order. Lacking wife and parents, and bereft in England of any family ties, Conrad proposes family and personal relationships as an alternative to the greed and hypocrisy that dominate Sambir life. Throughout Conrad's early work, he dramatizes the search for someone to legitimize one's activities by an empathetic response to one's motives and feelings. We see this in Jim's need to be understood by Marlow and Marlow's to be understood by his audiences, as well as Conrad's desperate early letters to Garnett.

In his exotic Malay landscapes, Conrad created mindscapes of his own concerns. As an orphan who felt guilty for betraying his personal and national paternal heritage by living in England, Conrad was concerned from the outset with the relationship between parent and child. In the Sambir novels each person seems to require someone else to share his confidence. This takes the form of a search for the missing family. Almayer and Willems lack a father and seek to compensate for the absence of someone in whom to confide. The Malays' search for the restored family parallels that of the white protagonists: Omar is a father figure to Babalatchi, and the latter plays that role for Lakamba.

Conrad's fascination with human decadence, begun in the Malay novels with Almayer and Willems and continued in "The Idiots" (1896), is the subject of his first Congo story, the powerful and underestimated "An Outpost of Progress" (1897), which was written during an interlude from *The Rescue* (1919). Because he was bogged down on *The Rescue,* writing a story in which the moral distinctions were clear and in which he was in complete control of his materials was extremely important to him. Conrad's letter to Fisher T. Unwin makes clear that the story is in part an intense response to his 1890 Congo experience: "All the bitterness of those days, all my puzzled wonder as to meaning of all I saw—all my indignation at masquerading *philanthropy* have been with me again while I wrote" (emphasis added).[8]

In "An Outpost of Progress," Conrad examines his 1890 Congo journey—the source of *Heart of Darkness*—for the first time. When we turn to *Heart of Darkness* after examining Conrad's 1890 Congo diary—reprinted in *Last Essays*— we see how Conrad's anterior reality informs his fictional text, and how his imagination creates the reality of place to meet the thematic needs of his fiction. Note the diary entries:

---

8. Letter to Fisher T. Unwin, 1896, quoted in John Dozier Gordan, *Joseph Conrad: The Making of a Novelist,* 242.

Friday, 4th of July. . . . Saw another dead body lying by a path in an attitude of meditative repose. At night when the moon rose heard shouts and drumming in distant villages. Passed a bad night.

Monday, 7th July. . . . Hot, thirsty and tired. At eleven arrived on the mket place. About 200 people. No water. No camp place. After remaining for one hour left in search of a resting place. Row with carriers. No water. . . . Sun heavy. Wretched.[9]

The phases of two white men's—Kayerts's and Carlier's—degeneration reflect Conrad's profound disillusionment from his own experience in the Congo. Despite their lip service to idealism, by the second day they have already ceased trying to export their civil-service version of European civilization. In fact, the outpost of progress quickly becomes an outpost of savagery. Rather than being agents of change, these men are changed: like Kurtz in *Heart of Darkness* they gradually regress to savagery. But while Kurtz actually *renounces* civilized values and boldly practices "unspeakable rites," Kayerts and Carlier forget their ideals and drift into anomie. If Eliot excluded Kurtz from his category of "hollow men" because Kurtz chose evil, he could well have had Kayerts and Carlier in mind as the hollow men who did not will their fate. In progressive stages, the trappings of civilization crumble. First, Kayerts and Carlier abandon their attempts to improve their outpost. Then, they abdicate the vestiges of their morality when they accede to Makola's trading of slaves for ivory. Finally, they revert to complete savagery when Kayerts, after he thinks that Carlier intends to do the same to him, murders his companion.

That Marlow, the principal narrator of "Youth," *Heart of Darkness, Lord Jim,* and, later *Chance,* is a vessel for some of Conrad's doubts and anxieties and for defining the problems that made his own life difficult is clear not only from his 1890 Congo diary and the 1890 correspondence with Madame Poradowska, but, even more so, from the letters of the 1897–1899 period. *Heart of Darkness* expresses his attitude toward the 1890 voyage to the Congo Free State and his response to the imperialistic excesses of Leopold II of Belgium.

The subject of *Heart of Darkness* is primarily Marlow, but the presence of Conrad is deeply engraved on every scene. Conrad dramatized Marlow's efforts to narrate his experience at a time when he himself was anxious that he might not be able to fulfill his artistic credo—as presented in the preface to *The Nig-*

9. Quoted in Jocelyn Baines, *Joseph Conrad: A Critical Biography,* 115, 116.

ger of the "Narcissus"—of making other men *see*. Conrad transfers to Marlow the agonizing self-doubt about his ability to transform personal impressions into a significant tale. Marlow's effort to come to terms with the Congo experience, especially Kurtz, is the crucial activity that engaged Conrad's imagination. Marlow's consciousness is the arena of the tale, and the interaction between his verbal behavior—his effort to find the appropriate words—and his memory is as much the *agon* as his Congo journey. Both the epistemological quest for a context or perspective with which to interpret the experience and the semiological quest to discover the signs and symbols that make the experience intelligible are central to the tale.

For the sake of making my argument about how Conrad uses exoticism to define his values, I shall draw upon some of my prior arguments about *Heart of Darkness* and *Nostromo* and, to a lesser extent, about *Under Western Eyes* and *The Rover*.

The Congo experience had plunged Marlow into doubt and confusion. Marlow's experience in the Congo invalidated his naive belief that civilization equaled progress. As Marlow engages in an introspective monologue, the catalyst for which is his recognition that the Thames, too, contained the same potential darkness for the Romans as the Congo does for him, he recalls how he had discovered the pretensions of European civilizations. The equation of the Roman voyage up the Thames and Marlow's up the Congo suggests an important parallel. That Marlow says "this also has been"—not "this also was"—"one of the dark places on the earth" denies the idea of humanity's progressive evolution, still a widely held view in the 1890s, by showing that the manifestation of barbaric impulses is a continuous possibility. The essential nature of Europeans and natives is the same: "The mind is capable of anything—because everything is in it, all the past as well as all the future" (96). Conrad stresses that illusions are not only a defense against reversion to primitive life, but the basis of civilization.

One of Conrad's characteristic themes is the relationship between experience and memory. When memory imaginatively transforms our actual experience—the experience of the self that has been "abroad"—what do we leave behind? Although every event is informed by his present attitudes, Marlow's meditation follows the order of the original experience until he reaches the circumstances surrounding his first meeting with Kurtz. He desperately wants to believe that his journey into the atavistic Congo and his climactic encounter with Kurtz have broken down his personality only to prepare him for a new, broader integration

and a deeper understanding of his relationship with—and responsibility to—
other people. Marlow defers recounting the meeting with Kurtz in order to leap
ahead to his meeting with the Intended, to comment on Kurtz's megalomania,
and to relate how he saw the shrunken heads. He has difficulty recollecting his
impression of the more gruesome details of his experience. Except for the
shrunken heads, he contents himself with merely alluding to "subtle horrors"
and "unspeakable rites." He claims he had almost expected to discover symptoms of atavistic behavior in his journey "back to the earliest beginnings of the
world." (He specifically says, "I was not so shocked as you may think" [130].)
Yet, now that Marlow is back within the civilized world, he recoils from the
grotesque memories.

Marlow's journey from Europe to the Congo helped prepare him to sympathize with Kurtz. From the outset he was offended by the standards and perspectives of the European imperialists, and gradually he began to sympathize
with the natives against the predatory colonialists. As an idle passenger on a boat
taking him to the Congo, he caught glimpses of the inanity he later encountered
as an involved participant. Even then, he saw the fatuity of the "civilized" French
man-of-war's shelling the bush. Marlow invests Kurtz with values that fulfill his
own need to embody his threat of the jungle into one tangible creature. While
Kurtz, the man who seemed to embody all the accomplishments of civilization,
has reverted to savagery, the cannibals have some semblance of the "restraint"
that makes civilization possible. While scholars have argued about possible
sources for Kurtz—and one can make a case for the parallel to the journalist/
explorer Henry Morton Stanley—it is best to see Kurtz as a composite figure
who symbolizes the pretensions of imperialism. Kurtz is a poet, painter, musician, journalist, potential political leader, a "universal genius" of Europe, and yet
once he traveled to a place where the earliest beginnings of the world still survived, the wilderness awakened "brutal instincts" and "monstrous passions." If
Kurtz is considered the center of the "heart of darkness," the business of following Kurtz and winning the "struggle" enables Marlow to believe that he had
conquered a symbol of the atavistic, debilitating effects of the jungle.

I V

Nostromo shows how Conrad became what Wallace Stevens might call a
figure of capable imagination who could use his reading and a brief visit to the

West Indies in 1878 to create an imaginary nation with its own history and landscape. The pain of exile and the feeling of marginality are important in Conrad. It is not necessary to agree with Jocelyn Baines that Costaguana is a disguised version of Poland to understand *Nostromo* as a sublimated act of self-justification on Conrad's part.[10] For Conrad was deeply troubled over accusations that he had abandoned Poland. He suspected his motives for settling in England and turning his back upon both his country and his family heritage. Once he left the sea and became a writer, the justification that Poland lacked the facilities for his chosen career was difficult to sustain.

It may be that *Nostromo* also reflects Conrad's subconscious resentment toward a father who neglected family for politics and ultimately left him an orphan, after inflicting exile, disgrace, and economic hardship upon his family. By castigating the possibility of change through politics, Conrad convinced himself of the rectitude of his own decision to desert Poland, to which his father had made a complete political commitment. Given his father's zealotry and Conrad's consciousness of it, it is hardly too much to say that politics becomes a paternal abstraction to which Conrad must atone, palliate, and explain himself. The means of palliation are his political novels. *Nostromo* justifies the choice of personal fulfillment over political involvement because it shows politics as a maelstrom that destroys those it touches and, more important, shows that one inevitably surrenders a crucial part of one's personality when one commits oneself to ideology.

Under Western Eyes depends on a juxtaposition of Geneva and Russia. Conrad had a deep abiding hatred for Russia because he believed it had exploited and terrorized Poland and was responsible for the death of his parents. Conrad followed events in Russia and knew, through his friends the Garnett family, Russian refugees and revolutionaries. In the author's note he wrote that the plot and characters "owe their existence to no special experience but to the general knowledge of the condition of Russia."

In Conrad's version of Russia, autocratic politics create a world in which personal lives are distorted by the political abstractions served by proponents and antagonists. Each of the Russians creates for himself the fiction of a receptive counterpart who understands his every thought and feeling. Russia finally emerges as primitive and atavistic, a kind of European version of the Congo, where possibilities exist that have all but been discarded by Western countries.

10. See ibid., 313–14.

Conrad's Geneva is a civilization where the libidinous energies and the atavistic impulses may be squelched, but violence and anarchy are under control. Conrad had visited Geneva in 1907 when he had taken his son Borys there for hydropathic treatment of suspected tuberculosis, the disease that had been the cause of death for both of Conrad's parents. He had been there once before in the 1890s on his own behalf. In a note in crude copy, he had written that he had been "induced to write this novel by something told me by a man whom I met in Geneva many years ago (Razumov's fate)."[11] It is very much to the point that the people, other than the revolutionaries, who reside in Geneva are engaged in shopkeeping, teaching, picnicking, walking; and that these quite ordinary activities can take place in Geneva, unlike in Russia, without bombs and intimidation. Geneva may have its materialistic aspect, epitomized by the rather tasteless Chateau Borel that now stands abandoned by its absentee owners, but it makes possible the cultivation of personal affections and the fulfillment of private aspirations, which the autocratic and violent Russian world blunts.

The narrator continually tests and redefines qualities that he associates with Russia and Geneva until, finally, he establishes the *moral* superiority of Western life. Like the narrator's fascination with Russian behavior, his repressed romantic interest in Natalie, and his imaginative excitement as he describes Razumov's self-flagellation in physical images, his muted dissatisfaction with Geneva indicates a repressed and sublimated longing for more intense experience than his lonely bachelor existence provides. Moreover, Geneva's willingness to accommodate the callousness and irrationality of the refugee revolutionary community within its midst offends his sense of morality. If, Conrad implies, the self-discipline of Western life has its cost in passion, it is nevertheless true that benign government gives people the choice of whether to write fictions, teach languages, or even pursue political visions. Geneva is a drab and pedestrian depiction of political stability, but it still remains a place where such a figure as the narrator may combine a highly civilized conscience with an individuality that, in its insistence on self-denigration, approaches the idiosyncratic and quirky.

In contrast to the narrator, who intuitively transforms every incident in his life into a matter of conscience, the Russians see their private lives in terms of a vague historical perspective. Thus the narrator's excerpts from Razumov's diary, Peter's autobiographical volume, and Tekla's life expand the novel's spatial-

11. Quoted in ibid., 370.

temporal dimensions. But the movement of the novel alternates between the
personal, limited, and subjective perspective of the narrator and the vast, im-
personal immensity of Russia with its countless anonymous citizens suffering
misery that can barely be implied:

> Razumov received an almost physical impression of endless space and of
> countless millions.
> He responded to it with the readiness of a Russian who is born to an in-
> heritance of space and numbers. Under the sumptuous immensity of the
> sky, the snow covered the endless forests, the frozen rivers, the plains of an
> immense country, obliterating the landmarks, the accidents of the ground,
> levelling everything under its uniform whiteness, like a monstrous blank
> page awaiting the record of an inconceivable history. (33)

Conrad deliberately depicts Geneva as tediously geometric and rather claustrophobic. Razumov is contemptuous of its decorum; he regards the view of the
lake as "the very perfection of mediocrity attained at last after centuries of toil
and culture" (203). While Russian political zealots such as Peter and Sophia—
and Mikulin and General T—speak of national destiny and political ideals, the
narrator's life is concerned with personal relationships in the "free, independent, and democratic" city of Geneva. The narrator speaks condescendingly of
the "precise" and "orderly" Genevan landscape, but the very precision of the narrator's description, as well as his personal subjective response to place, implicitly criticizes the unlimited, amoral space of Russia. The novel confirms the value of the mind's own interior space, personal communication, and private
relationships; it rejects historical and geographical explanations that seek to
place moral responsibility beyond the individual conscience. The humanity and
perspicacity that the narrator brings to his reminiscence "contain" and undermine the Russian conception of vast objective space that resists man's effort to
domesticate it.

V

Conrad's neglected masterpiece *The Rover* (1923) deals more with his re-
shaping of history to fit a dream of a heroic, self-sacrificing death and less with
the actual events of the Napoleonic war. In 1924, some months before he died,
Conrad spoke of *The Rover* in terms that suggested its special importance to

him: "I have wanted for a long time to do a seaman's 'return' (before my own departure)."[12] Peyrol's desire, in his final voyage, to merge his destiny with that of his nation may reflect Conrad's desire, as he approached death, to contribute meaningfully to Poland's destiny. His fantasy of a significant political act is embodied in Peyrol. If, like Nabokov's, Conrad's life was embodied in his imagination, he was never comfortable that he had turned his back on politics and the heritage of his father, whom he recalled as an idealistic patriot. The novel's title also refers to himself, the twice-transplanted alien who finally found a home in England and no longer felt himself something of an outsider. Peyrol re-creates himself at fifty-eight when circumstances connive with his own weariness to deprive him of his past; he creates a new identity just as surely as a younger Conrad did when he left Poland to go to sea and an older Conrad did later, when he turned from the sea to a writing career.

The Rover combines Conrad's fantasy of retreat with his lifelong fantasy of a heroic return home. (Neither his first visit to Poland in 1890, nor his second at the outbreak of the First World War, quite fulfilled his fantasy.) *The Rover* associates Peyrol's return with Conrad's own romantic desire to return to his past. In *A Personal Record*, writing of his first return to Poland, Conrad wrote how the faces "were as familiar to me as though I had known them all from childhood, and my childhood were a matter of the day before yesterday" (27). Similarly, upon arriving in revolutionary France, from which he had long absented himself while pursuing a career as an adventurer, Peyrol is struck by the parallel between himself and the people he encounters, including even the cripple. Gradually he feels that he belongs to France, represented in his mind by the tiny coastal hamlet in which he lives and the people he knows there:

> The disinherited soul of that rover ranging for so many years a lawless ocean . . . had come back to its crag, circling like a great sea bird in the dusk and longing for a great sea victory for its people: that inland multitude of which Peyrol knew nothing except the few individuals on that peninsula cut off from the rest of the land by the dead water of a salt lagoon. (142)

Peyrol embodies Conrad's lifelong relationship with Poland—the country he had left—and his desire to return to the land of the parents who had died while he was a young child. Finally Peyrol underlines the theme of this essay: that

---

12. Letter of February 22, 1924, in Jean-Aubry, *Joseph Conrad*, 2:339.

Conrad's exile and travels were not only sources of physical settings, but also imaginary places that were inextricably related to his own psyche. For Conrad—that figure of capable imagination—abroad was reshaped by his imaginatively transforming places, history, and politics for the purpose of emphasizing his themes and values.

Rereading "The Secret Sharer"

I. BIOGRAPHICAL CONTEXTS

In December 1909 Conrad interrupted his work on *Under Western Eyes* to write "The Secret Sharer." Commenting on Conrad's original plan to call the story either "The Second Self" or "The Other Self," Frederick R. Karl wrote, "His psychological need to share his situation with those close to him is a personal manifestation of what he had just been writing. . . . He displayed now his familiar pattern of dependency, seeking supports as he was being deserted, first by [Ford Madox Ford], then by [his agent, James] Pinker."[1]

"The Secret Sharer" owes its origins to events that took place on the *Cutty Sark* in 1880 when the first mate killed a man under his supervision. Conrad's "Author's Note" to the volume *'Twixt Land and Sea* explains that the story was based on a tale he heard less than two months after the crime on the *Cutty Sark* was committed. Indeed, in July–August 1882, he probably read about the trial in the London *Times,* since he was in Falmouth at the time. Norman Sherry's *Conrad's Eastern World* is a useful resource for contexts and backgrounds. In addition to Karl and Sherry, Zdzislaw Najder and Jocelyn Baines have examined the biographical aspects of "The Secret Sharer." For example, Jocelyn Baines wrote:

> The story is based on an incident which happened on board the *Cutty Sark* in 1880. The *Cutty Sark* had put in to Singapore on 18 September, three days after the chief officer of the *Jeddah* (the *Patna* in *Lord Jim*) had arrived there. In Conrad's adaptation of the *Cutty Sark* incident, Leggatt, the mate of the *Sephora,* kills a disobedient member of the crew during a storm and is put under arrest by his captain. But he escapes and swims to another ship of which the narrator of the story is captain. The captain is

Originally published in *Joseph Conrad's "The Secret Sharer,"* ed. Daniel R. Schwarz (1997), 63–78, 95–111.

1. *Joseph Conrad: The Three Lives: A Biography,* 675–76.

a young, comparatively inexperienced man who has just been given his first command—here Conrad seems to draw on his own experiences on the *Otago*—"a stranger to the ship" and "somewhat of a stranger to myself."[2]

Apparently Conrad had performed the kind of maneuver he describes—taking the ship perilously close to land before changing direction—as skipper of the *Otago* in 1888 during the first days of his only command.

Basil Lubbock's *The Log of the "Cutty Sark"* is an important background source. Excerpts from chapter 5 are reprinted in *Conrad's "Secret Sharer" and the Critics*, edited by Bruce Harkness. Harkness also reprints crucial articles from the *Times* of London about the arrest and trial of Sidney Smith, chief mate on the *Cutty Sark*, the character on whose murderous behavior Leggatt is based. In their essay "Morality and Psychology in 'The Secret Sharer,'" Royal Gettmann and Bruce Harkness stress the importance of both sources:

> In respect to the world of external appearances—the world of things, places, and actions—there are numerous parallels between the short story and the actual events aboard the *Cutty Sark* as narrated in Lubbock's "A Hell-Ship Voyage." The same is true of the possible source material from The London *Times*.

But they stress how Conrad's art transformed the story:

> Conrad felt obliged to penetrate much more deeply: to show that the universe and human nature are so constituted that any man innocently passing the time of night anywhere may have thrust upon him a moral dilemma that can be resolved only at the cost of a bitter struggle.

The source material enables them to argue that Leggatt represents atavistic, amoral behavior:

> This, then, is what Leggatt symbolizes: the instinct for violence in the Captain; his acknowledging Leggatt as his double means just that, for to acknowledge Leggatt is to acknowledge violence. . . . The hate then combines the expression of the Captain's pity and the dark impulse of Leggatt. It is, finally, a symbol of integration. It saves the present ship by permitting the

2. *Joseph Conrad: A Critical Biography*, 355.

Captain to navigate his ship safely past the rocks. The dark side of man saved the *Sephora,* as well as all hands aboard the new ship.[3]

'*Twixt Land and Sea* (1912) contains three long stories written for magazines in the 1909–1911 period. "The Secret Sharer" is one of the great tales in the English language, but, although not major works, the others—"Freya of the Seven Isles" and "A Smile of Fortune"—deserve to be read more than they are. All three tales explore a young captain under stress. Conrad returns to a world he had left behind—the lonely, bachelor world of the sea with its homosocial ship bonding, its absolute moral code. Although in this period of renewed personal and financial turmoil Conrad's imagination turns nostalgically to life at sea, the sea is no longer the simplified world of "Typhoon" (1902) or "The End of the Tether" (1902), where moral distinctions are clear.

In these 1909–1911 tales, a young captain is faced with circumstances and emotional traumas for which neither the maritime code nor his experience has prepared him. Both "Freya of the Seven Isles" and "A Smile of Fortune" provide evidence that Conrad is interested in the heterosexual relationships of inexperienced young adults. In each case an ingenuous and imperceptive male figure ceases to function effectively in his career because of his passionate involvement with an immature young woman. "A Smile of Fortune" is the most autobiographical and the most revealing of the two; in fact, it may suffer from Conrad's inability to separate himself from the captain-narrator.

II. CRITICAL HISTORY OF "THE SECRET SHARER"

I shall discuss in this section ways in which "The Secret Sharer" has been read before presenting my own reading. The critical history of "The Secret Sharer" reflects the history of Anglo-American criticism in the postwar period, a history I briefly discussed in my Introduction. In the late 1940s, when thematic criticism competed with more formal criticism, and concomitantly, when formal criticism was used to probe for thematic implications, Walter Wright stressed the theme of self-knowledge and community necessary on board ship:

But what causes the struggle here is that the very bond which should tie him to his fellowmen—the secret of man's emotional and impulsive na-

3. In Bruce Harkness, ed., *Conrad's "Secret Sharer" and the Critics,* 125, 127, 130, 131.

ture, of his fear and irresolution, of his unpredictability to himself—this bond is pulling him further away from the kinship which he must achieve with humanity as the master of a crew and a ship.[4]

One might note that the value of fellowship among a group of men pursuing a common purpose was in the forefront in the years during and immediately following World War II. Success on board ship, as in battle, depended on the efficiency of an interdependent community in which each male could be depended on to take care of his fellows. Following from that was the credo that each member of a unit had to know himself to do his duty and that such self-knowledge often derived from the Christian ethical imperative of placing the community's needs before one's own. Typical of the Christian humanism of some postwar criticism, Wright contends,

> The motif of the kind act's saving the doer is at least as old as Christianity. Conrad objected to Tolstoy for making the Christian religion his basis; yet he himself not infrequently arrived at a resolution of a paradox in accord with Christian sentiments . . . to do one's duty. It came when a man apprehended the mysterious nature of personality and destiny and found a dream that gave his world a center. When he did this, however far he might be estranged from actual men, he was true to the life of man.[5]

A later version of a thematic approach—fertilized by F. R. Leavis's stress on bracing moralism and tangible realism as the values to be discovered and valued by close reading—can be found in H. M. Daleski's characteristically humanistic and sensitive perspective in *Joseph Conrad: The Way of Dispossession*. Daleski sees the story in terms of the development and maturation of the captain as a result of his contact with Leggatt. One of the most interesting humanistic discussions in the 1980s was Steve Ressler's *Joseph Conrad: Consciousness and Integrity*. As have a number of other critics, including Sherlyn Abdoo, he argues:

> Conrad provides numerous signs that Leggatt is to be regarded as a symbolic manifestation of the captain's unconscious, his being a physical double both suggesting and reinforcing unconscious connections. . . . In the sense that the visitor corresponds uncannily to the wished-for male

4. Walter F. Wright, *Romance and Tragedy in Joseph Conrad*, 49.
5. Ibid., 50.

image, one might say that the captain has dreamed Leggatt into existence.[6]

But the problem with this position, that Leggatt is a figment of the captain's
imagination or is dream, is that unlike, say, Hawthorne's "Young Goodman
Brown," the dream is not embedded within the text as a suggestion that a dream
is taking place. And where does the dream begin and end? In other words, where
do we put the brackets that signify the dream, as opposed to the waking experience? Archbold would surely have to be part of the dream, and if the whole
story is a dream, how and why is it different from other works of fiction? It seems
odd to argue that because he is alone on deck and Leggatt wears his sleeping-
suit, it follows that the captain has fallen asleep. Within a text's system of language, we need specific formal indications that the text is a dream narrative. Perhaps one of the best early formalist (as opposed to thematic) studies is that of
R. W. Stallman, a significant figure in the New Critical movement, who asserts
in his essay "Conrad and 'The Secret Sharer'":

> The fact is that Conrad's theory of the novel is no other than the modern
> canon that every work of art is symbolic. Every great novel has a symbolic
> meaning, imparts a significance which transcends mere plot or fable. Sym-
> bolism, it has been aptly said, does not deny Realism; it extends it. . . . Be-
> cause a novel is a product of language, a novel depends for its very life upon
> the word. What we term the characters of a novel are nothing more than
> the author's verbal arrangements.

Stallman discusses the relationship between Leggatt and the captain, stressing
how they are counterparts or doubles of one another:

> It is this mutual, sympathetic understanding of what the other's plight
> means to him that bolsters and morally fortifies their spiritual being, Leg-
> gatt's no less than the captain's. . . . Through Leggatt that initial mood of
> calm and resolute self-confidence with which the captain begins and ends
> his arduous enterprise is gradually reinstated.

Stallman perceptively notes that each is the secret sharer of the other. He also
implies that were Leggatt to tell the tale, he would relate a vastly different ver-

---

6. *Joseph Conrad: Consciousness and Integrity,* 82. See Abdoo's "Ego Formation and the Land/Sea
Metaphor in Conrad's 'Secret Sharer.'"

sion of the events, and the reader would experience a vastly different structure of effects. Emphasizing, as so many of the New Critics do, the ethical and humanistic implications of formalist readings, Stallman continues:

> In terms of the ethical allegory, Leggatt is the embodiment of the captain's moral consciousness. . . . The captain's subconscious mind has anticipated, in the fiction of the symbolic flame, the idea of a second self—the appearance, that is, of someone untroubled, unyielding, self-confident. (The captain is just the opposite, being of a mind troubled and filled with self-doubt.) The symbolic flame materializes in human form. Leggatt bodies forth the very commonplace upon which the whole story is built: no man is alone in the world, for he is always with himself. Leggatt, this other self, becomes the psychological embodiment of the reality, the destiny, the ideal of selfhood which the captain must measure up to. He provides him the utmost test.[7]

Daniel Curley's 1962 essay "Legate of the 'Ideal'" is an important discussion of the doubling theme in formalist terms. While contending that Leggatt is not really guilty, Curley suggests, "He [Conrad] had to find a way of separating his protagonist's legal and moral responsibilities, and he had to invent for Leggatt an action that would be a crime in form but not a crime in fact."[8] But Curley's and Stallman's fine formalist readings show the problem of ignoring both the source material and the maritime code. They do not pay sufficient attention to the *Cutty Sark* or Conrad's maritime values. If one sees, as Curley does, the captain as a surrogate for Conrad, one tends to sympathize with the captain's identification with the murderous Leggatt. But later critics had difficulty seeing Leggatt as an ideal, particularly in view of Conrad's strict allegiance in his fiction to maritime ethics, which requires that the first mate be responsible for the welfare of those serving under him. Within the benign autocracy of the ship, the captain has the full allegiance and full responsibility for all those under his command, and the first mate, his second in command, is responsible in the same way for all but the captain. Put another way: Leggatt can no more be killing his crew members— no matter how much they misbehave—than a first-grade teacher can toss an unruly child down the stairwell during a fire drill. Louise K. Barnett views Leggatt as a social misfit rather than a murderer, more a primitive than a criminal.[9]

---

7. In Harkness, ed., *Conrad's "Secret Sharer,"* 95, 99, 100–101.
8. In ibid., 77.
9. Louise K. Barnett, "'The Whole Circle of the Horizon': The Circumscribed Universe of 'The Secret Sharer.'"

Stallman and Curley are typical of a generation of postwar formalists who, influenced by such figures as Dorothy Van Ghent and F. R. Leavis, used formal analysis to ask questions not merely about the structure and language of the text but also about the author's psyche and philosophy.

Among the landmarks of Conrad criticism is Albert Guerard's important study *Conrad the Novelist,* which provides what is still one of the most illuminating commentaries on "The Secret Sharer." Guerard wrote at a time when the archetypal-myth theories of Carl Jung were extremely influential. Using the concept of the Jungian "night journey," Guerard sees "The Secret Sharer," along with Conrad's two other great symbolist masterpieces, *Heart of Darkness* and *The Shadow-Line,* as quest journeys within the dark, dimly acknowledged parts of the psyche:

> I refer to the archetypal myth dramatized in much great literature since the Book of Jonah: the story of an essentially solitary journey involving profound spiritual change in the voyager. In its classical form the journey is a descent into the earth, followed by a return to light.

In addition to focusing on the archetypal dimension of "The Secret Sharer," Guerard writes compellingly about the narrative perspective:

> The point of view is not, as it happens, Conrad's usual one when employing the first person. His normal manner is to employ a retrospective first person, free to move where he wished in time, and therefore free to foreshadow his conclusion.

He stresses how the self-dramatizing telling is a critical issue for the captain-narrator understanding the story: "The nominal narrative past is, actually, a harrowing present which the reader too must explore and survive."[10] Although Guerard's view may not adequately account for the retrospective nature of the narrator in "The Secret Sharer," who tells us that he speaks at a distance of years, it began a process of seeing the telling as a central *agon* of the tale and of analyzing the teller's psyche and values in terms of his soliloquy.

Guerard discusses how *The Shadow-Line*—another of Conrad's first-person accounts of a captain on his maiden voyage—can be read as a sequel to "The Secret Sharer." Also wanting to see "The Secret Sharer" as a precursor to *The*

---

10. *Conrad the Novelist,* 15, 27.

Shadow-Line is Carl Benson, whose 1954 essay "Conrad's Two Stories of Initiation" is characteristic of humanistic formalism—an approach that, as noted before, demonstrates that literary criticism addresses the inextricable relation within texts of formal aesthetic issues and ethical implications. According to Benson, "The Secret Sharer" is not a story of full initiation into mature responsibilities. It is the beginning of the initiation, but it remains for *The Shadow-Line* to show the passage from egocentric youth to human solidarity. Unlike the pure New Critics who exclude the author from their discussion, Benson uses Conrad's other works to decode his "conscious interest" and to stress the relationship between Conrad and the captain:

> It is not, I think, remarkable that a reader who turns to the short novel after the long story should ask: For what reason, or reasons, did Conrad decide to handle the same problem (initiation), same ship, same crew, same captain twice? Is not *The Shadow-Line* in a sense a peculiarly significant rewriting, done because Conrad realized that the initiation of the captain of "The Secret Sharer" was humanly abortive—and this despite the last phrase, more applicable to the captain than to Leggatt, about "a free man, striking out for a new destiny"?[11]

At the time when the captain-narrator's telling was becoming a particular focus of readers in the 1950s and 1960s, Wayne Booth was formulating rigorous narratological methods for such an approach. In *The Rhetoric of Fiction* Booth shows that the "autonomous" text derives from the conscious or unconscious decisions made by the author to shape the reader's response: "Nothing is real for the reader until the author makes it so, and it is for the reader that the author chooses to make this scene as powerful as possible." Booth insists that an author affects the reader as the author intends and communicates human emotions and values to an audience. The reader in turn responds to the presence of a human voice within the text. In a retrospective essay on *The Rhetoric of Fiction*, Booth differentiates between a poetics ("study of what the work is, what it has been made to *be*") and a rhetoric ("what the work is made to *do*"): "*The kinds of actions authors perform on readers differ markedly, though subtly, from the kinds of imitations of objects they are seen as making*, in the poetic mode."[12]

---

11. "Conrad's Two Stories of Initiation," 46.
12. *The Rhetoric of Fiction*, 108, 152, 159; "The Rhetoric of Fiction and the Poetics of Fiction," 115.

Booth believed the New Critics focused on poetics—the ontology of a text as a well-wrought urn—and minimized rhetoric in the form of the author-reader relationship; by contrast, the neo-Aristotelian Booth defined the relationship among author, text, and audience.

One of Booth's major legacies is his distinction between reliable and unreliable narrators: "I have called a narrator *reliable* when he speaks for or acts in accordance with the norms of the work (which is to say, the implied author's norms), *unreliable* when he does not."[13] (I prefer the terms *perceptive* and *imperceptive,* since a narrator might be reliable and yet be unaware of the implications of his or her behavior.) Following Booth's insistence on asking "Who is speaking to whom?" and "For what purpose?" other critics have pursued the captain-narrator's motives. Although critics such as Michael Murphy have discussed the possibility of an unreliable narrator, it might be more to the point to understand the narrator as more imperceptive than unreliable. Other essays pursuing this line of discussion focusing on narrative point of view include J. D. O'Hara's "Unlearned Lessons in 'The Secret Sharer'" and Robert D. Wyatt's "Joseph Conrad's 'The Secret Sharer': Point of View and Mistaken Identities."

One of the best discussions of "The Secret Sharer" is Louis H. Leiter's 1960 essay "Echo Structures: Conrad's 'The Secret Sharer,'" which speaks of the way patterns of narrative formations—what he calls the "echo structures"—create meaning by displaying major similarities but crucial and revealing differences.

> Structures not only of character but also of narrative action, parable, metaphor, and the like, become a fundamental means for achieving aesthetic and thematic effects. . . . An echo structure implies one or more structures similar to itself. The tautology which is the echo structure may be a repeated symbol, metaphor, scene, pattern of action, state of being, myth, fable, or archetype. If viewed within the perspective of Biblical story or classical myth, either directly stated in the text of the story or implied, that perspective may suffuse the echo structures of similar construction with additional meanings.

In this dense essay influenced by Joseph Frank's famous 1945 three-part piece on spatial form in modern literature, Leiter concludes,

> The action of the echo structure implies, it seems to me, a moral judgment of Leggatt, although it does not state the judgment openly. It dramatizes it

13. Booth, *Rhetoric,* 158–59.

and by doing so makes the reader psychologically aware of it. At the same time the echo scene declares the moral superiority of the consciously aware narrator-captain who has come to face his secret inner self, to conquer it, and to control it.[14]

The scene in which the captain disciplines his first mate by shaking his arm departs radically from Leggatt's disciplining of his crew member by killing him and implies a strong judgment of Leggatt. Like Stallman, Leiter was influenced by the theories of Kenneth Burke—especially his *Philosophy of Literary Form*. Burke argues that

> a poem's structure is to be described most accurately by thinking always of the poem's function. . . . [A] poem is designed to "do something" for the poet and his readers, and . . . we can make the most relevant observations about its design by considering the poem as the embodiment of this act. In the poet, we might say, the poetizing existed as a physiological function. The poem is its corresponding anatomic structure. And the reader, in participating in the poem, breathes into this anatomic structure a new physiological vitality that resembles, though with a difference, the act of its maker, the resemblance being in the overlap between writer's and reader's situation, the difference being in the fact that these two situations are far from identical.[15]

Leiter also stresses mythopoeic parallels. In addition to following Guerard by drawing a parallel between the captain's descent into himself and the Jonah story, Leiter discusses the important Cain-Abel resonances:

> The Cain-Abel archetype circumscribes the narrator-Leggatt relationship as well, the longest pattern of action and most important relationship of the novel, for the narrator, in a role comparable to that of Cain, figuratively kills his Abel-Leggatt when he consigns him to the sea.[16]

Others who have discussed parallels between "The Secret Sharer" and the Bible include Mark A. R. Facknitz and Daphna Erdinast-Vulcan.[17]

14. "Echo Structures: Conrad's 'The Secret Sharer,'" 159, 162. See Frank's "Spatial Form in Modern Literature."
15. *The Philosophy of Literary Form*, 75–76.
16. "Echo Structures," 168–69.
17. Facknitz, "Cryptic Allusions and the Moral of the Story: The Case of Joseph Conrad's 'The Secret Sharer'"; Erdinast-Vulcan, *Joseph Conrad and the Modern Temper*.

The focus on mythopoeic issues reflects not only the influence of T. S. Eliot's mythic method (articulated in his famous 1923 review of *Ulysses* in *The Dial* and demonstrated in his poetry). It also reflects Northrop Frye's archetypal theories (related to but different from Jung's view that we share a collective unconscious) in the late 1950s and early 1960s. In his *Anatomy of Criticism* Frye creates a literary analogue to the Bible, which he describes as a "definitive myth, a single archetypal structure extending from creation to apocalypse." His description of the biblical cycle is useful in understanding his work:

> The Bible as a whole . . . presents a gigantic cycle from creation to apocalypse, within which is the heroic quest of the Messiah from incarnation to apotheosis. Within this again are three other cyclical movements, expressed or implied: individual from birth to salvation: sexual from Adam and Eve to the apocalyptic wedding; social from the giving of the law to the established kingdom of the law, the rebuilt Zion of the Old Testament and the millennium of the New.[18]

Like the work of Franz Kafka, Sigmund Freud, James Joyce, Bertolt Brecht, or Jackson Pollock, Frye's *Anatomy* attempts to question the possibility and significance of temporality, progress, and indeed any concept of unity that is dependent on movement.

Traditional formalism—biographical and contextual criticism and myth criticism—shares the assumption that the author has consciously, and on rare occasions unconsciously, made the narrative what it is and almost always *intended* the mythical, biblical, and biographical parallels the text contains. More recently, readers have sought perspectives of which the author may have been unaware, sometimes because his or her historical situation prevented such awareness. One model for such reading has derived from psychoanalysis. In their essay "Secret Sharing," Barbara Johnson and Marjorie Garber have used "The Secret Sharer" to explore varieties of psychoanalytic criticism. Influenced by Freud's *Interpretation of Dreams* and most notably by the work of Jacques Lacan, they examine the text in terms of "the pathology of the author," "the pathology of the protagonist," "the pathology (or symptomology, or symptomography) of the text," "the text as a theory of a symptom or complex," and "the text as an allegory of psychoanalysis." Johnson and Garber differentiate between psychological and psychoanalytic reading:

18. *Anatomy of Criticism: Four Essays,* 315, 316–17.

Psychological readings often posit intentions and beliefs in the author, and then apply them to the story told by the text. . . . A psychoanalytical reading, in contrast, sees conscious attitudes and beliefs as unstable constructions resulting from an ongoing struggle with conflicting forces within the self. Consciousness is only one part of a complex signifying dynamic. A hypothesis about Conrad's probable attitude toward Leggatt's crime can thus in no way be determining for an interpretation. This does not mean that the question of Leggatt's moral status is irrelevant, but that the question of morality in the story is more complex than can be accounted for through a simple innocent/guilty opposition.

They use "The Secret Sharer" as a paradigm of psychoanalytic process, arguing that the "relation between concealment and doubleness" articulated in the text is not the "relation between a mystery and its solution or a symbol and its meaning" but rather a "way of investigating that which psychoanalysis, too, investigates."[19]

Johnson and Garber's interest in the psychology of the captain-narrator as a model of psychoanalytic countertransference is hardly new to criticism of "The Secret Sharer," but they take it in new directions:

When we turn to the second paradigm of psychoanalytic reading, the pathology of the character, we discover a very similar Oedipal conflict in Conrad's "The Secret Sharer." If by Oedipal we mean competition with or rivalry with a father or father figure, or, by extension, threatening figures who wield power and seem to disempower the protagonist, the story has more than enough such conflicts to offer. There are several candidates for the role of father, notably the chief mate on the ship, an older man with "a terrible growth of whisker," "round eyes and frightful whiskers," like many emblems of castration in Freud (e.g., "The Head of the Medusa," "The Uncanny"), and, later, the skipper of the *Sephora,* also older, also whiskered, a married man whose name might be Archbold (a splendidly potent name) but the narrator isn't sure—he has repressed it, and explains away the repression: "at this distance of years I hardly am sure." . . . "Captain Archbold (if that was his name)." . . . In the end, having harbored and released the fugitive, the young captain can be alone with the ship, with the command. He has come out the other end of the Oedipal crisis by accepting the necessity of losing part of himself: his fantasy of guilty omnipotence. In essence he has arrived at a new, revisionary version of castration as *enabling.*

19. "Secret Sharing: Reading Conrad Psychoanalytically," 631, 629.

For them the ship represents the mother. When they discuss what they call the symptomology of the text, one sees how in the recent criticism the critic has become more of a focus figure than the author:

> There is another way to read the scene of Leggatt's appearance from the water, a way that accords more readily with what we have called the symptomology of the text than of the narrator. Viewed mythically or archetypally, the dangling rope ladder, though it may in one way signal vulnerability to castration, in another resembles an umbilicus, and the scene is a birth scene, the naked infant emerging from the water clinging to the cord.

They conclude their ingenious and subtle reading by suggesting,

> The narrator seems at last to have renounced both the potency and the terror of infantile omnipotence, and to be ready to recognize that control of his fate is neither his nor not his. Rather, his fate is somehow henceforth tied to the course of a floating signifier.[20]

We should realize that like formalists—or for that matter, myth critics—of a prior generation, Johnson and Garber look for patterns of iteration, including those of prior myths, such as the Oedipus story. Are they not emphasizing the ontological reality of the text—the sentences and words themselves as objects, units of energy, textures, sounds, visual surfaces, spaces, and even distinct letters—as well as the perceiver's role in making sense of that reality?

Yet for older generations of formalists, Johnson and Garber's speculations may be troubling. Their brilliant essay testifies to a fundamental shift *from* trying to render the author's conscious or unconscious intention and the effects the author was trying to create for readers *to* resistant readings that empower critics to create patterns of meaning of which the author was unaware. These critics use the text to illustrate psychoanalytic models even while deconstruing (or deconstructing) the *construed* text that the author intended for his audience. Garber and Johnson speak also to the extraordinary influence of Lacanian psychoanalysis in the past decade. In their deconstructive model, texts may be open, unresolved, and problematic, and readers need not choose one reading. An urge for order may falsify a text, and we need be attentive to gaps, fissures, and enigmas.

---

20. Ibid., 632, 634, 639.

Joyce Wexler, in "Conrad's Dream of a Common Language," uses Conrad's text to illuminate "Lacan's theory of the subject's entry into the Symbolic order." For her it is Leggatt who is the catalyst for the narrator's movement:

> In Lacanian terms, the captain does not project the double as an aspect of himself; instead, he views the other as his double so that he can introject him. According to Lacan, soon after birth a primordial form of subjectivity inaugurates the Imaginary, which dominates from six to eighteen months but never entirely disappears. In this early period, the child only partially and intermittently differentiates itself from the outside world. . . . Although most of Conrad's fiction recognizes the constraints of the Symbolic, in "The Secret Sharer," the narrator, a young captain uneasy with his first command, regains access to the Imaginary world of direct identification with the other. . . . [Finally,] relinquishing the Symbolic for a more primitive kind of connection with Leggatt, the captain relies on intuition and gesture to perform what words cannot do.[21]

Josiane Paccaud's Freudian and Lacanian reading underlines the story's kinship to *Under Western Eyes.* In language indebted to Lacan, she writes,

> My contention is that the ritual initiation performed in "The Secret Sharer" is no less than the subject's accession to the symbolic after inner divisiveness and the unbridgeable gap between desire and its impossible object, between signifier and signified, between the speaking "I" and the psychic self, have been acknowledged. Unlike Jim, the captain has realized that the step from the name to the thing must not be walked, for fear one should stumble into the realm of imaginary, albeit romantic, fantasies.[22]

As gender and gay studies and, more recently, queer theory have become important factors in reading, interest has turned to the male bonding in Conrad. Building on suggestions in Thomas Moser's excellent *Joseph Conrad: Achievement and Decline* and Bernard Meyer's idiosyncratic but valuable *Joseph Conrad: A Psychoanalytic Biography,* Robert Hodges suggests in "Deep Fellowship" that Leggatt represents the captain's homosexual side:

---

21. "Conrad's Dream of a Common Language: Lacan and 'The Secret Sharer,'" 599, 602, 603.

22. "Under the Other's Eyes: Conrad's 'The Secret Sharer,'" 62. Using the different approach of Jungian psychology, James White locates the theme of fertility in his "The Third Theme in 'The Secret Sharer.'"

A young ship's captain falls in love with the fugitive whom he hides in his cabin, and later risks both his ship and his career to help his lover escape. . . . The sexual connotations are prominent. Leggatt appears at night and is completely naked until the captain somewhat hastily finds clothing for him. He is always clad in a sleeping suit and is hidden in the captain's bedroom and bathroom. . . . The moment of their parting has intense sexual overtones. The two men crouch together in the sail locker from which Leggatt intends to drop into the sea unnoticed. The captain wants to give Leggatt a hat to protect him from the tropical sun. . . . The obvious suggestion here is of a sexual approach at first misunderstood, perhaps even construed as an attempt at murder, but finally accepted as a loving gesture of farewell.[23]

Our discussion demonstrates that the interpretative history of a text—in particular "The Secret Sharer"—is a trialogue among the text as object that critics write about, the subjective interests of individual critics, and the cultural context in which those critics write. The various strands of criticism coalesce around similar psychological, formal, and moral issues: how Leggatt and the captain behave and how they *should* behave; the narrator's point of view and how it is shaped by events of his life; and how the narrative iterations shape the reader's response. We see a continuing pattern of interest in "The Secret Sharer" as a tale of initiation, of individual guilt and collective responsibility, and as a journey into self from which the speaker emerges with great self-knowledge—a tale aesthetically organized to stress the transformation of the narrator. The critical history of "The Secret Sharer" is not only a critical history of Anglo-American criticism and of kinds of responses to literary modernism, but a continuing and vital conversation about how we make sense of a text that talks to us about our fear of failure, our need to communicate, and our desire to understand ourselves and be understood by others.

III. A PSYCHOANALYTIC PERSPECTIVE: "THE SECRET SHARER" AS AN ACT OF MEMORY

"The Secret Sharer" is personal in the way great lyrical poetry is personal, drawing from experience that is at once individual (Conrad's assuming

---

23. "Deep Fellowship: Homosexuality and Male Bonding in the Life and Fiction of Joseph Conrad," 384, 386.

the captaincy of the *Otago* in 1888) and representative of the deepest strains of human experience, especially fear and self-doubt in the face of challenge. Although in this period of renewed personal and financial turmoil Conrad's imagination turned nostalgically to life at sea, the sea is no longer the simplified world of "Typhoon" or "The End of the Tether," where moral distinctions are clear. Thus in "The Secret Sharer" the young captain is faced with circumstances and emotional traumas for which neither the maritime code nor his experience has prepared him.

Conrad's narrative reveals as it conceals, conceals as it reveals. The captain-narrator recounts a tale of initiation in which he successfully overcomes debilitating emotional insecurity to command his ship. The sensitive and intelligent captain discovers within himself the *ability to act* decisively. Initially the captain doubts himself, feels a "stranger" to his ship and crew, and wonders if he should "turn out faithful to that ideal conception of one's own personality every man sets up for himself secretly" (26).[24] His concern *now* in telling the story is to convey what Leggatt meant to him. Although he certainly knows that harboring an escaped murderer represents a threat to maritime civilization and violates his own legal and moral commitment, his retelling ignores this. In our psychological critique of "The Secret Sharer" we need to explore the complex psyche and values of the captain-narrator and to understand not only why he behaves as he does but also how the original experience is reflected, refracted, displaced, and projected in the retrospective telling.

The act of observing is a crucial focus of modernism. For example, borrowing from astronomy, James Joyce makes the theme of parallax (how the same phenomenon looks different depending on the angle of vision or perspective) central to *Ulysses* (1922). Cubism is about the need to see from multiple perspectives. Conrad's "The Secret Sharer," like Henry James's *The Turn of the Screw* (1898), is about seeing and being seen, which plays such an important role in impressionism and postimpressionism, especially in the tradition of still life. Leggatt likes to be looked at:

> "When I saw a man's head looking over I thought I would swim away presently and leave him shouting—in whatever language it was. I didn't mind being looked at. I—I liked it. And then you speaking to me so quietly—as if you had expected me—made me hold on a little longer." (37)

24. Page numbers in parentheses refer to *Joseph Conrad's "The Secret Sharer,"* ed. Daniel R. Schwarz.

As in this passage, the self-reflection and narcissism of "The Secret Sharer" are reflected in the verbal style of both the captain and Leggatt. The "I" is not here the "I" of a strong ego; rather, as the *object* of observation, "I" becomes the subject.

Conrad's experiments with the dramatized narrator show how, in the act of interpreting the subject, modernism has shifted the emphasis from the subject itself to the perceiver's mind. With some complaining irony, Virginia Woolf remarks in "Mr. Bennett and Mrs. Brown" that "where so much strength is spent on finding a way of telling the truth, the truth itself is bound to reach us in rather an exhausted and chaotic condition."[25] In the modern period, "finding a way"—the quest for values and for the appropriate style and form—becomes the subject. And is not finding our way another version of seeing?

In my discussion I want to examine the importance of seeing and being seen. When Conrad wrote eloquently in the preface to *The Nigger of the "Narcissus"* about his purpose as a writer, he wrote with the fervor of a man who believes in the capacity of art to shape our responses to life: "My task which I am trying to achieve is, by the power of the written word, to make you hear, to make you feel—it is, before all, to make you *see*." He was speaking of the power of the written word to create within the reader's mind an experience—a visual experience—that would belong to the reader but still be a version of Conrad's own:

> Fiction—if it at all inspires to be art—appeals to temperament. And in truth it must be, like painting, like music, like all art, the appeal of one temperament to all the other innumerable temperaments whose subtle and resistless power endows passing events with their true meaning, and creates the moral, the emotional atmosphere of the place and time.[26]

In many ways "to make you see" is also the subject of James's *The Turn of the Screw* (1898) another story that revolves around the psychological complexity of simultaneously observing and being observed. The governess learns how to see differently in part because of her need to be seen; Douglas wants to be the center of attention as narrator, and James is using his tale to discuss the subjective nature of optics. Using the governess as a paradigm of what happens when reality becomes subordinated to self-indulgence, James explores the way a teller becomes a painter of souls whose telling always has a strong autobiographical

---

25. "Mr. Bennett and Mrs. Brown," 117.
26. Preface to *The Nigger of the "Narcissus,"* 14, 13.

dimension. It may be that the governess—the unreliable narrator whose perceptions are psychotic—is James's self-parody of extreme and self-indulgent aestheticism.

Memory is another kind of seeing—retrospective seeing—and, as we know, memory creates its own distortions. The captain-narrator, separated by a "distance of years" from the meeting with Leggatt, delivers a retrospective monologue:

> On my right hand there were lines of fishing—stakes resembling a mysterious system of half-submerged bamboo fences, incomprehensible in its division of the domain of tropical fishes, and crazy of aspect as if abandoned for ever by some nomad tribe of fishermen now gone to the other end of the ocean; for there was no sign of human habitation as far as the eye could reach. (24)

But despite the past tense, the reader often forgets that the events have already occurred. To recall Guerard's insight, "The nominal narrative past is, actually, a harrowing present which the reader too must explore and survive."[27]

The oblique style disguises as much as it reveals: the "fishing-stakes resembling a mysterious system of half-submerged bamboo fences" anticipate the "headless corpse" that the captain pulls out of the water. When Leggatt appears he is "silvery, fish-like. He remained as mute as a fish, too" (29). Leggatt is aligned with the atavistic and primitive, whereas the captain is a hyperconscious modern man, retreating to his psychic laboratory to sift through his feelings. Appropriately, at the end Leggatt asks to be abandoned to the primitive world. Words such as *incomprehensible* and *crazy* are the available and feeble semiotic tools with which the captain is trying to come to terms with his behavior—behavior that even at the distance of years eludes explanation. He is well aware *now* of the stakes and knows that in the past he jeopardized his future by harboring an escaped murderer; Leggatt violated every tenet of the maritime code when he strangled a man under his command.

We need to understand that the narrative is a *painful* act of memory that has the potential to be deeply disruptive to the captain's current sense of self. In a way we are in the position of an analyst hearing about an incomprehensible, even traumatic experience. Indeed, we might recall that the act of telling is a version of "repetition compulsion," which Freud describes in his 1920 essay "Beyond the Pleasure Principle":

27. *Conrad the Novelist,* 27.

> It must be explained that we are able to postulate the principle of a repetition-compulsion in the unconscious mind, based upon instinctual activity and inherent in the very nature of the instincts—a principle powerful enough to overrule the pleasure-principle, lending to certain aspects of the mind their daemonic character, and still very clearly expressed in the tendencies of small children, a principle, too, which is responsible for a part of the course taken by the analysis of neurotic patients. Taken in all, the foregoing prepares us for the discovery that whatever reminds us of this inner repetition-compulsion is perceived as uncanny.[28]

Freud is describing a patient's need to repeat partly forgotten and repressed material. In "The Secret Sharer" the speaker has a burden of guilt because he has broken the seaman's code. His excuses make up much of the story, and his narrative iterates that he is still somewhat of a stranger to himself. In a sense, the captain's telling allows him to relive the original experience. As Neil Hertz has observed in his discussion of trauma in "Freud and the Sandman,"

> Repetition becomes "visible" when it is colored or tinged by something being repeated, which itself functions like vivid or heightened language, lending a kind of rhetorical consistency to what is otherwise quite literally unspeakable. Whatever it is that is repeated—an obsessive ritual, perhaps, or a bit of acting-out in relation to one's analyst—will, then, feel most compellingly uncanny when it is seen as *merely* coloring, that is, when it comes to seem most gratuitously rhetorical.[29]

Let us return to the act of watching and being watched is a theme that became increasingly prominent in the nineteenth century, as paintings such as Édouard Manet's *Déjeuner sur l'herbe* (*Luncheon on the Grass;* 1863) and works such as the aforementioned *The Turn of the Screw* and Thomas Mann's *Death in Venice* (1912) illustrate. Lacan has focused on the importance of the gaze:

> Is there no satisfaction in being under that gaze . . . that gaze that circumscribes us, and . . . which in the first instance makes us beings who are looked at, but without showing this. The spectacle of the world, in this sense, appears to us as all-seeing. . . . The world is all-seeing, but it is not

---

28. Freud quoted in Neil Hertz, "Freud and the Sandman," in *Textual Strategies: Perspectives in Post-Structuralist Criticism,* ed. Josué V. Harari, 300.
29. Ibid., 301.

exhibitionistic—it does not provoke our gaze. When it begins to provoke it, the feeling of strangeness begins too.[30]

Isn't the captain reenacting the developmental stage (called the "mirror stage" by Lacan) in which the baby recognizes the image in the mirror and gains a sense of wholeness and identity? Interestingly, Conrad entitled his reminiscence *The Mirror and the Sea* (1906).

Let us consider how mirrors function in modernism. The captain observes, "The shadowy, dark head, like mine, seemed to nod imperceptibly above the ghostly grey of my sleeping-suit. It was, in the night, as though I had been faced by my own reflection in the depths of a sombre and immense mirror" (31). Mirrors always distort, for we see only what we want to see; we see only the part of the body on which we focus. In *The Turn of the Screw,* the governess sees herself for the first time "from head to foot" in the mirror in the long, impressive room to which she is assigned (631).[31] Identity is dependent on what one sees, how one sees, and how one is seen. And does the mirror not focus on ourselves creating what we see and so call attention to the self-reflexivity of reading in the modern era and the continuity between reading texts and reading lives? Specter experiences may reveal that one is perceiving myopically *or* perspicaciously. There can be little doubt that the captain sees Leggatt—if he did not, where would the specter/dream experience begin? (After all, Captain Archbold comes looking for Leggatt.)

Let us consider Manet's *Déjeuner sur l'herbe* (1863), a parody of the pastoral as seen from an urban perspective. Manet's painting is a narrative of voyeurism, one that anticipates Henry James's *The Turn of the Screw* and the obsession in "The Secret Sharer" with seeing and being seen. Two young urban males—the tasseled cap was worn by students—are picnicking with a naked woman. Meanwhile, in the background—recalling ironically Botticelli's *Birth of Venus* (1480)—a woman emerges from a stream. But the flat background landscape might be another picture ironically commenting on the foregrounded picnic. Or we might say the "middle-grounded picnic" because foregrounded on the left is a still life; only the still life has a sense of depth. Isn't Manet calling attention to the painter's ability to mix genres however he pleases and to defy conventions of genre and perspective?

---

30. Jacques Lacan, *The Four Fundamental Concepts of Psycho-Analysis,* ed. Jacques-Alain Miller, trans. Alan Sheridan, 75.
31. Page numbers in parentheses refer to *The Great Short Novels of Henry James,* ed. Philip Rahv.

Édouard Manet, *Déjeuner sur l'herbe*, 1863. Paris, Musée d'Orsay. Photo by © RMN-Gérard Blot, réunion des musées nationaux.

Neither woman—the one sitting on her wrap or the one emerging from the stream—pays attention to the men or to each other. Each is in her own space. Note how the naked woman is unself-consciously looking away from her companions, perhaps to catch the attention of other men or women who are not within the scene. In a sense, we the audience are engaged frankly by her as voyeurs in a libidinal interchange in which she both looks and is looked at. If we think of *The Turn of the Screw*, the foregrounded woman is the governess's suppressed libidinal self and the self-absorbed woman in the background is the mysterious, ghostly presence that exists beyond the conscious level. In *Déjeuner sur l'herbe* we follow the phallic cane as it calls attention to her nakedness. As Françoise Cachin notes, "The still life accentuates the nudity of the woman, who becomes, in the presence of this heap of fashionable raiment, undressed rather than nude."[32] Yet the picnic lunch—with cherries of June, the figs of Septem-

32. *Manet, 1832–1883*, 169.

ber—is not realistic. We see the influence of Titian's *Concert Champêtre* and Raimondi's engraving—inspired by a Raphael composition—*The Judgment of Paris.* (Manet would have enjoyed the classical echo of his city's name.) But in Manet's realistic Paris sexual frankness dominates.

I want to consider "The Secret Sharer" in the tradition of Joris-Karl Huysman's *À Rebours* (*Against the Grain,* 1884) and Oscar Wilde's *The Picture of Dorian Gray* (1891). As Richard Sieburth notes, the bachelor has no place in a family-oriented culture:

> The bachelor cuts a somewhat pathetic figure in a nineteenth century given over to the ideological consolidation of the social and economic virtues of family life. Sexually, he is viewed with both condescension and trepidation, for while his legitimate recourse to prostitution is more or less condoned, he nonetheless threatens the social order as a possible agent of adultery, criminal seduction, or unnatural perversion. Economically, he is considered at most a marginal entity, for he plays no role in the transmission of property through inheritance or dowry. Civically, he is seen as an embarrassment to community values, a case of arrested development, narcissistically clinging to the prerogatives of his self-centered individualism.[33]

The bachelor motif plays a role in the sea tales of Conrad, in the male bonding between Marlow and Kurtz in *Heart of Darkness* and, in particular, between the captain and Leggatt in "The Secret Sharer," where the word *secret* (which implied sexuality—as in the anonymous text *My Secret Life*—to the Victorians) gives the male bonding a strong sexual implication. The captain-narrator never mentions a woman in his life, and Leggatt is disturbed that Captain Archbold of the *Sephora* has brought his wife aboard. The captain is a sometimes introverted bachelor, wedded to his routines, desperately lonely, and he creates his own company by reaching out for a lonely male figure—a supposedly empathetic other in the form of Leggatt.

"The Secret Sharer," like James's *The Turn of the Screw,* emphasizes looking and seeing as a mode of perception that reveals the inner workings of character; the captain's and Leggatt's loneliness helps to create what they see. The captain becomes imprisoned by a nightmare of his own choosing. Leggatt destabilizes the captain as the captain's obsession with Leggatt undermines his capacity to command his ship.

---

33. "Dabbling in Damnation: The Bachelor, the Artist and the Dandy in Huysman."

Among other things, homoeroticism is a metaphor for the inversion of art. In *The Turn of the Screw* the apparitions, particularly Quint's female companion and counterpart, Miss Jessel, become the governess's secret sharers, and she speaks of Quint as a stranger in the same way the captain-narrator speaks of Leggatt in "The Secret Sharer." Particularly to a contemporary reader, does the male bonding in Conrad's story not have a homoerotic aspect? After all, they are in bed together and communicate like lovers: "And in the same whisper, as if we two whenever we talked had to say things to each other which were not fit for the world to hear, he added, 'It's very wonderful'" (52). Note the parallel between the unmarried governess when she encounters her predecessor—or, rather, her ghost—in the schoolroom: "She had looked at me long enough to appear to say that her right to sit at my table was as good as mine to sit at hers" (707). The captain's looking at the naked Leggatt and realizing him as other—as a potentially fulfilling and sexualized other—is a male version of the kind of gazing we see in *Déjeuner sur l'herbe*. It is this looking at and being seen that suggest homoerotic interest on the captain's part. Like Gabriel Conroy, Joyce's paralytically self-conscious figure in "The Dead," the captain often regards himself as strangely detached, the object of his own gaze.

Let us return to the captain's act of memory. Perhaps we can draw upon Louis L. Martz's conception of a meditative poem to clarify what is happening. The intense reflective process in which the speaker's past comes alive in his memory and offers a moment of illumination by which he can order his life recalls Martz's definition of the meditative process: "The mind grasps firmly a problem or situation deliberately evoked by the memory, brings it forward toward the full light of consciousness, and concludes with a moment of illumination, where the speaker's self has, for a time, found an answer to his conflicts."[34] A meditative poem, such as George Herbert's "The Collar," recollects a vital episode in which the speaker experiences spiritual growth by conquering the secular demands of his ego. In both "The Collar" and "The Secret Sharer," the recollection is informed by insight that was lacking when the original event took place. That the captain can give meaning and structure to an experience which included neurotic immobilization demonstrates his emotional and moral development and his present psychic health.

One of Conrad's recurring themes is that each man interprets events ac-

34. *The Poetry of Meditation*, 2d ed., 330.

cording to his moral and emotional needs. Because one's version of events reflects an interaction between, on the one hand, experience and perception, and, on the other, memories and psychic needs, interpretation always has a subjective element. The captain's interpretation of his experience dramatizes the process of his coming to terms with what Leggatt symbolizes. In somewhat reductive but apt Freudian terms, Leggatt is a man of unrestrained id and underdeveloped superego. The captain is his opposite: a hyperconscious modern man who fastidiously thinks of the consequences of every action to the point where he cannot *do* anything. Self-doubt and anxiety create an illogical identification with Leggatt as his double. He risks his future to hide the man he regards as his other self. To avoid discovery, he begins to act desperately and instinctively without conscious examination of the consequences of each action. Leggatt's presence creates situations where the luxury of introspection is no longer possible. Symbolically, the captain completes himself. He finds within himself the potential to act instinctively and boldly that his double exemplifies. It can be said that his adult ego is created by appeasing the contradictory demands of the id and the superego. Listening to the narrator, we tentatively suspend our moral perspective and fail to condemn him for giving refuge to a suspected murderer. We react this way because as his words engage us and we become implicated as his confessor, we come to share his perspective.

Conrad wants us to perceive Leggatt and the captain as representatives of a modern split between mind and instinct. Leggatt's Conradian predecessors are Falk ("Falk: A Reminiscence"; 1903) and Kurtz, the demonic figure who reverts to savagery in *Heart of Darkness;* the captain recalls the narrators of "Il Conde," "The Informer," and "An Anarchist"—three of Conrad's political short stories collected in his *A Set of Six* (1908)—and anticipates the language teacher of *Under Western Eyes,* to which Conrad returned after finishing "The Secret Sharer." The effect of Leggatt's presence is to disrupt the ship's community and to raise further doubts in the minds of the captain's officers about his own self-control and sanity. The captain becomes more neurotic because he has to consider whether his every sentence might reveal his secret. He now has twin loyalties, mutually exclusive, to his ship and to the man he is harboring and with whom he identifies. Paradoxically, the desperation of his paranoia, of his belief that he is constantly being scrutinized by his subordinates, leads him to give his "first particular order." When threatened, he "felt the need of asserting [him]self." The pressure of circumstances makes it increasingly difficult for him to distinguish between himself and Leggatt:

> All the time the dual working of my mind distracted me almost to the point
> of insanity. I was constantly watching myself, my secret self, as dependent
> on my actions as my own personality, sleeping in that bed, behind that door
> which faced me as I sat at the head of the table. It was very much like being
> mad, only it was worse because one was aware of it. (40)

His distinction between self and other threatens to collapse; he had the "mental feeling of being in two places at once [which] affected me physically as if the mood of secrecy had penetrated my very soul" (48). Like Eliot's J. Alfred Prufrock and Joyce's Gabriel Conroy in "The Dead," the captain has a personality whose integrity is threatened by a disbelief in the authenticity of self. R. D. Laing's *The Divided Self* aptly describes this phenomenon of modern literature. The terms in which this existential psychologist describes schizoid conditions are directly related to the crisis of identity that Conrad analyzes:

> If one experiences the other as a free agent, one is open to the possibility of
> experiencing oneself as an *object* of his experience and thereby of feeling
> one's own subjectivity drained away. One is threatened with the possibili-
> ty of becoming no more than a thing in the world of the other, without any
> life for oneself, without any being for oneself. . . . One may find oneself en-
> livened and the sense of one's own being enhanced by the other, or one may
> experience the other as deadening and impoverishing.[35]

In retrospect it is clear that the captain has been "enlivened" by his experience of Leggatt, although at first Leggatt's appearance—like the presence of the threatening first mate, whose whiskers and manner intimidate the captain—has the effect of "deadening" the captain by making him doubt his own capacity.

The captain's *creation* of Leggatt is a major part of the original experience. By "creation," I do not mean that the captain invents or dreams up Leggatt but that he constructs Leggatt for his own psychological purposes. Before Leggatt's appearance, the captain is immobilized by self-consciousness and self-doubt: "My position was that of the only *stranger* on board. I mention this because it has some bearing on what is to follow. But what I felt most was my being a *stranger* to the ship; and if all the truth must be told, I was somewhat a *stranger* to myself" (26, emphasis added). That "stranger" carries the meaning of "alien" and "outsider" from the French word *étranger* is an instance of how the richness

---

35. *The Divided Self: An Existential Study in Sanity and Madness,* 47.

of Conrad's language is occasionally increased by his appropriating French definitions for similarly spelled English words.

Humorless, insecure, and claustrophobic, the captain needs to be on deck to avoid the discomfort and awkwardness fed by his feelings of inadequacy. Leggatt fulfills the captain's need for someone with whom to share the burdens of loneliness and anxiety. The captain's impulse is to completely integrate Leggatt into his social and moral fabric, and to totemize him as part of himself. But Leggatt is one of what Melville calls *Isolatoes,* one who "not acknowledging the common continent of men . . . [lives] on a separate continent of his own."[36] When the captain hears of Leggatt's alternatives (to keep swimming until he drowns or is welcomed aboard), he responds, "I felt this was no mere formula of desperate speech, but a real alternative in the view of a strong soul. . . . A mysterious communication was established already between us two—in the face of that silent, darkened tropical sea" (30). The captain recalls, "The voice was calm and resolute. A good voice. The *self-possession* of that man had somehow induced a corresponding state in myself" (30, emphasis added).

But this contrasts with his original assessment only seconds before: "He seemed to struggle with himself, for I heard something like the low, bitter murmur of doubt. 'What's the good?' His next words come out with a hesitating effort" (29). Jumping from one assertion to another without empirical data, the captain continues to convince himself of Leggatt's resemblance to himself on such flimsy grounds as that they are both "young." Although he tells us that they looked identical, he later admits that Leggatt "was not a bit like me, really" (34). His flattering description of Leggatt is continually modified until it is almost contradicted. Before Leggatt even begins to explain how he killed a man, the captain has excused him: "'Fit of temper,' I suggested, confidently" (31). Insisting on the value of his second self enables the captain to discover himself morally and psychologically; but the process of idealizing his double, his other self, into a model of self-control, self-confidence, and sanity is arbitrary and noncognitive. Perhaps we can better understand the extent of the narrator's surrender of self if we recall Laing's analysis of a man who suffered from what he calls "ontological insecurity": "In contrast to his own belittlement of uncertainty about himself, he was always on the brink of being overawed and crushed by the formidable reality that other people contained. In contrast to his own . . . uncertainty, and insubstantiality, *they* were solid, decisive, emphatic, and substan-

36. *Moby-Dick,* 108 (chap. 27).

tial."[37] Despite the evidence that Leggatt murdered another man in a fit of passion, the captain holds to a belief in Leggatt's control and sanity and insists that the killing was an act of duty. But the reader does not forget that Leggatt commits a horribly immoral act that *he does not regret.*

Conrad emphasizes how the destructive relationship between the doubting crew and the insecure captain shapes the captain's attitude toward Leggatt. The captain never criticizes Leggatt (despite his penchant for criticizing everybody else, from the ratiocinative first mate to the "impudent second mate" and "unintelligent" Captain Archbold) because, believing himself a stranger on the ship, he desperately needs an ally against self-doubt and the hostility of the crew. He identifies with Leggatt not as a criminal, but as an outcast: "I felt that it would take very little to make me a suspect person in the eyes of the ship's company" (37). Because in *the captain's own mind* Leggatt is the picture of resolute self-confidence, he becomes in some respects an ideal to be studied: "And yet, haggard as he *appeared,* he *looked* always perfectly self-controlled, more than calm—almost invulnerable" (48, emphasis added). The fetal position that Leggatt assumes as he hides in the cabin hardly suggests invulnerability. Indeed, it suggests his moral immaturity and his inability to distinguish between self and world, either from an ethical or from a psychological perspective. The now mature captain *believes* he learned from his second self qualities of courage, self-confidence, and psychological wholeness—qualities that became his means of achieving maturity.

Paradoxically, Leggatt disrupts the captain's psychic health, and hence the order of the ship, at the same time as he is a catalyst for a more efficient integration of both the captain's personality and his fitness to command. As we have seen, the captain projects onto Leggatt a confidence he himself lacks and an ability to face crises he does not yet possess. Yet Leggatt's struggle with the crewman came when he was himself highly excited, and he shows considerable emotion several times in discussions with the captain.

The captain is as much Leggatt's secret sharer as Leggatt is the captain's: each plays the role of analyst and analysand. Indeed, each of the two men has a partial understanding of the other, but each *believes* the other's partial understanding to be complete. In this sense, too, Leggatt is the captain's double. Leggatt says, "As long as I know that you understand," before adding, "But of course you do" (52), because he too needs to believe he is understood. Leggatt desper-

---

37. *The Divided Self,* 48.

ately reaches out for someone to share his psychic burden. He likes to be looked at and spoken to, and even stammers when recalling their first meeting. At one point he says, "I wanted to be seen, to talk with somebody, before I went on" (38). As Stallman says, "it is this mutual, sympathetic understanding of what the other's plight means to him that bolsters and morally fortifies their spiritual being."[38] They both create a buffer to protect themselves from their feelings of excruciating loneliness in a hostile world. In each other, they find the intimacy of a captain-mate relationship that they both pathetically lack. The first mate's suspicion of the captain echoes Leggatt's opinion of *his* captain. And Archbold, the captain of the *Sephora,* the boat on which Leggatt killed a man, is the type of captain—or, rather, Leggatt's and the captain's version of him—that the narrator might have become, if he had not engaged in this process of self-development. Archbold, whose name has resonances of traditional descriptions of Satan as *arch fiend* or *arch bold,* is an embodiment of the maritime tradition of authority. He represents a father figure whom the captain oedipally rejects.

Leggatt hides in the captain's L-shaped room. As Johnson and Garber remark,

> The cabin is L-shaped. It is shaped like a signifier, and what it signifies is what it contains and what contains it, the man whose name begins with L: Leggatt. Even Leggatt's name is doubled, two g's, two t's, two vowels—only the L stands alone, and it too is doubled in the form of the cabin. The capital L stands for Leggatt, but also for letter, for the "agency of the letter in unconscious" (Lacan), for the fact that what is innermost (concealed) in the mind is in a sense its other.[39]

While experiencing Leggatt's objective world—that is, seeing the world through Leggatt's perspective—the captain adopts Leggatt's perspective. Therefore he has no hesitation or ambivalence in his attitude toward Archbold. Not only does he compare Archbold, who stands, however poignantly, as an upholder of the moral order, to a criminal, but in addition he describes him as "a tenacious beast." Speaking of an exchange with Archbold, the captain recalls, "I had been too frightened not to feel *vengeful;* I felt I had him on the run, and I meant to keep him on the run. My polite insistence must have had something menacing in it because he gave in suddenly" (45, emphasis added). However,

38. "Conrad and 'The Secret Sharer,'" in Harkness, ed., *Conrad's "Secret Sharer,"* 99.
39. "Secret Sharing," 636.

the reader knows that the captain's judgment of Archbold is really Leggatt's and cannot exclude the possibility—indeed the probability—that Archbold is everything *he* says he is.

Nor can we accept the captain's belief that Leggatt deserves the allegorical identity of Truth, and Captain Archbold that of Falsehood. His recollection of Leggatt's captain is consistent with his present mythmaking. Although he does not remember his name, he assigns a pejorative name that we realize would be far more appropriate to Leggatt, a figure whose *arch boldness* defies conventional morality: "He mumbled to me as if he were ashamed of what he was saying; gave his name (it was something like Archbold—but at this distance of years I hardly am sure), his ship's name, and a few other particulars of that sort, in the manner of a criminal making a reluctant and doleful confession" (41). Although the captain is certain that Archbold suspects him, he offers no real evidence to support this notion; since he has told us how *different* from Leggatt he looked, it is unlikely that he would be the object of Archbold's transference of the antagonism he feels toward Leggatt. When he implies that Archbold does not like him, he is describing perhaps his own guilt: "I had become so connected in thoughts and impressions with the secret sharer of my cabin that I felt as if I, personally, were given to understand that I, too, was not the sort that would have done for the chief mate of a ship like the *Sephora*. I had no doubt of it in my mind" (43). Conrad hardly expected his readers to believe the captain's assertion that he reminded Archbold of Leggatt.

If we regard "The Secret Sharer" as a drama about the problems and interrelationships of people, we must ask why Leggatt requests to be abandoned. Does he sense that the captain cannot continue to operate as a split personality? Probably, but defined by his murderous, impulsive act, Leggatt also needs to assert his own independence and to accept the role of exiled wanderer, as outcast to the universe where civilized values, embodied by the benign autocracy of maritime life, prevail. The narrator, of course, puts the best possible interpretation on Leggatt's behavior and implicitly invites us to do the same. Certainly, when the character with whom we identify and whose judgment is practically beyond reproach enlists our sympathy, it is not surprising that our first response is to accept his evaluation. He admires Leggatt both as a self-controlled man who can accept the consequences of his actions and as a man whose instinctive behavior saved the *Sephora*. For him, Leggatt is not a mutineer and a murderer, but an effective officer who is the victim of circumstances beyond his control.

The captain's final view of Leggatt is significant: "I was in time to catch an evanescent glimpse of my white hat left behind to mark the spot where the se-cret sharer of my cabin and of my thoughts, as though he were my second self, had lowered himself into the water to take his punishment: a *free* man, a *proud* swimmer striking out for a new destiny" (60, emphasis added). The only way for the captain to satisfy his conscience now that he has released Leggatt is to create the myth of a triumphant departure, for even retrospectively he cannot admit that he might have sacrificed Leggatt in order to preserve his own posi-tion. Yet for the reader, Leggatt is a tragic, lonesome figure, branded as an out-sider destined to wander the earth not only by the standards of civilization but by the captain himself.

Why does the captain take Leggatt so close to land? For one thing he needs to assuage his conscience; for another, he has to prove to himself that he has grown into the role of captain; he needs to assert himself in the role of com-mand. Indeed, the telling is that of a retrospective analysand probing into a cru-cial crossing from youth to maturity. Although we cannot be sure of the tale's authenticity, its value to the speaker is incontestable.

It is the teller who has fulfilled the implied prophecy of a new destiny. He has lived up to an ideal conception of himself by proving his ability to command and by establishing his hierarchical position as captain. And Leggatt, abandoned to a world where the captain's epistemology is irrelevant, no longer exists with-in the civilized community except as part of the captain's consciousness. As soon as Leggatt has departed, the captain "hardly thought of my other self, now gone from the ship, to be hidden for ever from all friendly faces, to be a fugitive and a vagabond on the earth, with no brand of the curse on his sane forehead to stay a slaying hand . . . too proud to explain" (59). It is almost as if the captain can now cast aside the man who once threatened his identity (although the telling shows that he regards the experience as crucial to his personal development). With hindsight it seems that Leggatt represents his own potential for evil, which must be expurgated before he can become morally, as well as psychologically, whole. The narrator clearly knows that he has behaved quite differently from the man he regarded as a double when confronted with a similar situation. When we as readers finish the story we understand the story's iterative struc-ture. As Leiter perceptively argues,

> Leggatt seizes the man by the throat at the climax of his archetypal trial by
> storm and kills him in a fit of uncontrolled passion; the narrator also seizes
> the Chief Mate under similar circumstances, his archetypal trial by silence,

but by controlling himself, controlling the frightened, disbelieving man, he controls the ship and consequently saves her from destruction, while saving his reputation and winning the respect of his crew.[40]

The captain finds within himself the confidence to act entirely without the paralytic self-consciousness that interfered at the outset with his ability to command the ship.

Leggatt is flippantly conscious of his similarity to Cain: "The 'brand of Cain' business, don't you see. That's all right. I was ready enough to go off wandering on the face of the earth—and that was price enough to pay for an Abel of that sort" (35). Ironically, although Leggatt proclaims indifference to legal and religious standards, he cannot avoid responding to them:

> "You don't suppose I am afraid of what can be done to me? . . . [Y]ou don't see me coming back to explain such things to an old fellow in a wig and twelve respectable tradesmen, do you? What can they know whether I am guilty or not—or of *what* I am guilty, either? That's my affair. What does the Bible say? 'Driven off the face of the earth?' Very well. I am off the face of the earth now." (52)

It disturbs the conventional morality of the captain to be on the side of Cain. "The very trust in Providence was, I suppose, denied to his guilt. Shall I confess that this thought cast me down very much?" (46). Most of the time he acts as an Abel figure—his brother's keeper—in protecting Leggatt. Yet it is soon clear that the two men contain elements of both Cain and Abel. Leggatt plays the role of Abel when he willingly leaves the ship and thus helps the captain through the crisis. The captain's Cain identity derives from our realization that, to fulfill his own aspirations, he must abandon Leggatt.

The captain's use of Leggatt has its analogy in the creative process of art. Leggatt comes into the captain's experience as a fact of the objective world; the captain transforms Leggatt into a fiction only partially congruent with the objective data of Leggatt's real identity; and then the captain releases him back into the objective world. Unwilling to risk his future, the captain *sacrifices* Leggatt for the unity of his own personality, just as the artist may sacrifice moral engagement for his artistic purposes. Conrad believed that all men have a Cain aspect to their personalities in the sense that physical and psychic survival is depen-

40. "Echo Structures," 142.

dent on conscious and unconscious decisions that jeopardize the best interests of others. Likewise the artist withdraws into the imagination at the expense of immediate participation in the community. The persistent allusions to the Cain-Abel myth suggest that each man must continually confront an unresolvable conflict between self-fulfillment and commitment to others. In an early letter to his aunt, Marguerite Poradowska, Conrad writes, "Charity . . . is a gift straight from the Eternal to the elect. . . . For Charity is eternal and universal Love, the divine virtue, the sole manifestation of the Almighty which may in some manner justify the act of creation." But later in the same letter he writes:

> Abnegation carried to an extreme . . . becomes not a fault but a crime, and to return good for evil is not only profoundly immoral but dangerous, in that it sharpens the appetite for evil in the malevolent and develops (perhaps unconsciously) that latent human tendency towards hypocrisy in the . . . let us say, benevolent.[41]

The captain understands that it would be "sham sentiment"—what Conrad calls "abnegation carried to an extreme"—to sacrifice his future by indefinitely harboring Leggatt.

41. John A. Lee and Paul J. Sturm, eds., *Letters of Joseph Conrad to Marguerite Poradowska, 1890–1920*, 42.

The Continuity of Conrad's Later Novels

The accepted view of Conrad's later fiction—the fiction following *Under Western Eyes* (1911)—is that it represents a radical break with Conrad's prior fiction. In recent years, Conrad's later novels—*Chance* (1912), *Victory* (1915), *The Shadow-Line* (1916), *The Arrow of Gold* (1919), *The Rescue* (1919), and *The Rover* (1923)—have been discussed as symbolic tales and allegories, as if they belonged to a different genre from his previous work. Thematically, they have been seen as symptoms of Conrad's inability to deal with love and sexuality on a mature level. Yet there is scant evidence, either in the "Author's Notes" written in 1919–1920, in his letters, or in his nonfiction, that in his later years Conrad thought he was writing drastically different kinds of fiction or that his values had fundamentally changed. I believe that Conrad's later writing is best understood as an evolution and development of his prior methods, themes, and values. While we should not ignore the differences between these novels and his prior work, it may be time to stress the biographical, thematic, and formal continuities with Conrad's previous work.

The later novels, like their predecessors, need to be understood as expressions of Conrad's psyche and imagination. They continue to test and explore ways of feeling and ways of knowing and to reflect his quest for values and self-definition. Conrad was interested in dramatizing states of consciousness to the last, and the later Conrad novels, like his prior work, explore how men cope in an amoral cosmos more than how they argue for a system of values. Conrad still shows that each person sees reality according to his own needs. For example, *Chance* depends on the elaborate presentation of multiple points of view. Conrad has the omniscient narrator of *Victory* give perspectives other than Heyst's to undermine ironically that apparently strong figure and to show the reader an alternative view of Heyst. *The Arrow of Gold* consists of an appealing but im-

Originally published in *Conrad Revisited: Essays for the Eighties,* ed. Ross Murfin (University of Alabama Press, 1985), 151–69.

perceptive speaker, George, and a dramatic monologue between two notes provided by an editor. Conrad's later novels continue his interest in exploring heterosexual and family ties, often in the context of futile and morally bankrupt political activity. These novels are not divorced from the social and historical context in which the characters live, and they are usually as much concerned with psychological realism and social observation as was his previous work.

Conrad's letters provide evidence for the continuity of his work. For example, the following passage from a 1918 letter could have been written to Edward Garnett twenty years earlier: "That is the tragedy—the inner anguish—the bitterness of lost lives, of unsettled consciences and of spiritual perplexities. Courage, endurance, enthusiasm, the hardest idealism itself have their limits. And beyond those limits what is there? The eternal ignorance of mankind, the fateful darkness in which only vague forms can be seen which themselves may be no more than illusions." In a 1913 letter to Francis Warrington Dawson, he echoes the language of the preface to *The Nigger of the "Narcissus"* (1897) when describing the artist's lonely, agonizing struggle to create: "Suffering is as an attribute almost a condition of greatness, of devotion, of an altogether self-forgetful sacrifice to that remorseless fidelity to the truth of his own sensations at whatever cost of pain or contumely which for me is the whole Credo of the artist."[1] Conrad is still a skeptical humanist who believes that man's best hope rests in personal relationships. He resented those who neglected his humanism and who implicitly accused him of "brutality" and "lack of delicacy";[2] he insisted that, as he wrote in an August 1908 letter to Arthur Symons, "I have always approached my task in the spirit of love for mankind."[3] Of course, despite the considerable continuity of his career, Conrad still seeks the appropriate form and style for each subject and never ceases in his search for new subjects.

In 1910 Conrad was in his fifty-third year. He had lived and written in England for sixteen years and was very conscious that he was aging. While he had become recognized as an important novelist, he had not achieved financial success. He was regarded as an oddity even by his admirers, an outsider who wrote in English but whose temperament and values were not quite English. His self-image oscillated between, on one hand, pride in his achievement and artistic in-

1. Letters of February 6, 1918, to John Quinn, and June 20, 1913, to Warrington Dawson; quoted in Frederick Karl, *Joseph Conrad: The Three Lives: A Biography,* 807–8, 730. I am indebted to Karl's account of Conrad's later years.
2. For example, see an August 28, 1908, letter to Garnett, quoted in ibid., 650n.
3. In Gérard Jean-Aubry, *Joseph Conrad: Life and Letters,* 2:73.

tegrity to, on the other hand, disgust with his difficulties in completing his work and despair about his severe financial problems. He suffered from lack of public recognition and was still plagued by personal and artistic self-doubt. As always, writing was extremely trying for Conrad. He feared that he would leave both *Chance* and *The Rescue* unfinished and that he would not reach the goal of twenty volumes that he had set for himself.[4] His relations with Ford Madox Ford and his agent, James Pinker, were strained, and he was beset by anxiety, hypochondria, and gout. In this frame of mind he suffered a nervous breakdown.

Bernard Meyer has written that, after the 1910 breakdown, Conrad "could not longer afford these introspective journeys into the self." But this ignores the introspective journeys of *The Shadow-Line, The Arrow of Gold,* and *The Rover.* One cannot agree with Meyer that "the doubting, troubled men, like Marlow of *Heart of Darkness,* and hapless souls Jim or Decoud, caught in a neurotic web of their own creation, gave way to simple innocent creatures who, as pawns of fate, struggle with indifferent success against external influence, external accidents, and external malevolence."[5] The later fiction, like the prior work, shows that man is ineffectual in his effort to shape permanently the larger rhythm of historical events, but is able to form personal ties and sometimes to act boldly in his own or others' interest. In *The Shadow-Line* and *The Rover,* temporary personal victories give life meaning. And the act of telling in *The Shadow-Line* and *The Arrow of Gold* is a kind of affirmation; by using assertive, energetic first-person narrators to structure important aspects of his own past, Conrad becomes, as he had been in the 1898–1900 Marlow tales and in "The Secret Sharer" (1910), an active presence within his works. In the later works, passionate love and deep feeling temporarily rescue life from meaninglessness, even if they—to recall Eliot's *The Waste Land*—only provide fragments to shore against one's ruins.

Indeed, in the years that followed the breakdown, Conrad began to achieve financial stability and some measure of personal security. Selling manuscripts to John Quinn helped alleviate his debts. On occasion, Conrad would compromise his artistic integrity by writing potboilers for *Metropolitan Magazine.* Finally, beginning with *Chance,* his books began to sell. Gradually, he began to create a public mask. In particular, he was concerned not only with marketing

---

4. See Karl, *Joseph Conrad,* 639.
5. *Joseph Conrad: A Psychoanalytic Biography,* 243, 221.

his works but also with how he should appear as a literary presence. He developed a public personality for interviews and dialogues with critics, and adopted surrogate sons such as Richard Curle, Gérard Jean-Aubry, André Gide, and Warrington Dawson, all of whom propagated his reputation in the world of letters and in the marketplace. He became more of an urbane Englishman and cultivated a stance of moderation and worldliness. Although in his last years he was somewhat shunted aside by the surge of literary modernism, represented by the works of Joyce, Pound, Eliot, Lawrence, and Woolf, he occupied a prominent place in the world of letters until his death in 1924.

Any consideration of the later novels must take seriously Thomas Moser's splendid *Joseph Conrad: Achievement and Decline,* because Moser's arguments have shaped discussion of these novels since his book appeared in 1957. In order to clarify my own position, let me recapitulate those arguments and then briefly respond.

(1) Moser claims, "The heroes and heroines of the later Conrad are sinned against, themselves unsinning."[6] On the contrary, Heyst, George, Lingard (in *The Rescue*), Réal, and even Peyrol act self-righteously and arrogantly as they respond to their own motives and needs. If one must choose between sinning and being sinned against (an admittedly reductive polarity), one must choose the former. In these works Conrad is more interested in the psychosexual needs of his characters, and the situations those needs create than he is in moral categories. That he wishes us to understand that Peyrol, Lingard, Anthony (in *Chance*), and Heyst usually make not moral decisions but psychological decisions disguised as moral ones establishes continuity with his prior work.

(2) According to Moser, Conrad demonstrates that "we are basically sound. When trouble comes to us, we are in no way responsible for it. The fault lies elsewhere, in other people."[7] But is this true? Lingard, Heyst, Anthony, Réal, and George are shown to be people who on occasion behave illogically, irrationally, inadequately, and ineptly; certainly their behavior does not reveal them as fundamentally sound even if, like Jim, they *wish* to behave correctly. But although they are not involved in situations where their conduct can be measured by rigid external standards of conduct, they must choose between basic values—such as loyalty to a comrade or lover versus loyalty to oneself. Conrad continued to be

6. *Joseph Conrad: Achievement and Decline,* 141.
7. Ibid., 140.

concerned with the way in which man's passions, instincts, and needs trigger behavior that has unfortunate consequences. Because Conrad is obsessed with psychosexual problems, he is more interested in particulars and *less* concerned with ideals and values than in his prior work. Yet contrary to Moser's assertion, individual guilt does not disappear. Except for *The Shadow-Line,* some of the situations involving personal relations are puzzling to Conrad, and hence his standards may be less explicit. Each novel depends on a character's recognizing an ethical imperative in a difficult moral situation. Paradoxically, except for *The Shadow-Line,* the later novels are, to an extent, novels of manners, but without a *norm* of manners in which Conrad believes.

(3) Moser contends, "The perceptive hero disappears."[8] But, where is the perceptive hero in Conrad? As I argue in prior chapters, even the Marlow of "Youth," *Heart of Darkness,* and *Lord Jim* is quite imperceptive; in any case, in most of the later novels an omniscient narrator, a surrogate Conrad, is the perceptive figure even if he provides alternative behavioral standards to those of the major characters, standards that are not as lucid as they might be.

(4) According to Moser, "By the end of 1913, Conrad's surrender to the association between love and death is fairly complete."[9] It is true that Conrad's later protagonists face an external menace (like most of the earlier ones), and most of them (unlike the protagonists of the earlier novels) are in love. These facts, however, hardly establish an unnatural relationship between love and death. While death is a frequent presence in Conrad's later plots, is the mortality rate of his major characters really any greater than in his earlier fiction? Heyst is the only central figure in the novels whose death is directly related to sexual love. The example Moser cites, Renouard in "The Planter of Malata," is depicted as a pathological personality.

(5) According to Moser, Conrad is a misogynist. While there is some truth to Moser's contention, it is an hyperbole that has become an accepted critical shibboleth. The major evidence for misogyny is the views of Marlow in *Chance;* but Marlow, although an objectification of an aspect of Conrad, is, as he had been in the previous three works in which he appears, a dramatized character. Mrs. Fyne's peculiar masculinity and lesbianism may derive from her compensating for an exploitive tyrannical father; her brother, Captain Anthony, compensates in equally unusual ways, namely by his inability to respond physically to Flora's

8. Ibid., 163.
9. Ibid., 144.

need because of overfastidiousness and lack of self-regard. Surely, Flora's idyllic relationship with Anthony and forthcoming marriage to Powell raise questions about Moser's statement that "the later Conrad's hostility to feminine self-assertion results in the immediate destruction of his women as soon as they embark on a plan of action."[10] Arlette's initiative does not destroy her but leads to her happy marriage to Réal. And Peyrol's heroic death is not the act of a misogynist. Lena's death derives not from her failure to obey Heyst or the inadequacy of her plan, but from the failure of Heyst to respond boldly and bravely when he is threatened and, in the climactic scene, from his failure to prevent the shooting.

(6) Moser contends, "The productions of Conrad's last years [*The Arrow of Gold, The Rover*, the fragmentary *Suspense*, and the later half of *The Rescue*] are virtually without a redeeming feature. They reveal that Conrad has exhausted his creative energy. He has no longer anything to write about and must rework old materials."[11] Yet Moser hereby ignores the psychological complexity of his later novels and the structural brilliance of *The Rover*.

Let me turn now to the commonly held assumption that Conrad's later fiction is different in *kind* from the prior fiction. In his important study, *Joseph Conrad's Fiction*, John Palmer argues that Conrad's later works should be discussed as romances with strong symbolic and allegorical components.[12]

But had Conrad sought to write allegories, we would expect a writer as self-conscious as he to comment upon that. Yet one only has to reread his letters to understand the continuity of his subjects, themes, and art. His letters and author's notes show that not only verisimilitude but also the factual origins of his work were important to him. Of *The Shadow-Line*, he wrote on February 17, 1917: "The whole thing is exact autobiography. . . . That experience is transposed into spiritual terms—in art a perfectly legitimate thing to do, as long as one preserves the exact truth enshrined therein." And in 1917, Conrad contended that throughout his career "all my concern had been with the 'ideal' value of things, events and people."[13]

Allegory depends upon the artist's imagining a moral tale and *then* creating a story to illustrate the fable. Conrad's later novels do not dramatize an ethical

10. Ibid., 162.
11. Ibid., 180.
12. *Joseph Conrad's Fiction: A Study in Literary Growth*, 168–69.
13. Letter of February 17 and March 8, 1917, in Jean-Aubry, *Joseph Conrad*, 2:182–83, 185.

system. Throughout his career, Conrad's focus is on the psychic needs, motives, and eccentricities that separate one man from another. The representative aspect of his novels derives not from the situation but from the character's archetypal aspirations. Jim wants to be a courageous hero, and Razumov needs public recognition as an intellectual figure. Gould wishes to be a powerful figure who uses material wealth in the service of progress. If there is a difference in the later novels, it is that Conrad deals with obsessions and repressions that are peculiarly singular to one individual character. Because Heyst, George, Anthony, Lingard, and Peyrol have their own unique psyches, they may be at times less representative of moral and cultural issues than Conrad's prior protagonists. Because his later protagonists have motives with which most readers identify, we are drawn to them; because their unacknowledged needs and obsessions are often eccentric (although eccentric in a way that to our discomfort suggests *our* repressed selves), we draw away to a distance that approximates the stance of the omniscient narrator, with whose emotional and moral standards of behavior we as readers are more comfortable.

I would like to propose an alternative view of Conrad's later novels, a view that, while acknowledging differences in emphasis from the earlier work, stresses continuities. We can divide Conrad's career after 1910 into three distinct phases. In the first, comprising *Chance* and *Victory,* Conrad wanted to demonstrate that he was an English novelist, not a Slav writing in English, as some reviewers implied. He had to prove to his audience and perhaps to himself that he had become an English writer. *Chance* and *Victory* represent Conrad's attempts to write English novels of manners and to explore the intricacies of personal relationships in the context of contemporary customs and values. He regarded *Victory* as a "strictly proper" work "meant for cultured people," and he thought that "The Secret Sharer" was English "in moral atmosphere, feeling and even in detail."[14]

In *Chance* and *Victory,* Conrad's subject matter is less his own life than the external world. But the second phase of Conrad's later novels, comprising *The Shadow-Line, The Arrow of Gold,* and *The Rescue,* derives more from a personal impulse. In these works, unlike the Marlow tales, Conrad re-creates emotions of the past more than he objectifies his present inner turmoil. As Conrad aged,

---

14. Letter to Pinker, October 7, 1912, quoted in Karl, *Joseph Conrad,* 717; letter to Edith Wharton, December 8, 1912, quoted and paraphrased in ibid., 725.

he sought subjects in his personal past and literary past, and his fiction less frequently addressed his immediate personal problems or current public issues.
The Shadow-Line and *The Arrow of Gold* reach back into his personal past, while
The Rescue is completed primarily to settle his long-standing, personal anxiety
about a work that had been stalled for two decades. *The Shadow-Line* is a fictional memoir of his initiation into command, while *The Arrow of Gold* is a fictional version of initiation into sexual maturity. *The Rescue* is a nostalgic look
at both his personal past and his literary past. These texts provided something
of an escape from Conrad's present anxieties and harsher memories. *The Rescue* enabled him to recapture the romance world of Malay and of his literary
youth—the period of *Almayer's Folly* and *An Outcast of the Islands,* and his fa-
vorite work, *The Nigger of the "Narcissus."* In all three works he is, like Marlow
in "Youth," placing his back to the future and looking longingly into the past
with the hope of recapturing past feelings of energy, vitality, and success.

In the final phase, he looks back (in *The Rover* and the incomplete *Suspense*)
to the Napoleonic period and creates large historical canvases that recall his
great political novels. While we do not know what he would have done in *Suspense,* his real concern in *The Rover* is coming to terms with his own approach-
ing death. In *The Rover,* the Napoleonic era provides the occasion for a moving
lyrical novel about the possibility of facing death heroically. The major character, an aging seaman and an outsider, is a fictional counterpart of Conrad.

Continuing a trend begun in the novels about politics (*Nostromo, The Secret
Agent,* and *Under Western Eyes*), Conrad's post-1910 novels are concerned with
family and personal relationships, with how and why people love one another.
They address how historical and social forces limit and define the possibilities
for love and action. Conrad never put behind him the conviction that man was
caught in a web of circumstances beyond his control. But he also believed in
man's capacity to grow, to love, and to know himself. Conrad contends that
within an indifferent if not hostile universe, man's indomitable will enables
him to survive despite setbacks and individual failures. Thus, he is not the nihilist and the prophet of darkness that he has been depicted in much recent
criticism.

Except for *The Shadow-Line,* Conrad's later novels usually have three not
completely integrated organizing principles: (1) a basic adventure tale, often a
voyage, dominated by a self-sufficient, independent, one-minded male figure;
(2) the heterosexual interaction between the protagonist and the woman he
loves; and (3) the historical and social setting in which the events take place.

These structural principles often stand in an uneasy relationship, particularly in the novels' second halves, where the love relationships intensify and often overwhelm the potential moral consequences of the males' behavior in the adventure. In *Chance,* for example, from the time Flora and Captain Anthony elope, the structure revolves around their relationship and undermines the baroque narrative technique. Conrad's fundamental interest in the characters' psychosexuality reasserts itself in spite of the intervention of Marlow and the nameless narrator. In fact, Powell, the nominal source of the last phase, is subsumed into the love motif because of his passion for Flora. Again in *Victory,* the external views of Heyst and the double narrator—Davidson and his anonymous listener—become less important after the elopement; the novel becomes concerned with the lovers' interaction. In *The Rover,* Peyrol undertakes his final mission less from commitment to a political cause than out of his affection for Arlette and his inability to face defeat for her hand.

In these novels Conrad's conception of heterosexual love is often bourgeois and conventionally Edwardian, but wasn't this the case in his earlier work? Moments of passion and displays of physical affection are still often depicted as extraordinary events that violate society's taboos. Conrad is ambivalent to those whose love takes place in remote settings and unusual situations and whose love thus challenges the validity of traditional manners and mores. We see a typical moment in *The Rover* when Réal suddenly kisses Arlette's hand and fastidiously interprets the kiss as a violation of not only decorum but also morality. He excoriates himself for the kiss; a man of "pedantic conscience," Réal thinks of that kiss as if it had been a rape. That in *The Arrow of Gold* so much is made of Rita's reputation and her illicit relationship with Henry Allegre, and that Jóse Ortega and then Blunt become her nemeses as if in response to her passion for George, testify to the fastidious conscience of the author. The editor's patronizing view of George indicates Conrad's desire to separate himself from a protagonist who is a version of his passionate, impulsive younger self. At times the reader feels Conrad's longing for absolute standards with which to judge the passions that constitute the major subject of his later work.

To sustain my argument about the continuity of Conrad's career, I propose to return to 1910 and to look briefly at *Chance.* Conrad had the kind of writing block when working upon *Chance* that he had had several times earlier in his career, most notably while working on *The Rescue* in 1896–1897. Not only did he have the severe breakdown in 1910 and a relapse in early 1911, but he also suffered several episodes of hypochondria before completing *Chance* in 1912. As he had done when faced with writer's block before writing *The Nigger of the "Narcissus,"* Conrad used the process of beginning a voyage as a means of beginning a novel. Starting with *The Nigger of the "Narcissus"*—as I mentioned before—Conrad often used the voyage with its movement from beginning to end, its defined cast of characters, and, for him, its memories of successful action as a means of ordering his own writing process. Imagining the completion of a quest or a voyage released Conrad from the agonies of writing. As with *The Nigger of the "Narcissus,"* he thought of *Chance* as a voyage to be completed, and wrote of "having got a slant of fair wind with *Chance.*"[15] Again he relied upon his sea experience to overcome self-doubt as an author.

As he had in 1898–1900, Conrad uses Marlow when he has difficulty writing because he can transfer the problems of writing and understanding to an alter ego within the world he is trying to create. Like his creator, Marlow has retired from the sea but sustains himself with the possibility—surely a fiction in Conrad's case—that he might somehow return to that life. The subject matter of *Chance* becomes a means for Conrad to imaginatively escape the disappointments of land and the difficulties of writing. Conrad has Marlow consistently allude to a land-sea dichotomy in reductive terms. Criticism of the land is Conrad's aggressive, if childish, response to his frustrations with his personal and professional life.

Chance, the first novel after the three major political novels, sustains and intensifies the stress on private life and passionate love. Within Conrad's imagined world, empathy and understanding from a lover, child, parent, or compassionate counselor are the only alternatives to the invidious and insidious threats of materialism, political ideology, and uncontrollable historical forces.

The novel proposes the alternative achieved by Flora and Anthony and endorsed by Marlow when he arranges the union between Powell and Flora. Yet the ending should not betray us into believing that Conrad the optimist has triumphed over Conrad the skeptic or that Conrad's basic perception of man's place in the cosmos has fundamentally changed. Does marriage really ease the pain of living in a purposeless universe, in a world of meanness and pettiness? Once one perceives the prominence of the prison metaphor within the texture of the novel, one realizes that Conrad's indictment of English life has the harshness and bitterness of *The Secret Agent. Chance* discovers a heart of darkness beneath the civilized exteriors of Edwardian London, just as *The Secret Agent* dis-

15. Letter of May 1911, in Jean-Aubry, *Joseph Conrad,* 2:128.

covers it in the political machinations not only of anarchists and reactionaries but also of those charged with upholding the status quo. In *Chance,* the London of *The Secret Agent* still exists in all its shabby, ugly decadence: mankind is separated by individual dreams and illusions.

Let us turn to *The Rover,* the final novel Conrad completed, to pursue my argument for continuity. Throughout Conrad's career, he spoke of the search for solidarity with his kind and made clear that he did not want to write for a coterie. *The Rover* was written with the idea of reaching that part of the mass of mankind which was literate. In important respects, it is a synopsis of a number of major themes in his previous work. Peyrol, the rover, is a heroic version of the kind of man Conrad sought to reach. Every aspect of the novel—the style, voice, and structure—reflects his attempt to reach beyond a limited audience to those who would recognize a kinship with a forceful, competent, shrewd, but not intellectual hero. Conrad's technique is appropriate for the barely verbal and unself-conscious characters of *The Rover.* That is why the voice sometimes seems to be an articulate version of Peyrol; why the style deliberately eschews the elaborate syntax of Marlow's meditative, introspective voice or the hyperbole and imprecision of such later works as *The Arrow of Gold* and the short story "The Planter of Malata"; and why the structure avoids disrupted chronology and elaborate narrative technique. *The Rover* is a spare, bold, minor masterpiece even if it does not integrate plot, character, and historical context with the subtlety and intensity of *The Secret Agent* and *Heart of Darkness.* In *The Rover,* as in *Chance,* the small number of individuals in an isolated setting enables Conrad to insulate the characters from outside factors and to limit tangential interactions. In this way, the novel's fictional materials resemble the voyage experience with which as an artist he felt most comfortable.

For Conrad, life at sea was romance and epic, and the successful completion of a voyage such as Peyrol's climactic one is equivalent to discovering or regaining identity. *The Rover* is not only a version of the Ulysses myth, but a fictional version of *A Personal Record;* with its elegiac tone, its sense of forthcoming death, and its emphasis on returning home to discover the self that has been created abroad, Conrad's autobiographical volume anticipates major concerns of *The Rover. The Rover* is Conrad's *Death in Venice.* Every element combines to provide the orchestration for Peyrol's death. As in *Death in Venice,* the narrator's distance from his protagonist fluctuates; as in Mann's novella, an author is partly objectified in a character. Peyrol is the inarticulate, courageous man of action Conrad might have become. Motivated not by commitment to political dogma but by love of country, he is the man who finally makes a difference in the affairs of his nation. *The Rover* is about coming to terms with age and dying. Peyrol fulfills Conrad's fantasy of an elegant death in a heroic action.

In *A Personal Record,* writing of his first return to Poland, Conrad noted how the faces "were as familiar to me as though I had known them all from childhood, and my childhood were a matter of the day before yesterday."[16] Upon arriving in France, Peyrol is struck by the parallel between himself and the people he encounters, including even the cripple. Gradually, he feels that he belongs to France, represented in his mind by the tiny coastal hamlet in which he lies and by the people he knows there.

Peyrol is the obverse of Conrad's meditative, introspective aspect, the aspect dramatized by Marlow. Rather he represents Conrad the man of action, the man who, even while mistrusting democracy, sought solidarity with the rest of mankind. Peyrol is also a surrogate for the aging Conrad. He retires after success as a man of action and regrets the life he has left behind. He has difficulty finding a comfortable niche in his new life and, like Conrad, sustains himself with the dream of resuming his sea life. Despite formal omniscience, the distance between Conrad and Peyrol often dissolves because Peyrol is the fictional counterpart for Conrad's fantasies of a significant death to climax a heroic old age. Conrad's sympathies move back and forth from narrator to character, from his observer to his subject. Conrad's analysis of Peyrol often oversimplifies his behavior to the point of distorting it; that is, his comments do not do justice to the subtlety of his character. In a sense, Conrad is trying to write an adventure story in the Kipling and Stevenson tradition, but in the final scene his moral imagination resists the necessary structural simplicity, partly because he cannot fully separate himself from his protagonist. Peyrol need not have committed suicide to be captured; by having Peyrol take not only Scevola but also Michel to their deaths, Conrad shows once again the ambiguity of decisive action.

Since Conrad would have expected us to remember that France lost the Napoleonic Wars, Peyrol's efficacy must be measured in other than political or military results.[17] Arlette's and Réal's happy marriage derives from Peyrol's gen-

---

16. *A Personal Record,* 27. All quotations from Conrad's works are from the Kent edition.

17. In "Autocracy and War," Conrad had written: "The subtle and manifold influence for evil of the Napoleonic episode as a school of violence, as sower of national hatreds, as the direct provocator of obscurantism and reaction, of political tyranny and injustice, cannot well be exaggerated" (*Notes on Life and Letters,* 86).

erosity. The fantasy of quiet retreat from responsibility fulfills Conrad's own dreams. Both Peyrol and Réal wish to escape the mesh of public events. As in *Nostromo, The Secret Agent,* and *Under Western Eyes,* political partisanship is the enemy of human relationships; even Peyrol's zealous suicidal act illustrates this. Yet Peyrol's sacrifice for Réal is Conrad's final version of the recurring moral dilemma that a man faces when he must choose either self-interest or self-abnegation. By his heroic act, Peyrol shows the meaning of fraternity as self-sacrifice with a purity and clarity that few Conradian deeds permit.

I should like to conclude with a brief evaluation of Conrad's work after 1908. "The Secret Sharer," written immediately before *Under Western Eyes,* and *The Shadow-Line* rank with Conrad's masterpieces—*Nostromo, Heart of Darkness, Lord Jim,* and *The Secret Agent.* Not so incidentally, in both works Conrad uses his characteristic technique of a meditative mind probing the significance of a crucial past experience. While *Victory* and *The Rover* are quite splendid, even they share four flaws that occasionally disrupt the later fiction. (1) Often Conrad does not give himself as completely to the narrative voice or to his other major characters; at times, his withholding of the full range of his psychic involvement is responsible for a more flaccid form. (2) As Conrad sought a larger audience, he began to use a more conventional chronology and abandoned the nonchronological movement that depended upon the striking juxtaposition of incidents. In the work before *Chance,* Conrad's unique juxtaposition of events had enabled him to present the reader with a complex moral context for judging the actions of central characters. (3) His later novels focus on fewer characters and fewer dramatic situations and lack the moral density of the prior works. (4) He did not always successfully integrate his protagonist's private life into the historical or social background. In its way, *The Rover* addresses the French Revolution, as *Heart of Darkness* addresses imperialism, but its characters do not typify or epitomize their historical moment. *Nostromo* and *Heart of Darkness* penetrate to our deepest levels because they are representative of their zeitgeist in the same way that Odysseus's journey is. What makes Conrad's major novels so compelling are the tensions between public issues and private lives and between representative aspirations and idiosyncratic characters, and these tensions are often missing in the later works.

Conrad's later work contains qualities that typify the work of many older artists: the revival of forms and themes of past artistic successes, references to earlier works, nostalgia for an earlier period of life, emphases on turning points in life, and intermittent sensuality. But what is usually lacking in Conrad's later work is the creative rage of the older Yeats, the subtlety of the late James, the willingness to take the chances taken by the aging Claude Monet, the bold disregard for precedents of the Joyce who wrote *Finnegans Wake,* and the Olympian turning away from mere nominalistic details to focus on essential truths that characterizes the later work of Matisse.

Abdoo, Sherlyn. "Ego Formation and the Land/Sea Metaphor in Conrad's 'Secret Sharer.'" In *Poetics of the Elements in the Human Condition: The Sea: From Elemental Stirrings to Symbolic Inspiration, Language, and Life-Significance in Literary Interpretation and Theory*, ed. Anna-Theresa Tymieniecka. *Analecta Husserliana* 19 (1985): 67–76.

Achebe, Chinua. "An Image of Africa." *Massachusetts Review* 18 (1977): 782–94.

Aristotle. *Poetics*. Trans. S. H. Butcher. In *Criticism*, ed. Mark Schorer, Josephine Mies, and Gordon McKenzie, 199–217. New York: Harcourt, Brace and World, 1958.

Armstrong, Paul B. *The Challenge of Bewilderment: Understanding and Representation in James, Conrad, and Ford*. Ithaca: Cornell University Press, 1987.

Baines, Jocelyn. *Joseph Conrad: A Critical Biography*. New York: McGraw, 1960.

Bakhtin, Mikhail M. *The Dialogic Imagination*. Ed. Michael Holquist. Trans. Caryl Emerson and Michael Holquist. Austin: University of Texas Press, 1981.

Barnett, Louise K. "'The Whole Circle of the Horizon': The Circumscribed Universe of 'The Secret Sharer.'" *Studies in the Humanities* 8.2 (1981): 5–9.

Benson, Carl. "Conrad's Two Stories of Initiation." *PMLA* 69 (March 1954): 46–56.

Berlin, Isaiah. "Philosophy and Life: An Interview." *New York Review of Books*, May 28, 1992, pp. 46–55.

Booth, Wayne C. *The Rhetoric of Fiction*. Rev. ed. Chicago: University of Chicago Press, 1983.

———. "The Rhetoric of Fiction and the Poetics of Fiction." *Novel* 1.2 (1968): 105–17.

Bradley, F. H. *Appearance and Reality: A Metaphysical Essay*. London: Sonnenschein, 1893.

Brantlinger, Patrick. *Crusoe's Footprints: Cultural Studies in Britain and America.* New York: Routledge, 1990.

———. *Rule of Darkness: British Literature and Imperialism, 1830–1914.* Ithaca: Cornell University Press, 1988.

Bretell, Richard. *The Art of Paul Gauguin.* Washington, D.C.: Board of Trustees, National Gallery of Art, 1988.

Burke, Kenneth. *The Philosophy of Literary Form.* Rev. ed. New York: Vintage, 1957.

Cassirer, Ernst. *The Logic of the Humanities.* Trans. Clarence Smith Howe. New Haven: Yale University Press, 1961.

Clifford, James. *The Predicament of Culture: Twentieth Century Ethnography, Literature, and Art.* Cambridge: Harvard University Press, 1988.

Conrad, Joseph. *Collected Letters of Joseph Conrad, vol. 1, 1861–1897.* Ed. Frederick Karl and Laurence Davies. New York: Cambridge University Press, 1983.

———. *Complete Works.* 26 vols. Kent edition. Garden City, N.Y.: Doubleday, 1926.

———. *Lord Jim.* Ed. Thomas Moser. New York: Norton, 1968.

———. *"The Secret Sharer."* Ed. Daniel R. Schwarz. Boston: Bedford, 1997.

Curley, Daniel. "Legate of the Ideal." In *Conrad's "Secret Sharer" and the Critics,* ed. Bruce Harkness, 75–82. Belmont, Calif.: Wadsworth, 1962.

Daleski, H. M. *Joseph Conrad: The Way of Dispossession.* New York: Holmes, 1976.

Demory, Pamela H. "*Nostromo:* Making History." *Texas Studies in Literature and Language* 35.3 (fall 1993): 315–46.

Ducharme, Robert. "The Power of Culture in *Lord Jim.*" *Conradiana* 22 (1990): 3–24.

Eliot, T. S. "Ulysses, Order, and Myth." *The Dial* 75 (1923): 480–83.

Erdinast-Vulcan, Daphna. *Joseph Conrad and the Modern Temper.* Oxford: Clarendon, 1991.

Facknitz, Mark A. R. "Cryptic Allusions and the Moral of the Story: The Case of Joseph Conrad's 'The Secret Sharer.'" *Journal of Narrative Technique* 17.1 (winter 1987): 115–30.

Flam, Jack. *Matisse: The Man and His Art, 1869–1918.* Ithaca: Cornell University Press, 1986.

Fleishman, Avrom. *Conrad's Politics: Community and Anarchy in the Fiction of Joseph Conrad.* Baltimore: Johns Hopkins University Press, 1967.

Fogel, Aaron. *Coercion to Speak: Conrad's Poetics of Dialogue.* Cambridge: Harvard University Press, 1985.

Frank, Joseph. "Spatial Form in Modern Literature." *Sewanee Review* 53 (1945): 221–40, 433–56, 643–53.

Frye, Northrop. *Anatomy of Criticism: Four Essays.* Princeton: Princeton University Press, 1957.

Gordan, John Dozier. *Joseph Conrad: The Making of a Novelist.* Cambridge: Harvard University Press, 1940.

Gordimer, Nadine. "The Arts in Adversity: Apprentices of Freedom." *New Society* 24/31 (December 1981): ii–v.

Graff, Gerald. *Professing English: An Institutional History.* Chicago: University of Chicago Press, 1987.

———. "The Pseudo-Politics of Interpretation." In *The Politics of Interpretation,* ed. W. J. T. Mitchell, 145–58. Chicago: University of Chicago Press, 1983.

Guerard, Albert J. *Conrad the Novelist.* Cambridge: Harvard University Press, 1958.

Harkness, Bruce, ed. *Conrad's "Secret Sharer" and the Critics.* Belmont, California: Wadsworth, 1962.

Hartman, Geoffrey. "The Culture of Criticism." *PMLA* 99.3 (May 1984): 371–97.

Hay, Eloise Knapp. *The Political Novels of Joseph Conrad.* Chicago: University of Chicago Press, 1963.

Hertz, Neil. "Freud and the Sandman." In *Textual Strategies: Perspectives in Post-Structuralist Criticism,* ed. Josué V. Harari, 296–321. Ithaca: Cornell University Press, 1979.

Hodges, Robert. "Deep Fellowship: Homosexuality and Male Bonding in the Life and Fiction of Joseph Conrad." *Journal of Homosexuality* 4.4 (1979): 379–87.

Hofstadter, Douglas. *Gödel, Escher, Bach: An Eternal Golden Braid.* New York: Basic Books, 1979.

James, Henry. *The Great Short Novels of Henry James.* Ed. Phillip Rahv. New York: Dial, 1965.

Jameson, Fredric. *The Political Unconscious: Narrative as a Socially Symbolic Act.* Ithaca: Cornell University Press, 1981.

Jean-Aubry, G. *Joseph Conrad: Life and Letters.* 2 vols. Garden City, N.Y.: Doubleday, Page and Co., 1927.

Johnson, Barbara, and Marjorie Garber. "Secret Sharing: Reading Conrad Psychoanalytically." *College English* 49.6 (1987): 628–40.

Karl, Frederick R. *Joseph Conrad: The Three Lives: A Biography.* New York: Farrar, Straus, and Giroux, 1979.

Kelly, Aileen. "Tolstoy in Doubt." *New York Review of Books,* June 29, 1978, pp. 22–26.

Lacan, Jacques. *The Four Fundamental Concepts of Psycho-Analysis.* Ed. Jacques-Alain Miller. Trans. Alan Sheridan. New York: Norton, 1981.

LaCapra, Dominick. "On the Line: Between History and Criticism." *Profession* 89 (1989): 4–9.

Laing, R. D. *The Divided Self: An Existential Study in Sanity and Madness.* Baltimore: Penguin, 1965.

Langland, Elizabeth. *Society in the Novel.* Chapel Hill: University of North Carolina Press, 1989.

Lee, John A., and Paul J. Sturm. *Letters of Joseph Conrad to Marguerite Poradowska, 1890–1920.* New Haven: Yale University Press, 1940.

Leiter, Louis H. "Echo Structures: Conrad's 'The Secret Sharer.'" *Twentieth Century Literature* 5.4 (1960): 159–75.

Manet, 1832–1883. New York: Metropolitan Museum of Art, 1983.

Marcus, Steven. *The Other Victorians: A Study of Sexuality and Pornography in Mid-Nineteenth-Century England.* New York: Basic Books, 1974.

———. Review of *Obedience to Authority,* by Stanley Milgram. *New York Times Book Review,* January 13, 1974, pp. 1–3.

Martz, Louis. *The Poetry of Meditation.* 2d ed. New Haven: Yale University Press, 1962.

McNelly, Cleo. "Natives, Women, and Claude Lévi-Strauss: A Reading of *Tristes Tropiques* as Myth." *Massachusetts Review* 16 (1975): 7–29.

Melville, Herman. *Moby-Dick.* 1851. Reprint, New York: Holt, Rinehart, and Winston, 1948.

Meyer, Bernard C. *Joseph Conrad: A Psychoanalytic Biography.* Princeton: Princeton University Press, 1967.

Miller, J. Hillis. *Fiction and Repetition: Seven English Novels.* Cambridge: Harvard University Press, 1982.

———. *Poets of Reality: Six Twentieth Century Writers.* Cambridge: Belknap Press of Harvard University Press, 1965.

Moser, Thomas C. *Joseph Conrad: Achievement and Decline.* Cambridge: Harvard University Press, 1957.

Mueller, Martin. "The Yellow Stripes and Dead Armadillos." *Profession* 89 (1989): 23–31.

Murfin, Ross, ed. *Heart of Darkness: A Case Study in Contemporary Criticism.* New York: St. Martin's Press, 1989.

Murphy, Michael. "'The Secret Sharer': Conrad's Turn of the Winch." *Conradiana* 18.3 (1986): 193–200.

Najder, Zdzislaw. *Joseph Conrad: A Chronicle.* New Brunswick: Rutgers University Press, 1983.

Nussbaum, Martha. "Perceptive Equilibrium: Literary Theory and Ethical Theory." In *The Future of Literary Theory,* ed. Ralph Cohen, 58–85. New York: Routledge, 1989.

O'Hara, J. D. "Unlearned Lessons in 'The Secret Sharer.'" *College English* 26 (1965): 444–50.

Paccaud, Josiane. "Under the Other's Eyes: Conrad's 'The Secret Sharer.'" *Conradian* 12.1 (1987): 59–73.

Palmer, John. *Joseph Conrad's Fiction: A Study in Literary Growth.* Ithaca: Cornell University Press, 1968.

Pollack, Griselda. *Avant-Garde Gambits, 1888–1893: Gender and the Color of Art History.* New York: Thames and Hudson, 1992.

Ressler, Steve. *Joseph Conrad: Consciousness and Integrity.* New York: New York University Press, 1988.

Rosenfield, Claire. *Paradise of Snakes: An Archetypal Analysis of Conrad's Political Novels.* Chicago: University of Chicago Press, 1967.

Rosenzweig, Saul. "Freud, Jung and Hall the King-Maker." *New York Times Book Review,* January 24, 1993: 1, 20.

Roussel, Royal. *The Metaphysics of Darkness: A Study in the Unity and Development of Conrad's Fiction.* Baltimore: Johns Hopkins University Press, 1971.

Said, Edward. *Beginnings: Intention and Method.* New York: Basic Books, 1975.

———. *Culture and Imperialism.* New York: Knopf, 1993.

Schwarz, Daniel R. *The Case for a Humanistic Poetics.* London: Macmillan; Philadelphia: University of Pennsylvania Press, 1991.

———. *Conrad: "Almayer's Folly" to "Under Western Eyes."* London: Macmillan; Ithaca: Cornell University Press, 1980.

———. *Conrad: The Later Fiction.* London: Macmillan, 1966.

———. "Culture, Canonicity and Pluralism: A Humanistic Perspective on Professing English." *Texas Studies in Language and Literature* 34 (spring 1992): 149–75.

———. "The Ethics of Reading: The Case for Pluralistic and Transactional Reading." *Novel* 12 (winter–spring 1988): 197–218. Reprinted in *Why the Novel Matters,* ed. Mark Spilka and Caroline McCracken-Flesher. Bloomington: Indiana University Press, 1990.

———. *The Humanistic Heritage: Critical Theories of the English Novel from James to Hillis Miller.* Philadelphia: University of Pennsylvania Press, 1986.

———. *Imagining the Holocaust.* New York: St. Martin's Press, 1999.

———. *Narrative and Representation in the Poetry of Wallace Stevens.* London: Macmillan; New York: St. Martin's Press, 1993.

———. "Reading as Moral Activity: Wayne Booth's *The Rhetoric of Fiction.*" *Sewanee Review* 93 (summer 1985): 480–85.

———. *Reconfiguring Modernism: Explorations in the Relationship between Modern Art and Modern Literature.* New York: St. Martin's Press, 1997.

———. "Searching for Modernism's Generic Code: Picasso, Joyce, and Stevens as a Cultural Configuration." *Weber Studies: An Interdisciplinary Humanities Journal* 10 (winter 1993): 66–86.

———. "Teaching *Heart of Darkness:* Towards a Pluralistic Perspective." *Conradiana* 24.3 (1992): 190–206.

———. *The Transformation of the English Novel, 1890–1930: Studies in Hardy, Conrad, Joyce, Lawrence, Forster, and Woolf.* 1989. 2d ed. New York: St. Martin's Press, 1995.

Sherry, Norman. *Conrad's Eastern World.* London: Cambridge University Press, 1966.

Sieburth, Richard. "Dabbling in Damnation: The Bachelor, the Artist and the Dandy in Huysman." *Times Literary Supplement,* May 29, 1992, pp. 3–5.

Stallman, Robert W. "Conrad and 'The Secret Sharer.'" In *The Art of Joseph Conrad: A Critical Symposium,* 275–88. East Lansing: Michigan State University Press, 1960.

Stevens, Wallace. *Collected Poems.* New York: Alfred A. Knopf, 1954.

———. *Poems by Wallace Stevens.* Selected by Samuel French Morse. New York: Vintage, 1959.

Van Ghent, Dorothy. Introduction to *Nostromo.* New York: Holt, Rhinehart and Winston, 1961.

Visser, Daniel. "Crowns and Politics in *Nostromo.*" *Mosaic. A Journal for the Interdisciplinary Study of Literature* 23.2 (spring 1990): 1–15.

Wadley, Nicholas, ed. *Noa Noa: Gauguin's Tahiti.* Oxford: Phaidon, 1985.

Watt, Ian. *Conrad in the Nineteenth Century.* Berkeley and Los Angeles: University of California Press, 1979.

Wexler, Joyce. "Conrad's Dream of a Common Language: Lacan and 'The Secret Sharer.'" *Psychoanalytic Review* 78.4 (1991): 599–606.

White, James F. "The Third Theme in 'The Secret Sharer.'" *Conradiana* 21.1 (1989): 37–46.

Wiesel, Elie. *Night.* Trans. Stella Rodway. New York: Hill and Wang, 1960.

Woolf, Virginia. "Mr. Bennett and Mrs. Brown." In *The Captain's Death Bed and Other Essays.* New York: Harcourt, 1950.

Wright, Walter F. *Romance and Tragedy in Joseph Conrad.* Lincoln: University of Nebraska Press, 1949.

Wyatt, Robert D. "Joseph Conrad's 'The Secret Sharer': Point of View and Mistaken Identities." *Conradiana* 5.1 (1973): 12–26.

Daniel R. Schwarz is Professor of English and Stephen H. Weiss Presidential Fellow at Cornell University, where he received Cornell's College of Arts and Sciences Russell Award for Distinguished Teaching. He is the author of numerous books, including *Imagining the Holocaust, Reconfiguring Modernism: Explorations in the Relationship between Modern Art and Modern Literature, Reading Joyce's "Ulysses," Conrad: "Almayer's Folly" to "Under Western Eyes,"* and *Conrad: The Later Fiction.* He has edited "The Dead" and "The Secret Sharer" in the Bedford Case Studies in Contemporary Criticism Series and is coeditor of *Narrative and Culture.*